RESEARCH METHODS FOR CRIMINAL JUSTICE AND THE SOCIAL SCIENCES

PRACTICE AND APPLICATIONS

Connie Ireland and Bruce L. Berg
Department of Criminal Justice
California State University–Long Beach

Robert J. Mutchnick
Department of Criminology
Indiana University of Pennsylvania

Prentice Hall
Boston • Columbus • Indianapolis • New York • San Francisco • Upper Saddle River
Amsterdam • Cape Town • Dubai • London • Madrid • Milan • Munich • Paris • Montreal • Toronto
Delhi • Mexico City • Sao Paulo • Sydney • Hong Kong • Seoul • Singapore • Taipei • Tokyo

Vice President and Executive Publisher: Vernon Anthony
Senior Acquisitions Editor: Tim Peyton
Editorial Assistant: Lynda Cramer
Media Project Manager: Karen Bretz
Director of Marketing: David Gesell
Marketing Manager: Adam Kloza
Senior Marketing Coordinator: Alicia Wozniak
Project Manager: Holy Shufeldt
Creative Director: Jayne Conte
Cover Designer: Margaret Kenselaar
Inhouse Cover Artist: Karen Noferi
Full-Service Project Management/Composition: Niraj Bhatt, Aptara®, Inc.
Printer/Binder: Bind-Rite Graphics
Cover Printer: Demand Production Center

Library of Congress Cataloging-in-Publication Data

Ireland, Connie.
Research methods for criminal justice and the social sciences: practice and applications / Connie Ireland, Bruce L. Berg, Robert J. Mutchnick.
p. cm.
Includes bibliographical references.
ISBN-13: 978-0-13-501877-4
ISBN-10: 0-13-501877-3
1. Criminology—Research. 2. Criminal justice, Administration of—Research. 3. Social sciences—Methodology. I. Berg, Bruce L. (Bruce Lawrence), 1954- II. Mutchnick, Robert J. III. Title.
HV6024.5.I74 2010
364.042—dc22

2009025729

10 9 8 7 6 5

Prentice Hall
is an imprint of

www.pearsonhighered.com

ISBN-10: 0-13-501877-3
ISBN-13: 978-0-13-501877-4

Dedication

To the Memory of

Bruce Berg
1954–2009

Friend, colleague, professor, mentor, scholar, husband, and father

To my family—Jim, Sarah, Dean, and Dane

C.I.

To the love of my life, Jill; and my children, Kate and Alex

B.L.B.

To my family—Bea, Barbara, Kathryn, and Sarah

R.J.M.

To our students, from whom we continually learn

C.I., B.L.B., and R.J.M.

CONTENTS

PREFACE

Bruce Berg and Robert Mutchnick were having coffee one afternoon while attending a meeting of the American Society of Criminology, and the talk turned to work. Both had been teaching research methods for a number of years and had begun to grow weary of the usual lecturing style and traditional textbooks. In the course of the conversation, a great idea was born: What if someone were to combine traditional research textbook material with exercises that allow students to experience research in a controlled environment?

Berg and Mutchnick acted on their idea and wrote the first edition of this book, a companion methods/manual for use with most traditional social scientific research textbooks. Their intention was to create a book that offers readers basic information about various methodological concerns; a series of brief readings (or *abstracted reprints*, as we call them), taken from published research articles; and a variety of practice exercises related to the readings.

The strategy condensed lengthy research articles to produce brief abstractions, which are largely methodological. The results are shorter, edited versions of the original articles. Efforts were made to maintain the integrity of the articles, and no new or additional material was added to these; and we remain true to the presentation of information used in the abstracted reprints.

In this current edition, Dr. Connie Ireland has been invited to assist in updating many of the articles and passages to ensure inclusion of both contemporary material and many of the more timeless or classical pieces used in the first edition.

We believe that our book can be used to supplement a more comprehensive methods textbook or as a brief methods and applications practice during shorter summer semesters. We also believe that our book might be used to introduce inexperienced researchers to basic research concepts and practices.

PLAN OF THE TEXT

The plan of this text is simple. Each chapter begins with a discussion of the elements relevant to a basic understanding of research methods. This material is intentionally brief because we are primarily interested in emphasizing the application of ideas expressed in each chapter. Numerous lengthy texts are available that will describe aspects of research methods more comprehensively. Although these other texts are informative, they do not provide students with the opportunity to actually experience research. A unique feature of our book is that students actually *do research.*

Following the informational section of each chapter are several abstracted reprints. These readings contain the basic introductions of published articles, along with their methodological descriptions and findings. The articles were selected because they illustrate certain kinds of methodological strategies or techniques.

Each reading is followed by an Application Exercise that relates to the methodological procedure described in the abstracted reprint. All the exercises were designed to be completed by college students, bearing in mind that some of these students will be inexperienced in research methods. Completing these exercises will allow students to "get their hands dirty with data."

Reading the text and abstracted reprints and completing the exercises in this book will help fledgling researchers become more proficient in research methods. More important, we hope this book will show inexperienced researchers that there is nothing mystical or scary about designing or conducting research.

We thank Sofia Peralta, Jennifer Stumpp, and Rebecca Nash of California State University–Long Beach, who helped compile documents, reviewed drafts of this edition, and provided useful suggestions to us. We also thank the folks at Prentice Hall who had the confidence in us to produce a text worthy of publication. Specifically we want to thank our editor Tim Peyton, his assistant Lynda Cramer, and our marketing manager, Adam Kloza.

CHAPTER 1

Introduction

OBJECTIVES

This textbook/workbook provides both students and instructors with various options to learn and practice basic research methods/techniques for criminology and criminal justice. Most traditional research methods texts provide students with some information about a wide range of topics by adding a few questions at the end of each chapter; however, the application for the knowledge presented in these texts is insufficient. The practice/study questions are rarely integrated throughout the text, leaving students to bridge the gap between printed text and application on their own. In the last few decades, approaches to education have begun incorporating interactive kinesthetic activities, or "learning-through-doing" techniques. The authors believe that it is time to provide students and instructors of research methods with an option that incorporates a more hands-on, interactive approach to the subject.

This textbook/workbook is focused on the fields of criminology and criminal justice and is designed to work with many of the popular social science research methods texts currently available. Instructors can use this textbook/workbook in a variety of ways: (1) as a supplement to a standard methodology text; (2) as a stand-alone text supplemented with class lectures and some outside reading; or (3) as a self-paced text for students studying research methods on an individual or independent basis.

The material in this textbook/workbook is provided to assist inexperienced students in better understanding and completing the practice assignments. Students can use the material to augment information provided in their core texts.

The main focus of this textbook/workbook is on creating an environment where students learn various methodological techniques through a process that includes imitation, replication, and/or experimentation. Using the standard textbook approach, this textbook provides a brief presentation of a methodological topic or technique, followed by a number of current research examples culled from the criminological and criminal justice literature. The research examples represent applications of specific methodological techniques. Each journal article has been abstracted to present a brief but informative demonstration of the methodological topic or technique while maintaining the integrity of the article. In some instances, more than one research article has been abstracted for a given methodological technique to provide instructors with options for instruction and application, depending on the perspective from which they wish to teach.

In addition to the selected journal articles used as examples in this book, this edition includes reports from official criminal justice agencies such as the Bureau of Justice Statistics, Department of Justice, National Institutes of Health, and the like. Official agency publications are incorporated for several reasons. First, research questions often stem from official reports of crime and justice statistics. Many criminal justice scholars look frequently to these official reports to determine what issues are emerging in the field and what changes need further study. Thus, examining these data is likely to spark curiosity in the young scholar. Second, such reports are often deliverable products of grant-funded research. Thus, they are generally the result of a stringent research protocol or evaluation study and are thus empirically sound. Many such reports and publications supported by these agencies, such as the annotated *Monitoring the Future* report (Johnston, O'Malley, Bachman, & Schulenberg, 2008) in Chapter 5, are eventually transformed into journal articles. We thought it important to include reference to the original analyses of widely disseminated criminal justice data. Third, many young researchers are given mixed signals about the appropriate use of various types of scholarship in their literature reviews. While peer-reviewed articles are the gold standard in the discipline, official agency reports and documents are essential to scientific inquiry because they ground the research in tangible social problems. Fourth, it is essential to introduce students to the maze of government resources and hurdles related to criminological research. For example, the exercises in Chapter 2 include a notorious research project that sparks ethical concerns (Humphrey's *Tea Room Trade*, 1970) as well as the most current U.S. government standards on the Institutional Review Board (IRB; 46 CFR 45) and application/instructions for a Federal "Certificate of Confidentiality." Thus, students read an example of a questionable study alongside federal guidelines for ethical research today. Fifth, the use of such public domain documents helps keep the publishing costs down, making this a more affordable book for students.

Immediately following each abstracted article is an application exercise, which is designed to provide students with an opportunity to practice and apply the technique being demonstrated. Some of the application exercises present readers with a set of questions that allow students to demonstrate their understanding of the methodological technique. Other exercises give students the opportunity to actually use the technique, either through replicating or adapting it using the data provided or collected.

The authors believe that the approach of abstracting journal articles and providing application exercises allows students to engage interactively in learning the research process. As indicated earlier, in a number of instances, more than one abstracted article and exercise is provided for a given technique. While students may not be expected to demonstrate their knowledge of a technique using more than one of the abstracted articles and exercises, the additional materials are available to reinforce a particular methodological procedure, when necessary. The additional abstracted articles and exercises allow instructors and students some choice in selecting how to study and learn a particular methodological technique and offer a variety of examples of varying interest. Articles from a broad range of referred criminological and criminal justice journals, as well as official government publications and public domain examples included herein, allow this textbook/workbook to be used by criminal justice students with a variety of interests in several subspecialty areas, such as corrections, law enforcement, theory development, forensics, and public policy.

This textbook is also designed to be used as a workbook, similar to those most of us used when we were students in elementary and middle school. Spaces are provided for students to respond directly to exercises, and the pages are perforated to facilitate removal, in case instructors want to review the exercises for grading. The manual also can be used for self-paced, individualized instruction by allowing students to work on their own, completing and turning in exercises when they feel that they have mastered particular methodological techniques. As a supplemental text, this manual can be used to highlight specific topics through the exercises or to allow students to demonstrate proficiency in specific methodological techniques before moving forward with additional concepts. The pages of the exercises can be removed from the textbook and incorporated in a loose-leaf, three-ring binder; students can then add notes on specific methodologies.

This textbook/workbook is designed to work with approaches that incorporate qualitative as well as quantitative methodologies. Exercises addressing the main aspects of each of these methodologies are provided.

We assume that you are motivated, intelligent individuals who have little or no exposure to the subject of research methods. With a little effort on your behalf and the guidance of your instructor, you should have no difficulty mastering the content of this textbook.

TABLE READING

A wealth of information can often be obtained from tables if only readers know what to look for and how to look for it. The following material on table reading is designed primarily for readers with no regular table-reading experience. Those of you with some experience will also benefit from this section because of the systematic presentation of material on the subject. This section serves as a guide to the general components of a table. It should be noted that not all tables contain all the information presented in the example below, and the specific location of material might vary from table to table. Even so, the general principles remain the same and are important to know. Knowing how to read a table can save your valuable time in reading and understanding research.

It has been suggested that if you read the tables contained in a manuscript, you could call from them the information necessary for understanding the whole research project. While this claim is not entirely true, it points to the value of reading and understanding tables.

Title

First, students should read the title of the table. Often, readers dive directly into the body of the table, bypassing the title. This can be a mistake. Among the things the title of a table can inform us about are

1. the content of the table,
2. the names and types of variables included,
3. the time frame for the data presented, and
4. the form in which the data are presented.

By reading the title of Table 1.1, we learn that the table is about decreased civil liberties to combat terrorism and the data are derived from a public opinion survey. The title also tells us that the dependent variable in the table (i.e., the variable that is changed) reflects the percentage of people who believe decreased civil liberties are necessary to combat terrorism. The independent variable (i.e., the variable that precipitates any change we see in the dependent variable) is the year in which people were asked the question. In addition, we can learn from this title that the data represent the results of surveys conducted between 1996 and 2007.

The title of Table 1.1 has provided us with five pieces of important information before we have looked at the actual data. Knowing this information guides us in reading the content of the table and forming statements about the content. For instance, we know before looking further that we will probably discover information about the relationship (if any) between public opinion about decreased civil liberties and the year in which people were surveyed.

TABLE 1.1 Respondents reporting whether they think it will be necessary to give up some civil liberties to curb terrorism in the United States

United States, selected years 1996–2007
Question: "In order to curb terrorism in this country, do you think it will be necessary for the average person to give up some civil liberties, or not?"

Year	Yes, It Will be Necessary (%)	No, It Will Not be Necessary (%)	Don't Know/ Refused (%)
1996	30	65	5
1997	29	62	9
Mid-September 2001	55	35	10
January 2002	55	39	6
June 2002	49	45	6
2003	44	50	6
2004[a]	38	56	6
2005[a]	40	53	7
2006	43	50	7
2007	40	54	6

Note: Sample sizes vary from year to year; the data for 2007 are based on telephone interviews with a randomly selected national sample of 2,007 adults, 18 years of age and older, conducted December 12, 2006, to January 9, 2007.
[a]In 2004 and 2005, the question was worded: "In order to curb terrorism in this country, do you think it is necessary for the average person to give up some civil liberties, or not?"

Source: Data adapted from "Trends in Political Values and Core Attitudes: 1987–2007," *Sourcebook of Criminal Justice Statistics* (Washington, DC: Pew Research Center for the People & the Press, 2007), 106.

Headnotes

Some tables present readers with headnotes, which are designed to provide information that helps clarify the data or variables in the table. In the case of our sample table (see Table 1.1), the headnote tells us about the range of years in which the survey was administered (between 1996 and 2007). It also tells us the specific question that was asked in the survey: "In order to curb terrorism in this country, do you think it will be necessary for the average person to give up some civil liberties, or not?" This information will be very useful when we try to interpret the data. Knowing the years in which the survey was administered will allow us to assess how public opinion has changed over time, particularly in regard to historic events that occurred during this period, such as the 9/11 attack, the war in Iraq, and the 2004 presidential election. The headnote for Table 1.1 also tells us that the survey was administered in the United States.

Footnotes

Footnotes clarify the uses of terms, categories, and atypical or unusual aspects of a table. Sometimes, a footnote will be used to explain a whole column or row of data. In Table 1.1, there are two footnotes. The first advises readers that the sample sizes vary by year and that the most recent survey was administered by phone. While this provides some information, it leaves some questions unanswered. For example, is the reader to assume that previous administrations of the survey were done in face-to-face interviews or via pencil-and-paper methods? Was the previous sample much larger or smaller than the 2,007 respondents noted in 2007?

The second footnote explains an irregularity in the survey used, as the form of the question changed in 2004 and 2005. Specifically, the original question was changed from future tense ("In order to curb terrorism in this country, do you think it *will be* necessary for the average person to give up some civil liberties, or not?") to present tense ("In order to curb terrorism in this country, do you think it *is* necessary for the average person to give up some civil liberties, or not?") (emphasis added). The question returned to its original form (future tense) in 2006.

While a change in verb tense may not appear to be a critical point, the change was deliberately made, probably for good reason. Arguably, the present tense used in 2004 and 2005 reflects a timely issue: the pending expiration of the 2001 Patriot Act. Thus, the present tense of the question in these years hints at a possible change in policy in 2004. Stated another way, the wording of the 2004 and 2005 question asks, "We may have needed to decrease civil liberties to combat terrorism *before,* but do we still need to do so *today?*" Keep in mind with this and other examples that altered wording of a question generally has far deeper meaning than simple semantics. Such changes are clues for trends and explanations in the data; thus, it is often best to read the footnotes before examining the content of the table.

Source

What is the source of the data for the table? What do we know about the reliability of the data? Is the source reputable? In the case of our example (Table 1.1), the table was taken from a recognized, official source of criminal justice data, the *Sourcebook of Criminal Justice Statistics*, under the auspices of the Bureau of Justice Statistics (BJS). Although the table was compiled by members of the *Sourcebook* staff, the original source of the specific data was the Pew Research Center for the People & the Press. All of these sources, the *Sourcebook*, BJS, and the Pew Center, have an excellent reputation for accuracy and reliability. However, since the table was compiled by Sourcebook staff (i.e., the data did not exist in this form in the materials published by the Pew Center), it is possible that an error could have been made: Were the data correctly produced? Were the numbers for the data correctly reproduced? Were the numbers for the columns or rows transposed? Even if the staff members who compiled the data and constructed the table were entirely accurate, could a mistake have been made by the typesetter? How do you know that what is being presented is accurate?

In most instances, these types of errors are unlikely to get by the individuals responsible for proofreading the materials, but sometimes errors are missed. For example, as you read this text, you may discover a few typographical errors. They are inevitable, given the process that writing goes through before ending up as a publication. This is also true for tables. Regardless of the number of times a passage is proofread, it is possible that an error will be made and go undetected and that some of the data in a table will be incorrect.

Therefore, before you can take the data in the table at face value, you need to assess the quality of the source. Generally, the more reputable the source, the more reliable the content and presentation of data. Evaluating the credibility of a source is similar to seeking a doctor to treat an ailment. You would be more likely to use the services of someone who came highly recommended by people you trust. You would also be more likely to use the services of someone who had a list of established, verifiable credentials. You would be less likely to put your faith in someone who had only recently arrived in town, had no references, and had credentials that could not be verified. The same is true with sources of data. The reliability of the information tends to increase with the credibility of the source. Therefore, knowing the source of the data is helpful in assessing the accuracy of the information.

It is not always possible to determine the data source from the information provided in the table. Sometimes, you need to read the text of the research to ascertain the source. If the source is an original collection of data, you should consider who collected the data and under what conditions the data were collected. If the answer is three high school students who were hired because they live in the researcher's neighborhood—not because of any data-collection experience—this should be a reason to pause and raise questions about the credibility of the data. If, however, the source is three college students who were specifically trained and supervised by a researcher with extensive data-collection experience, the confidence in the data should certainly increase. Similarly, if the source is a research scholar who is an expert in a given field, and the table appears in an article published in a highly regarded, refereed professional journal, confidence in the data would increase all the more.

Knowing the source helps readers have faith in data and interpret them with greater confidence.

Column Heads and Table Body

Once we have received the title, headnotes, and footnotes of a table, it is helpful to review the rest of the table to see how much information is actually contained within it. The table column heads show that subjects were allowed three possible responses about the need to reduce civil liberties to combat terrorism: "Yes, it will be necessary," "No, it will not be necessary," and "Don't know/refused." Note that subjects were not free to answer the question in their own words; they were restricted to these three responses. The columns provide the percentage of people who selected each of the three responses. The rows provide years in which the survey was administered. Reading the rows, you will see that the data is presented annually, with one glaring exception: the period around the 9/11 attacks. Note that the survey was administered in 1996 and 1997, but not in 1998, 1999, or 2000. Most likely, this survey was initiated after another noteworthy terrorist event, and the survey was "retired" in 1997, when fewer than one-third of all respondents thought that reduced civil liberties were necessary to combat terrorism. After 9/11, the survey was administered in three 6-month intervals, then annually thereafter.

Within the body of the table, we find from the first entry in 1996 that 30% of respondents thought that reduced civil liberties would be necessary to combat terrorism, whereas 65% of respondents thought it would not be necessary. These numbers dropped to 29% and 62%, respectively, the following year. Following 9/11, these numbers changed dramatically, with 55% of respondents believing that reduced civil liberties were necessary (survey administered within days of 9/11) and only 35% believing that it was not necessary. In the following years, these numbers gradually moved toward their 1997 point, where fewer people believe that reduced civil liberties are necessary and more than half believe that it is not necessary.

The last anomaly or "bump" in the data occurs in 2004, the year of a presidential election and also the year in which the Patriot Act was reconsidered. Note that in this year, few people believed that reduced civil liberties were necessary to combat terrorism.

These findings could cause the reader to consider several related issues:

1. Do public opinions on such issues generally change so dramatically in election years?
2. Do public opinions on such issues generally spike with a noteworthy event such as this? If so, how long does it take to return to pre-event levels?
3. Are the public opinions reported here driven by political party affiliation?
4. Are pubic opinions such as these changed only with domestic events, or would we see a similar spike corresponding to a noteworthy foreign event?
5. What would respondents of other nations have reported during the same period?

Given the limited information in this table, it is not possible to answer these questions. Instead, the information in the table would help us formulate the questions we might use in future research.

THE RESEARCH PROCESS/SCIENTIFIC METHOD

Knowing how to read tables is one method that assists readers in evaluating research, but it is not the only helpful tool available. In addition to table reading, a working knowledge of the typical steps involved in the research process is beneficial, as it not only allows you to evaluate existing research but also introduces you, as a potential researcher, to the skills necessary to develop a research project of your own.

Regardless of how individual writers diagram the research process, the basic elements are usually the same. Very simply, a problem or question is identified, and a methodology is selected or developed to attempt to answer the question. The goal of using the scientific method to engage in the research process is to establish a set of standards by which the research can be judged and interpreted.

The Research Wheel

Some writers have presented the writing process as a wheel or circle, with no specific beginning or end (see Figure 1.1). The elements of the research process are parts of the circumference of the wheel, and even though they appear in a particular order, you can begin almost anywhere on the wheel with the research process. Typically, the research process begins with the selection of a problem and the development of research questions or hypotheses (Babbie, 2007; Bachman & Schutt, 2007). It is possible that the results of previous research may generate new research questions and hypotheses for the consumer of the research. This suggests that research is a cyclical, vibrant, and continuous process. When the researcher answers one question, the result is often the generation of additional or new questions, which plunges the researcher right back into their process of answering questions.

IDENTIFYING RESEARCH QUESTIONS/PROBLEMS: THE IDEA STAGE The first step in the research process is usually the identification of a problem or question that the researcher is interested in studying. Research questions can arise from a wide variety of sources:

1. They can be generated by the findings of an existing study.
2. They can be questions that a government or private agency needs to have answered.
3. They can be the result of intellectual curiosity.
4. They can result from observations of the phenomenon in its natural state.

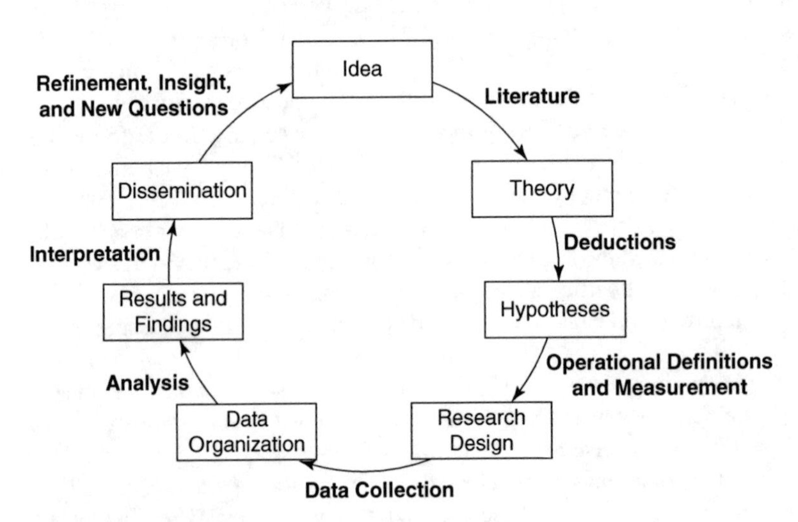

FIGURE 1.1 The Research Wheel

Often, when an existing research study is completed, more new research questions are raised than answered.

ASSESSING THE LITERATURE: THE THEORY STAGE Once the researcher has identified a particular problem or question, the next step in the research process is to assess the current state of literature related to the problem or question. The researcher will often engage in a considerable amount of library work to ascertain what the existing literature, if any is available, has to say about the subject. Has the subject already been studied to the point that the questions in which the researcher is interested have been sufficiently answered? If so, can the researcher approach the subject from a previously untested or unexamined perspective? Sometimes, research questions have been previously explored but not brought to closure. If this is the case, it may be appropriate to examine the question again. It even may be appropriate to replicate the previous study to assess whether the findings reported are due to some unrelated factor and whether the findings are applicable today.

FORMULATING HYPOTHESES: THE HYPOTHESIS STAGE After the researcher has determined that the research problem or question is appropriate for study, the next issue is directly related to the formulation of hypotheses. A hypothesis is "a specified testable expectation about empirical reality" (Babbie, 2007, p. 44) "involving a relationship between two or more variables" (Bachman & Schutt, 2001, p. 45). One of the most difficult problems faced by the researcher, especially one new to the research endeavor, is identifying a manageable research question. Often, the focus of research questions has to be narrowed so that they can be studied before hypotheses can be formulated. Also, after brainstorming, research questions can contain many subquestions that would be legitimate for study. The researcher needs to decide which questions to study first. A review of the existing literature on the subject can often shed light in this area. Once this has been established, hypotheses can be formulated for study.

Formulating hypotheses generally involves three steps: stating the research question, the null hypothesis, and the research hypothesis. First, the research question must be clearly stated; for example, *does drug treatment reduce recidivism for addict-offenders?* Second, the status quo of the question must be stated in the affirmative for the entire population to which your research could apply. In other words, before you do any research to demonstrate otherwise, what is the most accepted belief about this issue? This is the null hypothesis, or a statement that supports the truth of the status quo in the population. The null hypothesis for our research question above is as follows: *drug treatment does not impact recidivism for addict-offenders.* This statement predicts no relationship between the independent variable (drug treatment) and dependent variable (recidivism) in the population. This is the statement we must *dis*prove in our research, using a sample drawn from the population.

One important aspect of the null hypothesis is that it is "the truth" in the entire population. But, how can we ever know the truth about the entire population? How can we either prove or *dis*prove the null hypothesis if it applies to the entire population? Obviously, we cannot.

This leads to the third step: developing the research hypothesis. The research hypothesis is a predictive statement that contradicts the null hypothesis, but it can be tested on a sample of participants selected from the population. The research hypothesis can take two forms: nondirectional or directional research hypothesis. A nondirectional research hypothesis predicts a relationship between the independent and dependent variables, but it does not specify the direction of the relationship. The nondirectional research hypothesis in our example is as follows: *drug treatment does impact recidivism for addict-offenders.* If this were our research hypothesis, we would examine the possibility that treatment would impact (either reduce or increase) recidivism. Alternately, we could specify a directional research hypothesis if we can predict the nature of the relationship between the independent and dependent variables. For example, the directional research hypothesis would be as follows: *drug treatment reduces recidivism for addict-offenders.* The research hypothesis would be tested on a sample drawn from the population to *dis*prove the null hypothesis.

In addition to formulating hypotheses, this phase of the research process requires the researcher to define terms and concepts. The definitions of terms and concepts must allow the researcher to *operationalize* them for study. In this sense, the term *operationalize* means to define the term or concept so that it can be tested or measured. If a term or concept is defined in a manner that does not allow its operationalization, it cannot be tested, examined, or disproved.

Criticism regarding operationalization has been leveled at various theories in the social sciences. For instance, Edwin H. Sutherland's (1947) work on differential association has been criticized because Sutherland did not fully define or explain some of his concepts. In one of the nine propositions of his theory of criminal behavior, Sutherland posits that an individual needs an excess of definitions favorable to commission of a crime in order to become a criminal. While this seems logical on the surface, at no time does Sutherland specify what he means by *excess*. Is this 1, 20, or some ratio of unfavorable to favorable definitions promoting criminal behavior? Thus, researchers have expressed considerable consternation when they have tried to test his theory.

DEVELOPING THE RESEARCH PLAN: THE DESIGN STAGE After the research questions have been identified and supported with the existing literature, the hypothesis created, and the key concepts and terms defined, it is appropriate to move to the next component of the research process: development of the research design. In this phase, two specific questions are answered:

1. How will the variables of the study be measured?
2. What group or sample will be studied?

The variables for a research study usually include independent, dependent, and control variables. Research often examines "the effect of an independent variable on a dependent variable" (Babbie, 2007, p. 222). The *dependent variable* is the variable "we wish to explain" (Bailey, 1982, p. 47) or "predict" (Hagan, 1993, p. 15). It is also called the outcome variable. For instance, we may be interested in understanding why crime is higher in one particular community than in another, why certain people choose policing as a career, or why people vote for certain criminal justice ballot initiatives. In these examples, the dependent variables are crime, decision to become a police officer, and election results, respectively. The *independent variable* is the "variable that is hypothesized to cause, or lead to, variation in another (the dependent) variable" (Bachman & Schutt, 2007, p. 45). It is the variable that is independent to vary; in many research endeavors, this is the treatment variable or the intervention we use in order to observe some change in the dependent variable. Independent variables in the previous examples include community type (urban or suburban), personality traits (rule-oriented or high need for stimulation), and political party (Republican or Democrat). A *control variable,* sometimes called a *test variable,* is a third variable "that is held constant in an attempt to clarify further the relationship between two other variables" (Babbie, 2007, p. G11). For example, economic status may play a role in the three examples mentioned above; it is important to hold economic status constant to determine the relative effect of our independent variables (community type, personality traits, and political party) on our dependent variables (crime rate, policing career, and election results).

At the same time the variables are identified and operationalized, the specific technique or methodology for answering the questions is determined. The methodological technique should be driven by the type of research question asked. Certain types of questions are best answered by using quantitative strategies, such as a survey of a large number of individuals. Quantitative strategies generally rely on numbers to explain a phenomenon. For example, the study *Monitoring the Future* examines the drug and alcohol attitudes and behavior of adolescents over time; since the questions remain virtually the same, and we want to track changes over time, an annual survey of 8th-, 10th-, and 12th-grade students in the United States is an appropriate quantitative methodology to employ (Johnston et al., 2008).

Other research questions are best answered by employing qualitative methods, which generally rely on words or descriptive accounts to describe the phenomenon in question. Qualitative methodologies are also used when the subject of research is relatively new and the researcher wants to better understand the phenomenon before developing some quantitative measure. Examples include a case study of a single individual, such as the many treatises on serial killers published in the last three decades, or participation of a researcher in some activity under study, such as law enforcement literature that develops typologies of police during academy training from the perspective of a researcher going through the academy as a police cadet (Prokos & Padavic, 2002).

In many instances, a combination of quantitative and qualitative techniques is appropriate. (Methodologies are discussed in detail in Chapter 4.) The use of multiple methodologies is often referred to as *triangulation*. Simply put, triangulation is the "use of multiple methods to study one research question" (Bachman & Schutt, 2007, p. 352). The advantage of triangulation is that it "compared different interviews and perceptions of the same subject or behavior" across locations and time (Dooley, 2001, p. 249). (See Chapter 5 for additional information on triangulation.) The best method for answering the research questions should drive the selection of a methodological technique.

The second component in developing a research design is selecting the population from which the sample to be studied will be selected. How many people should be included, and what specific characteristics or minimum qualifying characteristics should they have? A variety of methods are available for selecting the group, or sample. Two general methods are random or purposive. (These two general methods are discussed at length in Chapter 5.)

COLLECTING AND ORGANIZING DATA: THE DATA ORGANIZATION STAGE The next phase in research involves the collection of data. If a survey instrument is being used, it would be field tested with a pilot group to assess the reliability (how consistent the results are in repeated administrations) and validity (how accurate it is in measuring what it is supposed to measure) of the instrument. These concepts are best illustrated using the example of a breathalyzer device. Suppose a 200-pound male subject has consumed four alcoholic drinks during a two-hour period. In repeated testings, a breathalyzer consistently shows a blood alcohol level of 1.2. This would be considered a *reliable* breathalyzer instrument. However, if the instrument continues to show a 1.2 blood alcohol level eight hours after the subject stopped drinking, the instrument would not be considered *valid*. In research, it is important that our instrument be pilot tested and demonstrated to be both reliable and valid. Once the survey instrument has been assessed to be reliable and valid, it can be used to gather data from the sample under study.

ANALYZING DATA: THE RESULTS AND FINDINGS STAGE After the data have been collected, the next phase of the research process requires coding and analyzing the data. At this point, various appropriate analysis techniques can be applied. For quantitative data, statistical techniques are most often used. For qualitative data, various methods of interpretive analysis, including thematic content analysis (Berg, 2007) or specialized software to analyze words along themes, such as Nudist and Atlas/ti (Barry, 1998), are generally employed. (See Chapter 3 for more detail.)

REPORTING AND INTERPRETING RESULTS: THE DISSEMINATION STAGE The final phase of the research process involves reporting and interpreting the results of the study. At this stage, the results are reported and an assessment is made regarding the support or lack of support for the research hypotheses tested. It is also at this stage that the researcher can posit additional research questions that may now need to be answered as a result of the research process. These revised questions often include some assessment of alternate research methodologies that may be more appropriate to study the phenomenon in question. Should that be the case, the research process can begin again.

Value-Free Research

One key element of the scientific research process is that it should be as void of personal biases or values as possible. Since every individual has preconceived notions of what causes behavior and events to take place, it is necessary that the research process neutralizes, as much as possible, the personal biases or values of the researcher.

In the natural, or "hard," sciences, the researcher often studies nonhuman subjects. In the social sciences, the subjects are often human, whether individuals or groups. At times, the researcher may be a member of the group under study, such as in the previous example of police academy training documented by researcher Prokos (2002), a police cadet who reports on gendered instruction during academy training. At other times, the researcher will not be a member of the group but will interact with the group. This is especially true if the researcher is using a participant observation method, which involves active participation of the researcher. An example of such research would include Humphreys *Tea Room Trade,* wherein the researcher acted as a lookout for men engaged in anonymous sex in public restrooms in the late 1960s (Humphreys, 1970). The researcher who is collecting data through administering a survey may not be actively involved in the subject of study, such as a researcher evaluating drug treatment services in a substance abuse program. In this case, however, he or she can still have some involvement with the research subjects as they interact and discuss the types of services they receive in drug treatment and their satisfaction with the overall experience, as in the case of the specialized court evaluations conducted by Deschenes and colleagues (see, for example, Cresswell & Deschenes, 2001).

While all of these are acceptable methods by which to gather data, the varying levels of intimacy involved in these contacts can have an influence on collecting data, interpreting results, and reporting conclusions. As the interactions between researcher and subject increase in frequency, duration, and intimacy, personal biases may become an issue. Some researchers have coined the term *going native* to illustrate the problem of losing one's objectivity after becoming too enmeshed with the research subject (Fuller, 1999; Kanuha, 2000). One way to reduce the impact of personal biases is to identify them at the onset of research and take regular inventory of any drift resulting from the study. When researchers acknowledge their biases and are cognizant of their values, they are more likely to prevent them from influencing the results of their research. This acknowledgement also benefits consumers of research, who are allowed to place the results in an appropriate context when they are told of researchers' biases and values.

The scientific method borrowed from the natural, or "hard," sciences, provides the social scientist with a vehicle relatively free of personal biases and values. In purest form, the physical sciences offer a model for the social sciences that incorporates elements of ethical neutrality and objectivity. In a classic article on the application of scientific techniques in social sciences, Bierstedt (1957) argues that objectivity "means that the conclusions arrived at as a result of inquiry and investigation are independent of the race, color, creed, occupation, nationality, religion, moral preferences, and political predispositions of the investigator" (p. 17). With regard to ethical neutrality, he states further, "(t)he scientist . . . does not take sides on issues of moral or ethical significance. . . . The scientist . . . has no ethical, religious, political, literary, philosophical, moral, or marital preferences. . . . As a scientist he is interested not in what is right or wrong or good or evil, but only in what is true or false (p. 10). In summary, Bierstedt argues that scientific researchers must detach themselves from their personal moral views and report only the objective reality of the phenomenon under study. The researcher is to report the facts, no matter how they turn out, and irrespective of his or her personal beliefs. This is a high standard to which scholarly researchers must aspire.

In addition to the elements of objectivity and ethical neutrality, relativism, skepticism, and parsimony are important to the scientific method. Fitzgerald and Cox (1987) argue that "relativism refers to the fact that scientists not consider their conclusions as permanent. . . . Instead, they assume their conclusions are tentative and limited" (p. 22). With regard to skepticism, Fitzgerald and Cox refer to the researcher's willingness to question almost everything, "especially common sense and common knowledge, accepting little at face value and looking beneath the surface in an attempt to determine for themselves the validity of an argument or conclusion" (p. 22). This is especially important in criminological and criminal justice research, where "common knowledge" about addition and rehabilitation has reversed itself multiple times in the preceding 25 years, thanks in part to the work of Martinson (1974), discussed in Chapter 2.

The last element of the scientific method discussed here is that of parsimony. The concept of parsimony means that the best theory about any phenomenon should involve the smallest number of variables to state the issue succinctly (Dooley, 2001). Simply put, parsimony means "short and sweet." As Fitzgerald and Cox argue (1987, p. 23), "Parsimony . . . holds that the numerous alternative explanations of a particular phenomenon should be reduced to the smallest number possible." Together, these elements of the scientific method help the researcher avoid value-laden and biased explanations with a neutral and succinct theory.

Value-Neutral Research and the Role of the Researcher

Some individuals consider it impossible for a researcher to be value free. Questions can be raised about the ethical behavior of researchers to the extent that, as human beings, they have values. Becker (1967), in his presidential speech to the Society of Social Problems (now a classic article titled "Whose Side Are We On?"), posits that it is impossible for researchers to engage in *value-neutral* or *value-free* research, which is "uncontaminated by personal and political sympathies" (p. 239).

Given this, Becker suggests that researchers should identify, as much as possible, their own personal and political beliefs so that these issues can be documented when research results are published. In closing his speech, he suggests that researchers should declare whose side they are on. By this, he means that researchers should say, "for instance, that we have studied the prison through the eyes of the inmates and not through the eyes of the guards . . . we warn people, thus, that our study tells us only how things look from that vantage point" (p. 247).

While this may be true, the scientific method at least points the social scientist in the right direction.

INDUCTIVE AND DEDUCTIVE REASONING

Some scholars debate where one should start in the research process. This issue concerns the methods of induction and deduction. Consider that some research "begins with a theory implying that certain data should be found" (Bachman & Schutt, 2007, p. 43) before any data are collected. This "a priori assumption (before-the-fact reasoning), wherein a theoretical idea precedes any attempt to collect facts" (Hagan, 1993, p. 16), is a deductive reasoning technique. In this case, the research is based on a theory or hypothesis, and the data are then collected and the results generalized to a larger population. Deductive reasoning moves from broad theory to specific prediction. An example of this kind of reasoning occurs when investigators consider the husband an initial suspect in his wife's murder. Nothing specific at the crime scene may point directly to the husband, except for the general theory that the most common homicide perpetrators are those closest to the victim; thus, it makes sense to consider the spouse from a deductive perspective.

Alternately, when the reasoning begins with an "a posteriori assumption (after-the-fact reasoning)" (Hagan, 1993, p. 16), the researcher is engaging in inductive reasoning. In this latter case, the facts are used to develop a theoretical explanation. Inductive reasoning moves from specific observation to board theory or generalization. For example, an investigator may observe that, in most of the homicide cases he or she investigates, the perpetrator had an intimate relationship with the victim; he or she then articulates a theory, based on inductive logic, that spouses are likely suspects in future homicide cases. When a researcher begins with a theory about behavior, formulates a research strategy, and then collects the data to test the theory (such as looking first at the husband in a woman's homicide), he or she is using deduction. When the researcher starts with a set of findings or results from a study and attempts to generate a theoretical explanation from the results (such as observing and then generalizing from crime scene investigation that most homicide offenders are intimate with their victims), he or she is engaging in induction. Both approaches are useful to the research process and can provide beneficial results.

RESPONSIBILITIES TO SUBJECTS, COLLEAGUES, AND THE COMMUNITY

When a social scientist undertakes a research project, questions are raised about the responsibility of the scientist to the subjects of the study, the scientist's colleagues, and the community at large as opposed to the subject of science itself. There have been significant changes in the laws governing the activity of research, especially as it relates to the use of live subjects, both human and nonhuman.

To maintain academic and research integrity, many professional organizations have established codes of ethics for researchers to provide them with sets of guidelines that include integrity in reporting results of research. In the discipline of criminology and criminal justice alone, researchers are guided by a handful of guidelines for the protection of human subjects, including the National Commission for the Protection of Human Subjects of Biomedical and Behavioral Research (1998), also called the "Belmont Report"; the United States Code of Federal Regulations (28 CFR 46 for Criminal Justice Research); The American Psychological Association's "Ethical Principles of Psychologists and Code of Conduct" (2002); and internal guidelines that govern research ethics specific to each university. In some instances, research also requires the approval of state-level IRBs and may need additional protections afforded with a U.S. "Certificate of Confidentiality," which provides subpoena protection in certain types of research. Such guidelines are especially important for the colleagues of researchers who rely on the academic integrity of others for purposes of their own research. The responsibilities of the researcher have been broadened even further to include the community at large, who often take the findings of research at face value. These issues are addressed in Chapter 2.

References

American Psychological Association. (2002). *Ethical principles of psychologists and code of conduct.* Retrieved October 1, 2008, from http://www.apa.org/ethics/code2002.html

Babbie, E. (2007). *The practice of social research* (11th ed.). Belmont, CA.: Thomson/Wadsworth.

Bachman, R., & Schutt, R. K. (2001). *The practice of research in criminology and criminal justice*. Thousand Oaks, CA: Pine Forge Press.

Bachman, R., & Schutt, R. K. (2007). *The practice of research in criminology and criminal justice* (3rd ed.). Thousand Oaks, CA: Sage Publications.

Bailey, K. D. (1982). *Methods of social research* (2nd ed.). New York: Free Press.

Barry, C. A. (1998). Choosing qualitative data analysis software: Atlas/ti and Nudist compared. Retrieved on November 5, 2008, from *Sociological Research Online, 3*(3), http://www.socresonline.org.uk/socresonline/3/3/4.html

Becker, H. S. (1967, Winter). Whose side are we on? *Social Problems, 14*, 239–247.

Berg, B. L. (2007). *Qualitative research methods for the social sciences* (6th ed). Boston: Allyn & Bacon.

Bierstedt, R. (1957). *The social order.* New York: McGraw-Hill.

Bureau of Justice Statistics. (2006). *Sourcebook of Criminal Justice Statistics*, Retrieved October 20, 2008, from http://www.albany.edu/sourcebook/pdf/t2162006.pdf

Committee for the Protection of Human Subjects. *State-level institutional review board.* Retrieved October 7, 2008, from http://www.oshpd.ca.gov/Boards/CPHS/committee_members.html

Creswell, L. S., & Deschenes, E. P. (2001). Minority and non-minority perceptions of drug court program severity and effectiveness. *Journal of Drug Issues, 31*(1), 259–292.

Department of Health, Education, and Welfare. (1979, 1998 update). The National Commission for the Protection of Human Subjects of Biomedical and Behavioral Research. *The Belmont Report.* Retrieved on October 7, 2008, from http://www.faculty.virginia.edu/capstone/docs/IRB-Belmont-Report-FDA-1998.pdf

Dooley, D. (2001). *Social research methods* (4th ed.). Upper Saddle River, NJ: Prentice Hall.

Fitzgerald, J. D., & Cox, S. M. (1987). *Research methods in criminal justice.* Chicago: Nelson-Hall.

Fuller, D. (1999). Part of the action, or 'going native'? Learning to cope with the 'politics of integration'. *Area, 31*(3), 221–227.

Hagan, F. E. (1993). *Research methods in criminal justice and criminology* (3rd ed.). New York: Macmillan.

Humphreys, L. (1970). *Tearoom trade.* Chicago: Aldine.

Johnston, L. D., O'Malley, P. M., Bachman, J. G., & Schulenberg, J. E. (2008). *Monitoring the future national results on adolescent drug use: Overview of key findings, 2007* (NIH Publication No. 07-6202). Bethesda, MD: National Institute on Drug Abuse.

Kanuha, V. K. (2000). Being native versus going native: Conducting social work research as an insider. *Social Work, 45*(5), 439–447.

Martinson, R. (1974). What works? Questions and answers about prison reform. *Public Interest New York, 35*, 22–54.

Miller, D. C. (1991). *Handbook of research design and social measurement* (5th ed.). Newbury Park, CA: Sage.

Prokos, A., & Padavic, I. (2002). There oughtta be a law against bitches: Masculinity lessons in police academy training. *Gender, Work and Organization, 9*(4), 439–459.

Sutherland, E. H. (1947). *Principals of criminology* (4th ed.). Philadelphia, PA: Lippincott.

United States Code of Federal Regulations. (2008). *Criminal justice information systems. 28 CFR 46.* Retrieved October 16, 2008, from http://www.access.gpo.gov/nara/cfr/waisidx_00/28cfr46_00.html

U.S. Department of Health and Human Services. *Certificates of confidentiality kiosk.* National Institute of Health: Office of Extramural Research. Retrieved October 15, 2008, from: http://grants.nih.gov/grants/policy/coc/

Exercise 1.1 Table Reading

Citizen complaint dispositions in large law enforcement agencies[a]

Type of Agency	Total with Disposition	Complaint Dispositions				
		Not Sustained	Unfounded	Exonerated	Sustained	Other Disposition
Total (%)	94	34	25	23	8	9
Local agencies	94	35	26	23	8	9
Municipal police	94	37	25	21	8	9
Sheriffs' offices	95	20	30	32	12	6
County police	93	25	17	35	6	17
Primary state police agencies	95	16	19	52	9	4
Full-time sworn officers						
Total	94	34	25	23	8	9
1,000 or more officers	93	42	23	19	6	10
500–999 officers	96	21	26	28	14	12
100–249 officers	97	22	31	34	10	3

[a]By type of agency and number of full-time sworn officers, United States, 2002.
Source: U.S. Department of Justice, Bureau of Justice Statistics. (2006, June). *Citizen complaints about police use of force, Special Report NCJ 210296.* Washington, DC: U.S. Department of Justice, p. 3. Table adapted by *Sourcebook of Criminal Justice Statistics* staff.

The table above is typical of those published in the *Sourcebook of Criminal Justice Statistics*. Using the data from the table above, and referencing the example from Chapter 1, answer the following questions.

Application Exercise 1.1

Name of Student:________________

Student ID No.:________________

Course/Section No.:________________

Date:________________

1. Read the title and headnotes for the table in Exercise 1.1. With just this information, what independent (predictor) and dependent (outcome) variables are shown in this table?

2. Looking only at the title and headnotes, what possible relationship between these variables might you expect?

3. What does the source information tell you, and do you feel confident on the quality and accuracy of these data? Why or why not?

4. Now look at the body of the table. What are the column heads?

5. Do these column heads reflect the independent or dependent variable in this table?

6. What are the row heads?

7. Do these row heads reflect the independent or dependent variable in this table?

8. What general trend do you see in this table? Are there any irregularities in this trend?

9. Which type of agency has the largest percentage of sustained citizen complaints against police officers? What percentage of sustained complaints are found in this type of agency?

10. Which type of agency has the largest percentage of citizen complaints ending in police exoneration? What percentage of complaints in this type of agency end in exoneration?

11. If you could design a follow-up study, what additional variables would interest you in further examining the relationship between type of agency and citizen complaints?

Exercise 1.2 Table Reading and Typology Construction

Bureau of Justice Statistics Special Report

Census of Publicly Funded Forensic Crime Laboratories, 2005

Matthew R. Derose, BJS Statistician

In 2005, the nation's forensic crime laboratories received evidence from an estimated 2.7 million criminal investigations. These cases included requests for a variety of forensic services, such as DNA analysis, controlled-substance identification, and latent fingerprint examination. A case not completed within 30 days was classified as backlogged. An estimated 359,000 cases were backlogged at the end of 2005—a 24% increase from the estimated 287,000 cases backlogged at year-end 2002. Other major findings on publicly funded forensic crime laboratories in 2005 included the following:

- Controlled-substance identification accounted for about half of all requests backlogged at year-end.
- DNA testing was performed by about half of the laboratories.
- About half of the public laboratories outsourced one or more types of forensic services to private laboratories.
- Eight in 10 laboratories were accredited by the American Society of Crime Laboratory Directors/Laboratory Accreditation Board.

These findings are based on data from the Bureau of Justice Statistics' (BJS) Census of Publicly Funded Forensic Crime Laboratories. Forensic crime laboratories are responsible for examining and reporting on physical evidence collected during criminal investigations for federal, state, and local jurisdictions. This report provides a comprehensive look at forensic services across the nation and the resources devoted to completing the work.

THE COMBINED ANNUAL BUDGET FOR ALL LABORATORIES EXCEEDED $1 BILLION

The 2005 census obtained budget data from 254 laboratories. The median budget among these laboratories was $1.7 million. The FBI laboratory had an annual budget of more than $130 million. The estimated budget for all 389 crime laboratories in 2005 exceeded $1 billion, nearly half of which was funded by state laboratories (Table 1.2).

Personnel costs, including salaries and fringe benefits, typically accounted for three-quarters of a laboratory's total budget. Median base annual salaries for laboratory directors ranged from $62,900 to $94,700, and for supervisors from $51,000 to $77,000 (Table 1.3). Analysts or examiners at both the state and local levels had a median maximum salary of about $70,000.

Laboratory expenditures also included supplies, equipment, and construction costs. In addition to their budgets, laboratories received funding from other sources, such as fees and grants. Twenty-eight percent of laboratories charged fees for forensic services in 2005, and nearly two-thirds (65%) received some funding from grants (not shown in Table 1.3).

CRIME LABORATORIES PROVIDED AN AVERAGE OF SIX DIFFERENT FORENSIC SERVICES

Crime laboratories are typically responsible for several analytical services. They receive evidence from criminal investigations submitted by a variety of sources, including law enforcement officials, prosecutors, and medical examiners. In 2005, laboratories provided a median number of six functions. Controlled-

TABLE 1.2 Total operating budget (in millions) for publicly funded crime laboratories in 2005 and 2002 by type of jurisdiction

Type of Jurisdiction	Total Operating Budget Reported (in Millions)		National Estimate (in Millions)[a]	
	2005	2002	2005	2002
All laboratories[b]	$821	$835	$1,155	$1,036
State	406	345	529	454
County	173	164	236	172
Municipal	94	83	130	112
Number of laboratories	254	267	389	351

Note. Budget totals were not adjusted for inflation.
[a]Based on imputations for laboratories that did not report budget data.
[b]Includes federal laboratories, not shown separately.

TABLE 1.3 Median base salaries of employees in publicly funded crime laboratories in 2005, by type of jurisdiction

Type of Position	Total*	State	County	Municipal
Director				
Maximum	$94,700	$92,500	$99,100	$89,800
Minimum	62,900	59,000	76,100	69,700
Supervisor				
Maximum	$77,000	$76,200	$84,800	$77,000
Minimum	51,000	50,100	58,600	58,000
Analyst/examiner				
Maximum	$67,700	$66,700	$71,600	$66,800
Minimum	37,800	35,400	42,300	40,700
Technical support				
Maximum	$42,200	$40,100	$45,000	$44,200
Minimum	27,400	26,400	29,800	30,700

*Includes federal laboratories, not shown separately.

TABLE 1.4 Forensic functions performed by crime laboratories in 2005, by type of jurisdiction

Forensic Function	Total (%)[a]	State (%)	County (%)	Municipal (%)
Controlled substances	89	88	94	85
Firearms/toolmarks	59	60	59	56
Biology screening	57	58	61	51
Latent prints	55	50	51	76
Trace evidence	55	57	59	44
DNA analysis	53	55	61	42
Toxicology	53	57	49	47
Impressions	52	50	53	56
Crime scene	40	36	46	56
Questioned documents	20	18	22	24
Computer crimes	12	9	16	15

Note: Detail sums to more than 100% because some laboratories reported performing more than one function. See Methodology section for definitions of individual functions.
[a]Includes federal laboratories, not shown separately.

substance identification was the analysis performed by the largest percentage (89%) of the 351 laboratories responding to the census (Table 1.4). Forensic work for computer crime investigations was the function reported to be performed by the smallest percentage of laboratories (12%).

About 6 in 10 crime laboratories examined firearms or toolmarks in 2005. Laboratories that performed this function were asked about their use of the Bureau of Alcohol, Tobacco, Firearms and Explosives' National Integrated Ballistic Information Network (NIBIN). Using this electronic system, forensic examiners can compare evidence (such as fired bullets and cartridges) from crime scenes to firearm evidence from other criminal investigations for matches (or hits). Seventy-six laboratories reported making about 95,000 NIBIN entries and searches in 2005. Almost 2,000 hits that year were reported by 56 laboratories.

More than half (55%) of crime laboratories analyzed latent (or hidden) fingerprints recovered from crime scenes. These laboratories were asked to report on their use of the FBI's Integrated Automated Fingerprint Identification System (IAFIS) in 2005. More than 100 laboratories reported making about 328,000 searches and finding 33,000 hits using IAFIS in 2005.

CRIME LABORATORIES RECEIVED AN ESTIMATED 2.7 MILLION CASES IN 2005

Laboratories have different methods for measuring workload, such as cases or requests. A *case* is defined as evidence submitted to a crime laboratory from a single criminal incident. A case may require more than one *request* for forensic services. For instance, a laboratory may receive samples of fibers and blood from the

TABLE 1.5 Cases received by publicly funded crime laboratories during 2005 and 2002, by type of jurisdiction

Type of Jurisdiction	Reported Cases Received		Cases Received by Comparable Laboratories Reporting in Both Years		National Estimate[a]	
	2005	2002	2005	2002	2005	2002
All laboratories[b]	2,106,478	2,399,468	1,654,023	1,862,009	2,712,000	2,891,000
State	1,166,786	898,642	837,154	803,545	1,302,000	1,230,000
County	495,665	798,118	466,017	555,456	727,000	847,000
Municipal	413,932	622,775	335,667	498,813	566,000	711,000
Number of laboratories	288	265	200	200	389	351

[a]Based on imputations for laboratories that did not report data on cases received.
[b]Includes federal laboratories, not shown separately.

same case that requires analysis by different discipline areas of the laboratory. This study examined workload in terms of both cases and requests.

The nation's 389 crime laboratories received an estimated 2.7 million new cases during 2005 (Table 1.5). Almost half—or 1.3 million—were submitted to state laboratories. Laboratories serving local jurisdictions received about 1.3 million cases in 2005, including 727,000 cases received by county laboratories and 566,000 by municipal laboratories. Federal laboratories received the fewest cases that year.

An estimated 359,000 cases were backlogged (not completed within 30 days) at the end of 2005, compared with 287,000 at year-end 2002 (Table 1.6). This represents a 24% increase in backlogged cases between 2002 and 2005. State laboratories accounted for more than half of the backlog in both years.

Among the 288 laboratories that reported this information, the median number of cases received in 2005 was about 4,100. Overall, laboratories ended the year with a median backlog of about 400 cases. Six percent of laboratories that received cases in 2005 reported having no backlog at year-end.

Two hundred laboratories provided data in both the 2002 and 2005 censuses on the total numbers of cases received during each year (Table 1.5). The number of cases received during 2005 (1,654,023) was less than the total received in 2002 (1,862,009). Of the 172 laboratories that reported backlog totals for the 2002 and 2005 censuses, the number of backlogged cases increased from 142,739 to 192,126 (Table 1.6).

TABLE 1.6 Cases backlogged by publicly funded crime laboratories at year-end 2005 and 2002, by type of jurisdiction

Type of Jurisdiction	Backlogged Cases Reported		Cases Backlogged in Comparable Laboratories Reporting in Both Years		National Estimate[a]	
	2005	2002	2005	2002	2005	2002
All laboratories[b]	260,821	212,676	192,126	142,739	359,000	287,000
State	166,337	117,092	126,162	90,056	203,000	155,000
County	40,314	49,954	35,859	29,555	65,000	55,000
Municipal	44,881	42,218	29,544	22,128	70,000	59,000
Number of laboratories	265	243	172	172	389	351

[a]Based on imputations for laboratories that did not report data on backlogged cases.
[b]Includes federal laboratories, not shown separately.

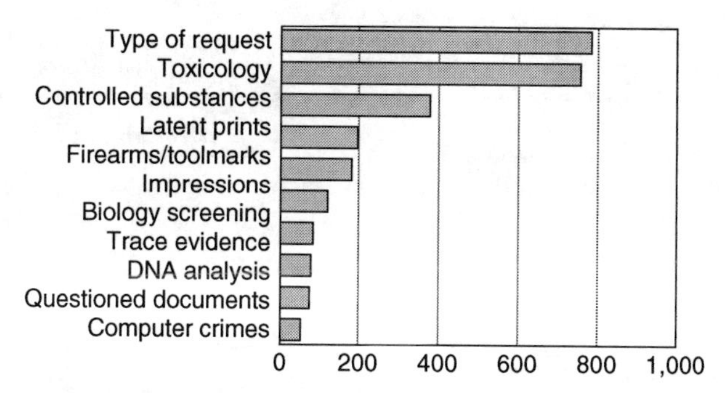

FIGURE 1.2 Mean Number of Requests Completed per Full-Time Examiner in 2005
Note: Numbers based on labs that provided complete data on request processing and employee performance. See appendix table 2 for more information.

GREATEST PERSONNEL NEED WAS DNA ANALYSTS

The ability to process a larger percentage of evidence depends on numerous factors, including the complexity of the procedures, use of innovative solutions, and availability of examiners and other resources. Overall, laboratories were able to complete about 80% of all outstanding requests in 2005. The remaining requests were backlogged at year-end. This completion rate was lower for more complex types of examinations, such as DNA analysis and biology screening.

Laboratories were asked how many full-time examiners or analysts were required to process their requests. The work of a single examiner varied depending on the type of request. DNA analyses were more time consuming and complex than the examination of controlled substances or toxicology.

A typical DNA analyst completed 77 requests in 2005 (Figure 1.2). By comparison, the average forensic examiner completed about 10 times the number of controlled-substance requests that year (752). These examiners compared drug-related evidence with standards of known origin to identify unknown substances.

ABOUT HALF OF LABORATORIES OUTSOURCED SOME FORENSIC WORK

To meet demands for forensic services, about half of the publicly funded forensic crime laboratories contracted private laboratories for at least one type of forensic service in 2005 (Table 1.7). Nearly 30% of laboratories reported outsourcing DNA casework, and 11% outsourced Combined DNA Index System (CODIS) samples.

A total of 190 laboratories provided outsourcing data for both censuses. A larger percentage of those laboratories outsourced forensic work in 2005 (54%) than in 2002 (44%).

METHODOLOGY

Data Collection

Data collection for the 2005 Census of Publicly Funded Forensic Crime Laboratories was conducted by Sam Houston State University (SHSU) for BJS. The National Forensic Science Technology Center and the American Society of Crime Laboratory Directors assisted in developing and administering the data collection instrument, which was pretested with 17 laboratories.

TABLE 1.7 Percentage of publicly funded crime laboratories outsourcing requests for forensic services in 2005 and 2002

	Laboratories Reporting (%)		Comparable Laboratories Reporting in Both Years (%)	
Type of Request	**2005**	**2002**	**2005**	**2002**
Any outsourcing	51	41	54	44
DNA casework	28	19	29	23
Toxicology	17	14	18	15
CODIS[a] samples	11	9	11	11
Controlled substances	6	4	5	5
Number of laboratories reporting	268	269	190	190

[a]Combined DNA Index System.

TABLE 1.8 Response rates for the census of publicly funded forensic crime laboratories, 2005 and 2002

Type of Jurisdiction	Number of Laboratories in Census		Laboratories Reporting to Census			
			Number		Percentage	
	2005	2002	2005	2002	2005	2002
All laboratories	389	351	351	306	90	87
State	210	198	207	171	99	86
County	84	67	79	62	94	93
Municipal	62	53	55	48	89	91
Federal	33	33	10	25	30	76

Note: Seventeen laboratories reported a different government affiliation in 2005 than 2002. To allow for jurisdiction-level comparisons between 2002 and 2005, the government affiliation of these laboratories was based on information from the most recent census.

In May 2006, the census form was mailed to 393 facilities that self-identified as crime laboratories. Some laboratories were part of a multiple laboratory system. The census attempted to collect information from each laboratory in the system. Four laboratories were subsequently dropped because they did not meet the project definition of a publicly funded forensic crime laboratory.

Completed forms were obtained from 291 of the 389 eligible laboratories. Follow-up telephone calls and e-mails encouraged nonresponding laboratories to participate. In a final effort to improve response, a shorter census instrument was developed to collect basic information about laboratory operations. An additional 60 laboratories responded to the short form, for a final response rate of 90% (Table 1.8). Of the 351 responses received for the 2005 census, 197 were submitted electronically and 154 were mailed or faxed.

The 389 eligible laboratories for the 2005 census included 210 state, 84 county, 62 municipal, and 33 federal laboratories. Ten federal laboratories responded to the 2005 census, compared to 25 for 2002. Because of the low response rate in 2005, summary statistics for federal laboratories were not presented in many of the tables.

Application Exercise 1.2

Name of Student:________________

Student ID No.:________________

Course/Section No.:____________

Date:________________________

1. Create a typology using the data on "Census of Publicly Funded Forensic Crime Laboratories, 2005," published by the Bureau of Justice Statistics. Your typology should inform the reader about current trends for the types of services currently provided by forensic laboratories.

2. What are some of the implications of the current trends based on these data? What future needs can you identify?

3. Given the data presented in this article, discuss implications of these data if demand for forensic analysis increases but forensic crime laboratories are funded at their current level?

Exercise 1.3 Going Native

Going native:

POTENTIAL SOURCES OF OBSERVER BIAS IN POLICE OBSERVATIONAL DATA

Richard Spano[1]

Social Science Research, Vol. 34, pp. 591–617, July 2004.

Abstract Much of our knowledge about police behavior "on the street" is based on in-person observation of the police. However, little research has examined how the observers can potentially bias observational data. In this paper, anecdotal accounts from a variety of field settings are categorized into four potential sources of observer bias. Secondary analyses of data from a large-scale observational study of police are used to assess the impact of three out of the four types of observer bias (reactivity, going native, and burnout). There is evidence of reactivity for arrest, but not use of force behavior and little support for going native and burnout. More generally, observer bias is categorized as: (1) threats to the validity of observational data collected at different stages of fieldwork; and (2) the potential for human error implicit in observational data. The incorporation of a semi-structured field diary is suggested to more systematically document all four types of observer bias in future research.

1. INTRODUCTION

Since the discovery of police discretion, researchers have recognized the potential for bias, inequities, and prejudice in the application of the law by the police (Walker, 1992). Police researchers have documented the limitations of organizational controls on police behavior "on the street" as well as the factors that influence the behavior of beat officers (Reuss-Ianni, 1993). There is also a growing appreciation for the role of field research and observational data in the study of discretionary decision-making given the limitations of other sources of information on police behavior.

Police observational data have strengthened our understanding of the determinants of police behavior by examining explanatory variables that encompass multiple units of analysis (e.g., officer and organizational characteristics) (Mastrofski and Parks, 1990). For example, police researchers have observed officer behavior during encounters with citizens and found that police behavior is strongly influenced by the structural characteristics of the situation or "situational factors" such as the nature of the problem, the characteristics and behavior of involved citizens, and the location of the encounter (Riksheim and Chermak, 1993).

In short, simply "being there" gives the researcher access to events, aspects of police behavior, and situational dynamics not recorded in police reports and arrest records (Emerson, 2002a, p. 2; Ferrell, 1998, p. 27). However, some researchers categorize field research as a "marginal methodology" that produces data of questionable quality (Denzin and Lincoln, 2000; Goodwin and Horowitz, 2002). The most serious challenge centers on the concept of observer bias. Since the observer is part of the context of observed behavior, observers can potentially "bias" or contaminate observational data and undermine its reliability and validity (Tedlock, 1991).

The purpose of this study is to identify potential sources of observer bias and to conduct a limited test of its impact on police observational data. Specific research questions will be developed utilizing concepts derived from the extant literature to operationalize three out of four types of observer bias (reactivity, culture shock, and burnout) and assess its impact on POPN observational data.

2. FOUR TYPES OF OBSERVER BIAS

2.1. Reactivity

One common criticism of observational data is that research subjects may react to the presence of an observer by changing his or her behavior. [*Note:* This section has been omitted.]

2.2. Culture Shock

Immersion into an alien environment can be an intense and unsettling experience (Emerson, 2002b). Culture shock refers to feelings of disorientation and anxiety that observers feel during the early stages of field research (see DeWalt and DeWalt, 2002, for a review). [*Note.* This section has been omitted.]

---

[1]Fax: 1-205-348-7178. E-mail address: rspano@bama.ua.edu

doi:10.1016/j.ssresearch.2004.05.003

2.3. Going Native

Gans (1982) argued that observers become sympathetic toward individuals under study for a number of reasons. One reason is that observers and research subjects work together in close quarters over the course of fieldwork. A natural consequence of the observer's task is a more sympathetic outlook toward individuals under observation. A second reason is that researchers feel a pull toward increased involvement while collecting observational data (see Adler and Adler, 1987, for an overview). Pollner and Emerson (2002) argued that research subjects could use observers as an assistant and a resource while conducting their work. This level of involvement can range from innocuous requests for observers to act as a "go-fer" to participation in more critical activities. For example, while studying drug dealers, Adler (1985) loaned drug dealers money, watched their children for extended periods of time, testified in court on their behalf, and allowed them to conduct drug deals in Adler's home. While observing police officers, Norris (1993) not only made tea for the shift, but also helped to chase and arrest suspects and administered first aid following suicide attempts. Since he did not look like a police officer, Skolnick (1966) aided police by walking into a bar to find a dangerous armed robber. Skolnick also helped some officers get past a lookout by driving a disguised truck up to a building.

A more general concern is that observing research subjects in their natural settings has the potential to resocialize the researcher. This process of resocialization has been described as "overapport" and conceptualized as the problem of "going native," since observers lose sight of their role as a researcher and, in extreme cases, begin to think of themselves as members of the group under study. Observers may become involved as participants and systematically influence the phenomenon under study (Manning, 1976; Pollner and Emerson, 2002). Reiss (1968, pp. 365–366) described one instance of observer socialization that occurred during an observational study of police. In a precinct located in a high crime area populated predominantly by African-Americans, a common practice in the stationhouse was to walk down the row of cells and flush the toilets when an inmate asked for water. One evening, an inmate asked for water and an observer imitated the officers by walking down the cellblock and flushing the toilets. On his last shift, one officer asked the observer what he learned over the summer. The observer shocked a fellow observer by replying "I learned to hate niggers." In extreme cases, observers could transfer their loyalty to research subjects, completely abandon data collection, and refuse to return from the field. Anthropologists who have gone native have stopped publishing material completely, rejected academia, and decided to live with indigenous people who were the topic of inquiry (Gronewold, 1972).

2.4. Burnout

Burnout refers to inaccurate documentation of observational data at later stages of fieldwork due to the mentally and physically demanding nature of data collection (Fine, 1993; Lofland and Lofland, 1995). [*Note:* This section has been omitted.]

3. DATA

This study utilizes POPN observational data of patrol officers collected in Indianapolis and St. Petersburg during the summers of 1996 and 1997, respectively. Shifts were selected for observation based on time of day and day of the week, but busier days (Thursday through Saturday) were oversampled to maximize the number of police–citizen encounters. Observers rode with patrol officers in 12 of Indianapolis's 50 patrol beats and 12 of St. Petersburg's 48 patrol beats. Beats in both sites were selected to capture variation in service conditions within each jurisdiction. In addition, an attempt was made to match service conditions for beats selected from St. Petersburg and Indianapolis (Mastrofski et al., 1998). Thirty-seven observers accompanied patrol officers during 729 shifts and documented a total of 2488 encounters with suspects. Observers accompanied patrol officers over the course of a shift and were trained to unobtrusively take brief field notes on their behavior.

4.1. Research Questions

4.1.2 GOING NATIVE This study will examine two research questions related to going native. First, are observers becoming socialized by officers and developing more positive attitudes toward the police over the course of fieldwork? Second, do these shifts in observer attitudes toward police (ATP) predict whether observers help police officers and/or participate in police work?

5. RESULTS

5.2. Going Native

In Table 2, the impact of going native in POPN observational data is assessed by examining: (1) shifts in observer's attitudes toward police (ATP) over the course of fieldwork and (2) the probability that an observer will participate during fieldwork by helping with police work. Panel A in Table 2 addresses the first issue by examining observer surveys ($N = 32$) that were completed before the start of fieldwork (T1—see column one) and immediately following fieldwork (T2—see column two). Observer's ATP became more positive between T1 and T2 for the first three out of four attitudinal measures, but this change is only statistically significant at the .05 level for one out of the three measures (see Panel A). For the fourth measure, there was no change in observer ATP.

TABLE 2 Assessing the impact of observer bias on police observational data: going native as a shift in observer's attitudes toward police and observer's level of participation in police work (observer effects)

	Before Fieldwork (T1)	After Fieldwork (T2)
(A) Observer's attitudes toward police (ATP): mean comparison		
Do police discriminate toward certain groups? (coded 0,1 where 1 = never or rarely)	.13	.28
Would you approve if an officer struck a citizen who was attacking the officer with his/her fists? (coded 0,1 where 1 = yes)	.84	.94
Would you approve if an officer struck a citizen attempting to escape custody? (coded 0,1 where 1 = yes)	.59**,[a]	.72
Would you approve if an officer struck a citizen who said vulgar or obscene things to the officer? (coded 0,1 where 1 = yes)	.00	.00
N (number of observers who completed both T1 and T2 observer surveys)	32	32
	Observer Effects	
	Observer Helps Police Officer[c]	Observer Helps with Police Work[d]
(B) The relationship between change in ATP[b] and observer effects: odds ratios from logistic regression		
Observers with more positive ATP (T2 > T1)	.50*,[e]	.54
Observers with no change in ATP (T2 = T1)	_f	–
Observers with more negative ATP (T2 < T1)	1.25	.69
Initial ATP (before fieldwork)	2.07**	2.46**
Model χ^2	19.3***	17.0***
N (number of shifts where observers completed both T1 and T2 observer surveys)	598	598

(A) Observer's attitudes toward police (ATP): mean comparison.
[a]Two-tailed significance level indicated by a χ^2 test of independence.
[b]Measures of change in ATP in Panel B were derived from an additive scale of the first three observer survey questions from T1 and T2 in Panel A. This more general measure of ATP at T1 and T2 ranged from zero to three. To determine if the observer's ATP became more positive (T2 > T1), stayed the same (T2 = T1), or more negative (T2 < T1), scores on this additive scale were compared as described above.
[c]Dichotomous coding derived from descriptive data on reactivity (1 = rides where the observer helps patrol officer) (see Spano, 2003 for a more detailed description).
[e]Level of statistical significance is derived from odds ratios from multivariate logistic regression.
[f]Observers with no change in ATP is the comparison group.
*$p < .1$ ** $p < .05$ ***$p < .01$

Panel B in Table 2 addresses the second issue by investigating whether observers with more positive ATP are more likely to "participate" during fieldwork by helping police officers. An additive scale was developed using the observer's first three attitudinal measures from Panel A from T1 and T2. Observer's ATP were categorized as more positive if this additive scale of ATP at T2 was greater than ATP at T1. If there was no change in ATP, then T2 and T1 ATP were equal. Finally, observer's ATPs were categorized as more negative if T2 was less than T1 ATP.

Two measures of observer participation (or observer effects) were derived from a dichotomous coding scheme derived from descriptive and quantitative data on reactivity (see Spano, 2002, 2003, for a more detailed description). Column one in Panel B contains rides where observers helped police officers in any capacity. This measure includes more mundane and innocent forms of participation (e.g., the observer tells the officer that s/he left his/her lights on or offers advice when asked about whether to pull over a vehicle) to instances when observers helped officers with police work (e.g., holding handcuffs or helping to fill out paperwork, arrest and/or detain suspects) (see column one in Panel B) (Spano, 2002). Column two in Panel B is a subset of cases from the qualitative coding in Column one where observers helped the officer with police work.

Panel B examines shifts where observers completed both T1 and T2 observer surveys ($N = 598$). Observers with more positive ATP (T2 > T1), no change in ATP (T2 = T1), and more negative ATP (T2 < T1) were regressed on the two dichotomous measures of observer effects discussed above using multivariate logistic regression after controlling for the observer's initial ATP before fieldwork. Observers with more positive ATP are about 50% less likely to help police officers (see column one in Panel B). Although this relationship is marginally significant ($p < .1$), the direction of the effect is not in the expected direction. Observers with more positive ATP are not more likely to help police officers or participate in police work, which would be consistent with going native. In fact, this finding suggests exactly the opposite.

6. IS RAPPORT A PROBLEM (GOING NATIVE) OR A SOLUTION (REACTIVITY)?

Another contradiction in the methodological field research literature relates to rapport. The development of rapport is essential to minimize reactivity to get research subjects to feel comfortable and trust observers, and to act naturally while under observation. Reactivity suggests that, for example, too little rapport between police officers and observers can cause police officers to engage in atypical behavior and thus undermine the validity of observational data collected during the early stages of fieldwork. In contrast, going native suggests the opposite: Too much rapport between observers and research subjects will affect the accuracy of data collected at later stages of fieldwork. Going native could be rationalized as a way of mitigating reactivity by establishing a high level of rapport with those being observed. However, Miller (1952) observed that friendship is based on an all-accepting outlook that can limit the depth of an observer's investigation into and criticism of the behavior of research subjects (see also Van Maanen, 1983a, 1983b). Thus, going native could limit the scope, the depth, and the accuracy of observational data.

7. SUMMARY AND CONCLUSION

Observers are a potential source of bias for two reasons. First, observers are part of the context of observed behavior. As a result, the research subject could react to the presence of the observer and behave atypically (reactivity). Second, observers are also data collection instruments. Thus, the quality of observational data could be undermined if observers become resocialized, contaminate observational data by participating in police work, and/or document inaccurate observational data (going native).

The relevance of these findings is not limited to the field of criminology and criminal justice. Ethnographers, researchers who conduct face-to-face interviews, and child development researchers who "unobtrusively" study the interactions between parents and children (to name a few) all collect and utilize observational data to further our scientific understanding of various real-world phenomenon and use of force behavior, needed to be statistically significant. Second, the direction of the relationship between measures of observer bias and the outcome measures also needed to be consistent with hypothesized effects specified as research questions for reactivity, going native, and burnout.

The analyses of POPN descriptive and quantitative data focused on observer bias (going native) and revealed key findings. One key finding is the very limited support for observer bias in the form of going native and burnout. On the surface, observers' ATP became more positive over the course of fieldwork in terms of absolute change, but the change in ATP was statistically significant for only one of four measures. In addition, findings from multivariate logistic regression were marginally significant ($p < .1$) and showed that observers whose ATP became more positive over the course of fieldwork were less likely to "participate" in the form of helping officers for one out of two measures of observer effects. In contrast, the literature and logic of going native would predict that these observers would be the most likely to participate in police work.

Future research should include additional control variables to rule out alternative explanations for patrol officer arrest and use of force behavior. To further explore the robustness of these findings, multivariate analyses should be conducted to determine if observer bias is a significant predictor of, for example, arrest and use of force behavior net of a variety of control variables (e.g., officer work orientation, suspect characteristics, and situational factors). If the significant effect is suppressed in the "full" multivariate model, then it is presumed that observer bias has not substantively affected the quality of police observational data.

References

Adler, P.A., 1985. Wheeling and Dealing. Columbia University Press, New York.

Adler, P.A., Adler, P., 1987. Membership Roles in Field Research. Sage Publications, Newbury Park, CA.

Denzin, N.K., Lincoln, Y.S., 2000. The discipline and practice of qualitative research. In: Denzin, N.K., Lincoln, Y.S. (Eds.), Handbook of Qualitative Research, second ed. Sage Publications, Thousand Oaks, CA, pp. 1–28.

DeWalt, K.M., DeWalt, B.R., 2002. Participant Observation: A Guide for Fieldworkers. AltaMira Press, New York.

Emerson, R.M., 2002a. Introduction: the development of ethnographic field research. In: Emerson, R.M. (Ed.), Contemporary Field Research: Perspectives and Formulations, second ed. Waveland Press, Prospect Heights, IL, pp. 1–26.

Emerson, R.M., 2002b. Fieldwork Practice: issues in participant observation. In: Emerson, R.M. (Ed.), Contemporary Field Research: Perspectives and Formulations, second ed. Waveland Press, Prospect Heights, IL, pp. 113–151.

Ferrell, J., 1998. Criminological verstehen: inside the immediacy of crime. In: Ferrell, J., Hamm, M.S. (Eds.), Ethnography at the Edge: Crime, Deviance, and Field Research. Northeastern University Press, Boston, pp. 20–42.

Fine, G.A., 1993. Ten lies of ethnography: Moral dilemmas of field research. Journal of Contemporary Ethnography 22/3, 267–294.

Gans, H., 1982. The participant observer as a human being: Observations on the personal aspects of fieldwork. In: Burgess, R. (Ed.), Field Research: A Sourcebook and Field Manual. George Allen and Unwin, London, pp. 53–61.

Goodwin, J., Horowitz, R., 2002. Introduction: the methodological strengths and dilemmas of qualitative sociology. Qualitative Sociology 25 (1), 33–47.

Gronewold, S., 1972. Did Frank Hamilton Cushing go native?. In: Kimball S., Watson, J. (Eds.), Crossing Cultural Boundaries: The Anthropological Experience. Chandler Publishing, London, pp. 33–50.

Lofland, J., Lofland, L.H., 1995. Analyzing Social Settings: A Guide to Qualitative Observation and Analysis I, third ed. Wadsworth, Belmont, CA.

Manning, P., 1976. The researcher: an alien in the police world. In: Niederhoffer, A., Blumberg, A. (Eds.), The Ambivalent Force: Perspectives on Police, second ed. Dryden Press, Hinsdale, IL, pp. 103–120.

Mastrofski, S.D., Parks, R.B., 1990. Improving observational studies of police. Criminology 28 (3), 475–496.

Mastrofski, S.D., Parks, R.B., Reiss, A.J., Worden, R.E., DeJong, C., Snipes, J.B., Terrill, W., 1998. Systematic observation of public police: applying field research methods to policy issues. National Institute of Justice, Washington, DC, NCJ 172859.

Miller, S.M., 1952. The participant observer and over-rapport. American Sociological Review 17 (1), 97–99.

Norris, C., 1993. Some ethical considerations on fieldwork with police. In: Hobbs, D., May, T. (Eds.), Interpreting the Field: Accounts of Ethnography. Oxford University Press, New York, pp. 123–143.

Pollner, M., Emerson, R.M., 2002. Constructing participant/observation relations. In: Emerson, R.M. (Ed.), Contemporary Field Research: Perspectives and Formulations, second ed. Waveland Press, Prospect Heights, IL, pp. 239–259.

Reiss, A.J., 1968. Stuff and nonsense about social surveys and observation. In: Becker, H. (Ed.), Institutions and the Person. Aldine, Chicago, pp. 351–367.

Reuss-Ianni, E., 1993. Two cultures of policing: street cops and management cops. Transaction, New Brunswick (USA).

Riksheim, E.C., Chermak, S.M., 1993. Causes of police behavior revisited. Journal of Criminal Justice 21 (4), 353–382.

Skolnick, J., 1966. Justice Without Trial. Wiley, New York.

Spano, R., 2002. Potential sources of observer bias in observational studies of police. PhD thesis, State University of New York at Albany.

Spano, R., 2003. Concerns about safety, observer sex, and the decision to arrest: evidence of reactivity in a large scale observational study of police. Criminology 41, 909–932.

Tedlock, B., 1991. From participant observation to the observation of participation: the emergence of narrative in ethnography. Journal of Anthropological Research 47 (1), 69–74.

Van Maanen, J., 1983a. The fact of fiction in organizational ethnography. In: Van Maanen, J. (Ed.), Qualitative Methodology. Sage Publications, Beverly Hills, CA, pp. 37–55.

Van Maanen, J., 1983b. On the ethics of fieldwork. In: Smith, R. (Ed.), An Introduction to Social Research: A Handbook of Social Science, vol. 1. Ballinger, Cambridge, MA, pp. 227–251.

Walker, S., 1992. The origins of the contemporary criminal justice paradigm: The American Bar Foundation Survey, 1953–1969. Justice uarterly 9 (1), 47–76.

Application Exercise 1.3

Name of Student:________________

Student ID No.:________________

Course/Section No.:________________

Date:________________

1. Based on the article, "Going Native: Potential Sources of Observer Bias in Police Observational Data," why is "going native" a threat to researchers who study police officers?

2. Given the information included in this article, what steps might a research take to avoid going native in criminal justice research?

3. What precautions might be used to protect against "going native" in criminal justice law enforcement research?

4. Consider one of the following areas of criminal justice research: prisons, gangs, and drug addicts. How might the process of "going native" be mitigated in participant observation in this area?

CHAPTER 2

Research Ethics

During the past few decades, ethical issues have become a major concern of many groups, including businesses and corporations, the military, government agencies, and the academy. So many instances of unethical behavior have surfaced in recent years that much of society now seems concerned with ethical issues. For instance, in 2004, troubling pictures taken at Guantanamo Bay were widely disseminated. These included photographs of U.S. military men and women, with jovial gestures and smiles, around prisoners posed in various demeaning poses. These photographs received considerable public scrutiny and resulted in disciplinary action for military personnel who were identified in the photos; these also called into question the overall ethical conduct in our military institutions (McGeary et al., 2004). Similarly, reports of the Rampart police scandal in 1999 detailed a complex ring of dirty cops in Los Angeles, five of whom were criminally prosecuted for making false arrests, filing false reports, committing perjury, planting evidence, shooting suspects, stealing weapons and drugs from police evidence, and killing two people during a botched drug deal. The implications were enormous: An estimated 30,000 criminal cases were reexamined in light of the debacle (Cable News Network [CNN], 2000). In 2005, an exposé of practices within the California Youth Authority (CYA) detailed the plight of several incarcerated youth who were kept in cages during school lessons while in state custody (Warren, 2005). While CYA authorities were quick to cite staff and client safety as the reason for this practice, it nevertheless caused great public concern and ultimately led to the systematic dismantling of CYA in California (Little Hoover Commission, 2008). Such examples abound of incidents that bring public scrutiny and concern over issues of ethics. This is especially problematic in the field of criminal justice, a cornerstone of which is professional integrity and justice for all.

Universities and colleges have not been exempt from unethical behavior. In the area of research, competition for grant monies has caused some researchers to engage in unethical practices. When researchers zealously believe in their approaches to solving problems and invest many years in their work, some falsify their results to secure continued funding in hopes of finally finding the breakthrough that will justify their means. In other instances, academicians feel so pressured to publish that they cut corners in their research and publish questionable results, often before it is appropriate to do so. The accuracy of these results is often suspect, as is the methodology or statistical test employed. This issue is not just related to individual researchers, but is also systemic to large research institutions and grant-funding agencies. In the spring of 2008, a U.S. congressional committee began investigating allegations that the U.S. Office of Juvenile Justice and Delinquency Prevention (OJJDP) "violated its bidding process in order to give competitive grants to favored organizations" (Boyle, 2008b). Talk of kickbacks and special favors tainted the objective research and review process that academia has touted for decades. In another recent case, the National Council of Juvenile and Family Court Judges agreed to pay an undisclosed fine (estimated at $300,000) amid allegations that the judicial group committed fraud to obtain grant money from the U.S. Department of Justice (Boyle, 2008a). These unethical breaches of trust by researchers underscore the fragility with which the research system operates.

Ethics and ethical behavior are of particular concern to social scientists, including criminologists and criminal justice researchers, specifically, as these issues relate to research and research methods (Braswell, McCarthy, & McCarthy, 1991; Davis, 1989; Longmire, 1991). In criminological research, ethical issues are compounded because research in these areas typically involves human subjects and is often focused on the very issues of ethics and justice themselves. Thus, both the manner in which research is conducted and the findings that are released have direct consequences for people's lives. Unfortunately, criminologists are not immune to unethical practices in research.

ETHICAL ISSUES IN RESEARCH

Numerous ethical questions have been raised about research and research methods of social scientists. While examples abound, a handful of cases received considerable attention within the discipline(s) and garnered tremendous public scrutiny. These fall into three categories: (1) ethical breaches that cause physical harm to subjects, (2) breaches that cause emotional/psychological harm, and (3) breaches that undermine and redirect the course of an entire academic discipline. A review of each case illustrates not only the seriousness and nature of the unethical questions and methods employed, but also the magnitude of the ethical dilemmas and far-reaching implications that follow.

Physical Harm to Subjects

UNIVERSITY OF CALIFORNIA, IRVINE, FERTILITY SCANDAL In 1995, the University of California, Irvine, had the premiere fertility clinic in the nation. The UCI Center for Reproductive Health boasted one of the highest success rates of all such clinics in the United States. In 1995, several irregularities were discovered. The full investigation revealed a web of deceit unparalleled in recent history. Motivated by a desire to maintain impossibly high success rates, doctors at the clinic knowingly implanted embryos from highly fertile clients into other clients not biologically related to the fetuses. The result was as follows: Dozens of children born to nonbiologically related parents, and dozens of childless couples who were, in fact, biologically related to children born to other clients. This baffled university administrators and legal professionals alike, as a medical debacle of this magnitude had never been exposed before. In fact, attorneys were not even sure what, if any, crime had been committed, as an embryo is not property (thus negating theft charges), nor is it deemed a person (thus negating kidnapping charges). In the end, criminal charges for assault (against the female clients) and fraud were filed. The debacle resulted in a class action lawsuit involving 113 parties (former clients and children); this was settled for an estimated $20 million. Meanwhile, multiple complicated custody battles ensued, and none of the parties could ever be truly satisfied or made whole again. Consider the plight of a 5-year-old child, raised by one set of parents, at risk for returning "home" to biological parents he or she never knew. The plight of the center was the least complicated aspect of this debacle: The center closed in disgrace, and the doctors fled the United States. Federal charges were brought against three of the physicians, two of whom fled the country to avoid prosecution (Becerra, 2000).

TUSKEGEE SYPHILIS CASE In 1932, the United States Public Health Service (PHS) began the Tuskegee Syphilis Study. This study was initiated to document the progression of untreated syphilis in humans. The subjects, a group of 399 poor black sharecroppers from Alabama, had latent syphilis. PHS researchers told the subjects that they were being treated for "bad blood." Over the next 40 years, the subjects were followed, and their physical health deterioration was catalogued. Throughout this time, researchers deliberately denied treatment to these syphilis-infected subjects and went to great lengths to prevent subjects from receiving treatment elsewhere. As compensation, infected subjects were provided with free meals, medical examinations, and burial insurance (Jones, 1993).

The study ended abruptly in 1972, but not due to some moral epiphany by the researchers. In fact, it ended when the story was reported in the Washington Star on July 25, 1972; the story was subsequently reported across the nation. The Tuskegee Case is probably the single most egregious case of ethical violation in research, and it serves as a powerful example of "racism in medicine, ethical misconduct in human research, paternalism by physicians, and government abuse of vulnerable people" (Legacy Committee, 1996, Paragraph #5).

THE OHIO PRISON EXPERIMENTS In 1955, 50 prisoners at correctional institutions in Ohio were research subjects to test "vaccines as part of the Army's bacteriological warfare program" (Lore, 1990, p. 2B). Although the inmates "volunteered" to participate, they were provided with no services to address any potential harm caused by the vaccines or biological agents they were given. Quite the contrary, no extended follow-up of medical treatment was provided for any of the inmates involved. In fact, the doctors who performed the medical research had no contact with the subjects after the study, nor did they know where the subjects were in the following years.

Between 1956 and 1961, doctors from two prestigious institutions used prison volunteers from the same institutions in Ohio to study whether healthy humans could be inoculated against cancer (Lore, 1990); in this case, uninformed subjects were injected with live cancer cells. As in the biological warfare vaccine project, no medical services were provided to the subjects beyond that which was given to all inmates; researchers had no contact with the subjects following the study, and there are no published reports of the long-term outcomes for the participants of this study.

Psychological Harm to Subjects

THE HUMPHREYS CASE Another type of unethical behavior related to the social sciences is demonstrated by Laud Humphreys's work titled *Tearoom Trade* (1970; also discussed in Chapter 6). Humphreys examined the use of public bathrooms and the people who frequented them to engage in deviant sexual behavior. Humphreys played the role of observing participant, facilitating the deviant activities by serving as a lookout.

Had Humphreys's research stopped here, it is likely that only three ethical issues would have been raised. First, he failed to identify himself as a researcher. Second, subjects were not given the opportunity to consent (or refuse) to be a subject of his research. Third, he observed, facilitated, and failed to report behavior that, in some jurisdictions, violates the law.

Humphreys went beyond the observations in public bathrooms discussed above. He copied down the license plates of individuals who participated in the deviant acts. Then, retrieved their names and addresses through a connection he had at the state department of motor vehicles. After obtaining these names and addresses, Humphreys visited the homes of these people, posing as a mental health researcher collecting data for a survey unrelated to the sex acts he observed in the public bathrooms. Humphreys asked the respondents personal questions, which he then correlated with his observations of them in public bathrooms. At no time did he seek the permission of these people for their involvement in the real purpose of his research.

The surreptitious acts—copying down license plate numbers to track the individuals he observed and then interviewing them under false pretenses—raise even more serious ethical issues than his initial transgression. While there were no specific reports of emotional or psychological harm to individual subjects, the possibility of harm was extreme, particularly given that fact that many of the subjects were married men, and their wives had no knowledge of their extramarital sexual proclivities.

THE MILGRAM CASE Stanley Milgram was interested in testing conditions under which a person will or will not follow directions that cause him or her to knowingly harm another individual. Milgram's study was motivated, in part, by actions of individuals who were victims of the Holocaust. During their imprisonment, supposedly normal individuals participated in hideous acts against fellow prisoners with the knowledge that they were hurting their fellow captives.

Milgram (1965) set up an experiment in which laboratory assistants, dressed in white coats, instructed subjects to send electrical shocks to individuals who answered questions incorrectly. Subjects sat at the controls of a machine and were told to turn up the current with subsequent incorrect answers, thereby increasing the supposed shock levels. Milgram hired actors to play the individuals receiving the shocks; they could be seen by the real subjects of the study and were instructed to act is if they were in pain as they were shocked. In some instances, the actors even clutched at their chests, complained of a heart condition, and begged the subject to stop.

In some instances, subjects refused to administer the shocks, especially when the dials of the machine indicated the electrical dose to be lethal. The laboratory assistants assured the subjects that they (the laboratory assistant) would accept responsibility for the consequences and urged the subjects to keep increasing the current. Many of the subjects were upset by the situation since they did not know that the recipients of the supposed shocks were actors and were not actually harmed.

Undermining the Course of a Particular Discipline

Of course, the physical and psychological harm done to specific research subjects is a travesty. However egregious, these harms can be quantified in terms of the number of individuals in danger of harm, or the specific individuals harmed, due to ethical breaches in research. It is difficult to compare this number with the elusive and far-reaching harm caused when an ethical breach changes the course of a discipline. If a researcher gives subjects a harmful medication, we can quantify the potential harm to some degree. This is not an easy task when the ethical breach changes the course of a discipline by leading other researchers down a false road paved with fabricated research findings. Consider the following examples.

THE MARTINSON CASE In 1974, Robert Martinson published his now infamous paper titled, "What works in rehabilitation?" In short, his answer was nothing. Martinson performed an analysis of multiple studies looking at various drug treatments and vocational and educational programs for criminal offenders. He was too quick to report his initial findings that nothing worked to rehabilitate offenders, and the media and public were just as quick to act on his faulty assertions. Following Martinson's publication, many states defunded rehabilitation programs. Their logic was sound: If no single type of rehabilitation worked to reduce recidivism, then why pay for rehabilitation at all? The result was a national move away from rehabilitation programs in state and local corrections agencies.

Within months of Martinson's publication, numerous scholars evaluated his methods and found them faulty. Several scholars (Palmer, 1975; Andrews, Zinger, Bonta, Gendreau, & Cullen, 1990) published rebuttals to his work, and Martinson himself later recanted (Lipton, Martinson, & Wilkes, 1975; Martinson, 1979). However, the damage was done; most states embarked on a 20-year journey away from rehabilitation programs.

While no single research participant was directly harmed, Martinson's premature, inaccurate report shifted funding away from rehabilitation, arguably harming thousands of inmates who could have benefited from vocational, educational, and drug treatment rehabilitation. With decreased focus on rehabilitation came increased focus on retributive forms of punishment, and the U.S. incarceration rate increased nearly five fold in 20 years. Arguably, this also impacted public safety, as felons lacking rehabilitation programs returned home from prison less prepared for successful reintegration in the community; the recidivism rate increased. The fiscal cost and human toll is unfathomable. Around the year 2000, correctional programs began to reinvest in rehabilitation programs once again, but this was after a quarter century hiatus initiated by Martinson's premature results. Martinson committed suicide in 1980 (Miller, 1989).

THE BURT CASE Cyril Burt was a famed psychologist who, in the late 1970s and early 1980s, was accused of falsifying data related to his study of twins dating back to 1943 (Broad & Wade, 1982). Burt, who was actively involved in the development of experimental psychology, devoted a considerable amount of his early research to the relationship between heredity and intelligence. Wade (1976) discovered that Burt reported the same correlations for each set of twins (Davis, 1989). In plain terms, this meant that Burt found exactly the same degree of relationship between biology and intelligence for every single pair of twins he examined over nearly 30 years of research. Statistically, this is just not possible.

A detailed examination of Burt's notes demonstrated that he had, in fact, simply invented the correlations he reported in his research. This discovery brought the results of his studies into question, especially those involving his work on twins. The only reasonable conclusion researchers could draw about the results was that the findings were falsified, and thus, were not reliable.

Arguably, Burt was so sure that his hypotheses were correct that he did not believe that he needed to follow the normal research route (Davis, 1989); yet any defense such as this of falsifying data or results is unacceptable. This type of unethical behavior is a serious violation of ethical research methods. Many researchers trusted in Burt's ethics; they accepted his results and built their own research on his findings, which make them victims of Burt's unethical behavior. The same is true of the many students who were taught erroneous knowledge, based in part on the results of Burt's work.

THE SUMMERLIN CASE The falsification of data and results is certainly not limited to the social sciences. Numerous examples can be found in other fields, especially the medical sciences.

The competition for getting research monies and positions can be fierce in the field of medical research. Further funding is often based on the results of the currently funded research. In practice, this means that research that shows promise or positive results continues to receive funding. The case of William Summerlin, a cancer researcher, points out the difficulty of needing to provide results (Davis, 1989).

Summerlin was working on the lack of rejection properties of culture-grown skin, a highly competitive area of medical research. Because of the pressure he felt to succeed, Summerlin "inked a black patch on two white laboratory mice to convince Good (his boss) that a skin graft between genetically different animals had been successful" (Davis, 1989, p. 7). One of Summerlin's assistants discovered the misrepresentation and brought it to the attention of proper authorities.

While this ethical breach was caught early, one can imagine how such a violation can impact an entire field of study. Suppose Summerlin's fraud had not been discovered and his fabricated findings were accepted by the scientific community as legitimate. Research would then focus on the skin-graft conditions Summerlin specified, possibly including human trials aimed at replicating Summerlin's success in human skin grafts. But for the fact that Summerlin's assistant reported his fraud, this erroneous line of research could have taken a ghastly human toll.

ASSESSMENT OF ETHICAL ISSUES

The Tuskegee, Ohio Prison, Humphreys, and Milgram experiments would be extremely difficult, if not impossible, to carry out today given the guidelines in place for informed consent. Briefly, the researcher must obtain informed consent to participate in research from the subjects after the researcher discloses any possible risks to the subject. Deceptions such as those employed in these examples would be viewed as inappropriate and not allowed under most circumstances.

Scholars generally agree that the cases presented here are at the negative extreme of a continuum of ethical behavior. However, not all cases are so blatant, and many are not simple issues of right and wrong. Many times, ethical issues regarding research questions and methods are somewhat clouded by various factors, including the relative benefit to subjects, which would be negated if the subject was fully aware of the research parameters. For example, most medical research involving new medications requires subjects to be unaware as to whether they receive a new medication, the standard treatment, or a placebo. This is necessary to ensure that any result is due to the properties of the medication, not the optimism of subjects who know they are getting the "better" treatment. The results demonstrating a superior cancer treatment, for example, can then benefit countless more patients. Thus, some level of deception is often necessary in the name of science, but it can never approach the level of outright deceit discussed in the previous examples.

RESPONSES OF ORGANIZATIONS AND AGENCIES TO ETHICAL ISSUES IN RESEARCH

In part because of the problems identified with doing research, a number of professional academic organizations have produced codes of ethics designed to serve as guideposts for researchers. For example, the Academy of Criminal Justices Sciences, the American Anthropological Association, American Forklore Society, American Judicature Society, American Political Science Association, American Psychological Association, American Sociological Association (ASA), Australian and New Zealand Society of Criminology, and the British Society of Criminology each has a distinct code of ethics governing research related to criminal justice–related study. There are equally numerous federal organizations and policies that govern ethics in research related to criminal justice, most notably the Department of Health, Education, and Welfare (which drafted the Belmont Report), the *United States Code of Federal Regulations,* and the U.S. Department of Health and Human Services (which issues federal Certificates of Confidentiality). Each state also has distinct policies that govern ethics in human subjects research. For example, the Committee for the Protection of Human Subjects (2008) oversees research pertaining to public data (such as inmates) in California. Further, each research institution, college or university, also has its own ethical guidelines for research. Books could be written cataloguing the various rules governing research ethics and approaches for protecting human research subjects today.

Leedy (1993) provides an excellent summary of the code of ethics of one such organization, the American Sociological Association (ASA):

1. Researchers must maintain scientific objectivity.
2. Researchers should recognize the limitations of their competence and not attempt to engage in research beyond such competence.
3. Every person is entitled to the right of privacy and dignity of treatment.
4. All research should avoid causing personal harm to subjects used in the research.
5. Confidential information provided by a research subject must be held in strict confidentiality by the researcher.
6. Research findings should be presented honestly, without distortion.
7. The researcher must not use the prerogative of a researcher to obtain information for other than professional purposes.
8. The researcher must acknowledge all assistance, collaboration of others, or sources from which information was borrowed from others.
9. The researcher must acknowledge financial support in the research report or any personal relationship of the researcher with the sponsor that may conceivably affect the research findings.
10. The researcher must not accept any favors, grants, or other means of assistance that would violate any of the ethical principles set forth in the above paragraphs (pp. 129–130).

Consider item 1: *Scientific objectivity.* If the researcher is well versed in the scientific method (discussed in Chapter 1), this will certainly facilitate maintaining objectivity. Closely following the different components of the scientific method will not absolutely guarantee that the researcher will maintain objectivity, but doing so will definitely improve the probability for those who want to be objective.

One component of the scientific method calls for the researcher to identify his or her biases and beliefs as early in the research process as possible. Taking this step gives the researcher the opportunity to control for the influence of his or her biases and beliefs. When these personal issues are included in the body of the research, the consumers of the results have the opportunity to make informed interpretations of what has been reported.

The issue of *honest presentation of results,* item 6 in the ASA code, can best be exemplified by the Cyril Burt case discussed above. When researchers present their results in a dishonest manner, as Burt did, they misdirect others who unknowingly use these tainted results as the basis for further research. Researchers often rely on the results of previous work to guide their current endeavors and to break new scientific groundwork laid by other scholars, rather than rehash existing findings (akin to reinventing the wheel). When statistically significant but fraudulent results are reported, they can wrongly influence research that is undertaken to pursue a similar line of thought. This can have costly, long-term, and widespread ramifications for the development and future directions of programs and research. Reporting false results can influence what people in the field believe and thus what textbooks teach, compounding the problem for the future of the discipline.

Federal Agencies

As referenced above, various federal agencies have promulgated ethical policies that include guidelines for research involving human subjects in addition to those developed within academic disciplines. The issues of confidentiality, informed consent, and avoidance of harm to subjects are also found in the *Code of Federal Regulations* today (discussed below); however, a number of past studies were unconcerned with protecting subjects from harm, and some studies actually brought harm to subjects.

Consider the Ohio prison experiments discussed above. Arguably, the prisoner subjects volunteered, and informed consent was obtained. However, one must ask if individuals such as prisoners, who are controlled by the state for extended periods of time, can willingly give their consent. Perhaps these volunteers felt coerced by the prison officials; alternately, perhaps captive volunteers believed that their participation would bring favored status, such as a shortened sentence or improved conditions of confinement. Even if subtle coercion or erroneous belief in some secondary benefit were not at issue, these subjects were injected with potentially deadly diseases. This would not be permitted under any circumstances according to ethical guidelines today. In the 1950s, however, there were no such restrictions or guidelines for involving prisoners in research. All states now have regulations for the protection prisoners, who are generally considered a vulnerable population in need of additional protection, that would prevent this type of abuse from occurring today.

In 1966, in one of the first federal efforts at ethical regulation, Surgeon General William Stewart issued the Public Health Service (1996) policy that called for institutional review of the research involving human subjects. Since that time, government policies and regulations have shifted from the level of policy to that of federal statute. Correspondingly, the requirements have become both more rigorous and complex. To make matters even more complicated, "the review requirements, which originally applied only to research funded by the Public Health Service, were extended by the National Research Act of 1974 to all research involving human subjects that is conducted at institutions that receive funds for research under the Public Health Services Act" (Gray, 1979).

The *Code of Federal Regulations* specifies ethical guidelines for human subjects in research (46 CFR 45). Part 46, "Protection of Human Subjects," was added to the *Code of Federal Regulations* by the Department of Health and Human Services under Title 45, further delineating the responsibilities of institutions and institutional review boards (IRBs). The updated policy applies to all research involving human subjects that is carried out by federal departments or agencies, their subsidiaries, or institutions subject to their regulation. Research conducted at colleges and universities that receive funds from the federal government is subject to the requirements of this policy.

According to the Department of Health and Human Services (2008), research done at colleges and universities that involves (1) normal educational practices; (2) the use of educational tests; or (3) the study of existing data, documents, and records that are publically available is exempt from standard IRB review and is subject only to an *expedited review.* In this type of review, the chair of the IRB reviews the research proposal to determine whether it fits into one of these categories; if it does, the proposal is approved. The chair of the IRB is then responsible for notifying other board members about the action taken.

Institutions engaging in research that comes under the auspices of the federal code are required to establish IRBs, which have the authority to review and approve all research proposals. The *Code of Federal Regulations* specifies the following criteria for IRB approval of research (46 CFR 45, §46.111):

1. In order to approve research covered by this policy, the IRB shall determine that all of the following requirements are satisfied:
   a. Risks to subjects are minimized: (i) by using procedures that are consistent with sound research design and that do not unnecessarily expose subjects to risk and (ii) whenever appropriate, by using procedures already being performed on the subjects for diagnostic or treatment purposes.
   b. Risks to subjects are reasonable in relation to anticipated benefits, if any, to subjects, and the importance of the knowledge that may reasonably be expected to result. In evaluating risks and benefits, the IRB should consider only those risks and benefits that may result from the research (as distinguished from risks and benefits of therapies subjects would receive even if not participating in the research). The IRB should not consider possible long-range effects of applying knowledge gained in the research (for example, the possible effects of the research on public policy) as among those research risks that fall within the purview of its responsibility.
   c. Selection of subjects is equitable. In making this assessment, the IRB should (i) take into account the purposes of the research and the setting in which the research will be conducted and (ii) be particularly cognizant of the special problems of research involving vulnerable populations, such as children, prisoners, pregnant women, mentally disabled persons, or economically or educationally disadvantaged persons.
   d. Informed consent will be sought from each prospective subject or the subject's legally authorized representative, in accordance with, and to the extent required by §46.116.
   e. Informed consent will be appropriately documented, in accordance with, and to the extent required by §46.117.

   f. When appropriate, the research plan makes adequate provision for monitoring the data collected to ensure the safety of subjects.
   g. When appropriate, there are adequate provisions to protect the privacy of subjects and to maintain the confidentiality of data.
2. When some or all of the subjects are likely to be vulnerable to coercion or undue influence, such as children, prisoners, pregnant women, mentally disabled persons, or economically or educationally disadvantaged persons, additional safeguards have been included in the study to protect the rights and welfare of these subjects.

When deemed necessary, IRBs can require that modifications be made in research proposals prior to approval, bringing them in line with these requirements.

References

American Psychological Association. (2002). *Ethical principles of psychologists and code of conduct.* Retrieved October 7, 2008, from http://www.apa.org/ethics/code2002.html

Andrews, D. A., Zinger, I., Bonta, J., Gendreau, P., & Cullen, F. T. (1990). Does correctional treatment work? A clinically relevant and psychologically informed meta-analysis. *Criminology,* 28(3), 369–404.

Becerra, H. (2000, May 13). Fertility clinic sold embryo, woman claims. *Los Angeles Times.* Retrieved June 30, 2008, from http://articles.latimes.com/2000/may/13/local/me-29720

Boyle, P. (2008a, March 28). Congress probes justice department grants: Did OJJDP play favorites with competitive bids? *Youth Today.*

Boyle, P. (2008b, April 29). Juvenile judges group secretly pays to settle U.S. Fraud Claim. *Youth Today.*

Braswell, M. C., McCarthy, B., & McCarthy, B. (1992) *Justice, crime and ethics.* Cincinnati, OH: Anderson.

Broad, W., & Wade, N. (1982). *Betrayers of the truth.* New York: Simon & Schuster.

Cable News Network. (2000, October 9). Los Angeles Police Department timeline. Retrieved June 11, 2008, from http://archives.cnn.com/2000/LAW/05/12/lapd.timeline/

Committee for the Protection of Human Subjects. *State-Level Institutional Review Board.* Retrieved October 15, 2008, from http://www.oshpd.ca.gov/Boards/CPHS/committee_members.html

Davis, M. S. (1989). *The perceived seriousness and incidence of ethical misconduct in academic science.* Unpublished doctoral dissertation, The Ohio State University, Columbus, Ohio.

Department of Health, Education, and Welfare. (1979). The National Commission for the Protection of Human Subjects of Biomedical and Behavioral Research. *The Belmont Report.* Retrieved September 12, 2008, from http://www.hhs.gov/ohrp/humansubjects/guidance/belmont.htm

Department of Health and Human Services (1991). *Protection of human subjects, title 45, code of federal regulations,* part 46. Washington, DC: National Institutes of Health, Office for Protection from Research Risks.

Humphreys, L. (1970). *Tearoom trade.* Chicago: Aldine.

Jones, J. H. (1993). *Bad blood: The Tuskegee Syphilis Experiment* (new and expanded ed.). New York: Free Press.

Leedy, P. D. (1993). *Practical research: Planning and design* (5th ed.). New York: Macmillan.

Legacy Committee. (1996). *Tuskegee Syphilis Study Legacy Committee Final Report.* Retrieved on November 4, 2008, from http://www.tuskegee.edu/Global/story.asp?S=1141982

Lipton, D., Martinson, R., & Wilkes, J. (1975). Effectiveness of correctional treatment: A survey of treatment evaluation studies. *New York Governor's Special Committee on Criminal Offenders.* New York Office of Crime Control Planning.

Little Hoover Commission. (2008). *Juvenile justice reform: Realigning responsibilities.* Retrieved August 17, 2008, from http://www.lhc.ca.gov/lhcdir/192/report192.pdf

Longmire, D. R. (1991). Ethical dilemmas in the research setting: A survey of experiences and responses in the criminological community. In M. C. Braswell, B. R. McCarthy, & B. J. McCarthy (Eds.), *Justice, crime and ethics* (pp. 279–296). Cincinnati, OH: Anderson.

Lore, D. (1990, August 26). The convicts who volunteered to be guinea pigs. *The Columbus Dispatch,* p. 2B.

Martinson, R. (1974). What works? Questions and answers about prison reform. *Public Interest New York, 35,* 22–54.

Martinson, R. (1979). New findings, new views: A note of caution regarding prison reform. *Hofstra Law Review 7,* 243–258.

McGeary, J., Crittle, S., Novak, V., Thompson, M., Waller, D., & Thornburgh, N. (2001). Pointing fingers. *Time Magazine.* Accesses on November 5, 2008, from http://www.time.com/time/magazine/article/0,9171,994233,00.html

Milgram, S. (1965). Conditions of obedience and disobedience to authority. *Human Relations, 18,* 57–76.

Miller, J. D. (1989, March). The debate on rehabilitating criminals: Is it true that nothing works? *Washington Post*. Retrieved November 5, 2008, from http://www.prisonpolicy.org/scans/rehab.html

Palmer, T. (1975). Martinson revisited. *Journal of Research in Crime and Delinquency, 12*(2), 133–152.

Public Health Service. (1996, July 1). PPO #129, Washington, DC: U.S. Government Printing Office.

Wade, W. (1976). *Great hoaxes and famous impostors.* Middle Village, NY: Jonathan David.

Warren, J. (2005). For young offenders, a softer approach. *L. A. Times.* Retrieved November 1, 2008, from http://articles.latimes.com/2005/feb/01/local/me-cya1

United States Code of Federal Regulations. (2008). *Criminal justice information systems. 28 CFR 46.* Retrieved October 1, 2008, from http://www.access.gpo.gov/nara/cfr/waisidx_00/28cfr46_00.html

U.S. Department of Health and Human Services. *Certificates of Confidentiality kiosk.* National Institute of Health: Office of Extramural Research. Retrieved October 7, 2008, from http://grants.nih.gov/grants/policy/coc/

Exercise 2.1 Tearoom Trade

Tearoom Trade

Laud Humphreys

While the agreements resulting in "one-night-stands" occur in many settings—the bath, the street, the public toilet—and may vary greatly in the elaborateness or simplicity of the interaction preceding culmination in the sexual act, their essential feature is the expectation that sex can be had without obligation or commitment.[1]

At shortly after five o'clock on a weekday evening, four men enter a public restroom in the city park. One wears a well-tailored business suit; another wears tennis shoes, shorts, and tee-shirt; the third man is still clad in the khaki uniform of his filling station; the last, a salesman, has loosened his tie and left his sports coat in the car. What has caused these men to leave the company of the homeward-bound commuters on the freeway? What common interest brings these men, with their divergent backgrounds, to this public facility?

They have come here not for the obvious reason, but in a search for "instant sex." Many men—married and unmarried, those with heterosexual identities and those whose self-image is a homosexual one—seek such impersonal sex, shunning involvement, desiring kicks without commitment. Whatever reasons—social, physiological, or psychological—might be postulated for this search, the phenomenon of impersonal sex persists as a widespread but rarely studied form of human interaction.

There are several settings for this type of deviant activity—the balconies of movie theaters, automobiles, behind bushes—but few offer the advantages for these men that public restrooms provide. "Tearooms," as these facilities are called in the language of the homosexual subculture,[2] have several characteristics that make them attractive as locales for sexual encounters without involvement.

According to its most precise meaning in the argot, the only "true" tearoom is one that gains a reputation as a place where homosexual encounters occur. Presumably, any restroom could qualify for this distinction, but comparatively few are singled out for this function at any one time. For instance, I have researched a metropolitan area with more than ninety public toilets in its parks, only twenty of which are in regular use as locales for sexual games. Restrooms thus designated join the company of automobiles and bathhouses as places for deviant sexual activity second only to private bedrooms in popularity.[3] During certain seasons of the year—roughly, that period from April through October that midwestern homosexuals call "the hunting season"—tearooms may surpass any other locale of homoerotic enterprise in volume of activity.

Public restrooms are chosen by those who want homoerotic activity without commitment for a number of reasons. *They are accessible, easily recognized by the initiate, and provide little public visibility.* Tearooms thus offer the advantages of both public and private settings. They are available and recognizable enough to attract a large volume of potential sexual partners, providing an opportunity for rapid action with a variety of men. When added to the relative privacy of these settings, such features enhance the impersonality of the sheltered interaction.

AVAILABILITY

In the first place, tearooms are readily accessible to the male population. They may be located in any sort of public gathering place: department stores, bus stations, libraries, hotels, YMCAs, or courthouses. In keeping with the drive-in craze of American society, however, the more popular facilities are those readily accessible to the roadways. The restrooms of public parks and beaches—and, more recently, the rest stops set at programmed intervals along superhighways—are now attracting the clientele that, in a more pedestrian age, frequented great buildings of the inner cities. . . . [M]y research is focused on the activity that takes place in the restrooms of public parks, not only because (with some seasonal variation) they provide the most action but also because of other factors that make them suitable for sociological study.

It is a function of some societies to make these facilities for elimination available to the public. Perhaps the public toilet is one of the marks of "civilization," at least as perceived by European and post-European culture. I recall a letter from a sailor stationed in North Africa during World War II in which he called the people "uncivilized" because they had no public restrooms and used streets and gutters for the purpose of elimination.

For the cultural historian, American park restrooms merit study as physical traces of modern civilization. The older ones are often appended to pavilions or concealed beneath the paving of graceful colonnades. One marble-lined room in which I have done research occupies half of a Greek temple-like structure, a building of beautiful lines and proportions. A second type, built before the Great Depression, are the toilet facilities located in park administration buildings, maintenance shops, or garages. For the most part, these lack the artistic qualities of the first type. Partly because they are not accessible from the roads and partly because they are too easily approached by supervisory personnel and other interfering "straights," these restrooms enjoy homosexual popularity only during the months when other outlets are closed.

With the depression of the 1930s a new variety of public toilet appeared on the park scene. Ten of the twelve tearooms in which I made systematic observations . . . were of this category. Although the floor plans and building materials used vary from city to city, the majority of restrooms I have seen were constructed during this period. These have been built by the Work Projects Administration and, in any one community, seem to have been stamped from the same die. In the city where most of my research took place, they are constructed of a native white stone with men's and women's facilities back-to-back under one red roof. They have heavy wooden doors, usually screened from public view by a latticework partition attached to the building's exterior. In most of these doors, there is an inset of opaque French panes.

Each of the toilet facilities in the building has two windows in the same opaque glass, situated at either side of the room. The outside of these apertures is always covered with heavy screen. Against the blank wall opposite the door, there are (from left to right) three urinals and two stalls, although smaller restrooms may provide only two urinals and one stall. Some of the facilities still have washbasins intact, situated in the corner to the left as one enters the door, but few of these are in working order. There is an occasional wastebasket. Paper towels are seldom provided, and there are no other furnishings in the rooms.

Few park restrooms date back to the 1940s, when the nation was concerned with building those other major outlets for homosexual activity, the military posts. Apparently, most public construction in the 1950s was connected with the rush to provide more athletic facilities—swimming pools, golf courses, skating rinks, and the like.

The past decade has witnessed the construction of new, functional, cement-block facilities. Most of these structures are located along the expressways, but a number are appearing in the parks and playgrounds of our cities. These relief stations may be viewed as an expression of the current interest in urban planning; some replace buildings no longer fit for use; others are located on the newly created urban playgrounds; and the bulk accompany the nation's answer to problems of mass transportation. However, one may interpret the new construction as a reflection of the course of American history, it should be a boon to the tearoom customers. Most of the newly built restrooms are isolated structures with ready access to the roads and thus meet the primary requisites of tearoom activity.

According to some older respondents, the real turning point for the tearoom trade arrived with the WPA. One man, who has been active in the homosexual subculture for more than forty years, put it this way:

> I suppose there has been such activity since the intervention of plumbing. I first started out in one of those pavilion places. But the real fun began during the depression. There were all those new buildings, easy to reach, and the automobile was really getting popular about then. . . . Suddenly, it just seemed like half of the men in town met in the tearooms.

Not all of the new buildings were easy to reach, but those that were soon found popularity for homosexual activity. Tearoom ecology, like that of society at large, is highly affected by the location of transportation routes. Whether by accident or design, most large city parks are located close to major thoroughfares and freeways. Because the activity in the tearooms reaches its peak at the close of the workday, restrooms will draw more customers if located near principal commuting routes of the metropolitan area. The two facilities that I found to attract the greatest numbers for homosexual relations were adjacent to four-lane traffic arteries. All others in which any noteworthy amount of activity was observed were located within five minutes' driving time on the expressways that circle and cross the city.

LOCATING THE ACTION

There is a great deal of difference in the volumes of homosexual activity that these accommodations shelter. In some, one might wait for months before observing a deviant act (unless solitary masturbation is considered deviant). In others, the volume approaches orgiastic dimensions. One summer afternoon, for instance, I witnessed twenty acts of fellatio in the course of an hour while waiting out a thunderstorm in a tearoom. For one who wishes to participate in (or study) such activity, the primary consideration is one of finding where the action is.

Occasionally, tips about the more active places may be gained from unexpected sources. Early in my research, I was approached by a man (whom I later surmised to be a park patrolman in plain clothes) while waiting at the window of a tearoom for some patrons to arrive. After finishing his business at the urinal and exchanging some remarks about the weather (it had been raining), the man came abruptly to the point: "Look, fellow, if you're looking for sex, this isn't the place. We're clamping down on this park because of trouble with the niggers. Try the john at the northeast corner of [Reagan] Park. You'll find plenty of action there." He was right. Some of my best observations were made at the spot he recommended. In most cases, however, I could only enter, wait, and watch—a method that was costly in both time and gasoline. After surveying a couple of dozen such rooms in this way, however, I became able to identify the more popular tearooms by observing certain physical evidence, the most obvious of which is the location of the facility. During the warm seasons, those restrooms that are isolated from other park facilities, such as administration buildings, shops, tennis courts, playgrounds, and picnic areas, are the more popular for deviant activity. The most active tearooms studied were all isolated from recreational areas, cut off by drives or lakes from baseball diamonds and picnic tables.

I have chosen the term "purlieu" (with its ancient meaning of land severed from a royal forest by perambulation) to describe the immediate environs best suited to the tearoom trade. Drives and walks that separate a public toilet from the rest of the park are almost certain guides to deviant sex. The ideal setting for homosexual activity is a tearoom situated on an island of grass, with roads close by on every side. The getaway car is just a few steps away; children are not apt to wander over from the playground; no one can surprise the participants by walking in from the woods or from over a hill; it is not likely that straight people will stop there at all. According to my observations, the women's side of these buildings is seldom used at all.

Active tearooms are also identifiable by the number of automobiles parked nearby. If two or more cars remain in front of a relatively isolated restroom for more than ten minutes, one may be reasonably certain that homosexual activity is in progress inside. This sign that the sexual market is in operation is an important one to the participants, who seldom enter a park restroom unless the presence of other unoccupied cars indicates that potential partners are inside. A lone arriver will usually wait in his auto until at least one other has parked nearby. That this signal is obscured when a golf course, zoo, or other facility that draws automobiles is located in close proximity may help explain the popularity of the isolated restroom.

Another means of recognizing the active tearoom requires closer inspection. Here, I refer to the condition of the windows and doors. Men who play the tearoom game must be able to know when someone is approaching. A door that squeaks or sticks is of great assistance; however, the condition of the windows is even more important. If they are of opaque glass, are nailed shut, or have no broken panes, the researcher may presume that the facility is seldom used for homosexual encounters.

In a western city, I have observed an exception to this rule. One of the popular meeting places, there was a restroom located beneath the pavement of a colonnade. There were vents but no windows. The only access to this tearoom, however, was by means of a circular, metal stairway, and clanging footfalls could be heard well before the intruder was far enough down to see into the room. Normally, popular tearooms have at least one pane broken from each window, unless the windows have been opened. Fragments of glass that remain between the window frame and an outside screen are indicative of destruction that was initiated from within the restroom rather than by outside vandals. As [one] account of a teen-age attack . . . indicates, occasional damage to the buildings comes from outside. But one of the first acts of participants after the spring opening or renovation of a facility is to break out a few carefully selected panes so that insiders can see who is approaching.

Graffiti were expected to provide some indication of restroom usage for deviant activity. On the basis of quantity alone, however, inscriptions vary most directly with the time since the latest repainting or cleansing of the walls or with the type of wall covering used. There also seems to be a relationship between the quantity of such markings and the neighborhood in which the facility is situated. Restrooms in lower class and commercial neighborhoods or close to schools tend to invite more of such writings than those in middle class or residential areas.

The *type* of graffiti found does correlate with use of the room for homosexual purposes. In the more active tearooms, I have often noticed inscriptions such as "show hard—get sucked," "will suck cocks—10/12/66—all morning," or "I have eight inches—who wants it?" One respondent says that the presence of recent markings such as these reassures him that he has come to the right place for action. Active homosexual locales are conspicuously lacking in initials, sketches of nude females, poetry, and certain of the classic four-letter words. Writings on the walls of the true tearooms are straightforward, functional messages, lacking the fantasy content of the graffiti in most men's rooms. Moreover, this research suggests that involvement in homosexual encounters may preclude the leisure time necessary for some of the more creative types of graffiti production.

Volume and Variety

The availability of facilities they can recognize attracts a great number of men who wish, for whatever reason, to engage in impersonal homoerotic activity. Simple observation is enough to guide these participants, the researcher, and perhaps, the police to active tearooms. It is much more difficult to make an accurate appraisal of the proportion of the male population who engage in such activity over a representative length of time. Even with good sampling procedures, a large staff of assistances would be needed to make the observations necessary for an adequate census of this mobile population.[4] All that may be said with some degree of certainty is that the percentage of the male population who participate in tearoom sex in the United States is somewhat less than the 16 percent of the adult white male population Kinsey found to have "at least as much of the homosexual as the heterosexual in their histories."[5]

Participants assure me that it is not uncommon in tearooms for one man to fellate as many as ten others in a day. I have personally watched a fellator take on three men in succession in a half hour of observation. One respondent, who has cooperated with the researcher in a number of taped interviews, claims to average three men each day during the busy seasons.

I have seen some wait in turn for this type of service. Leaving one such scene on a warm September Saturday, I remarked to a man who left close behind me: "Kind of crowded in there, isn't it?" "Hell, yes," he answered. "It's getting so you have to take a number and wait in line in these places!"

There are many who frequent the same facility repeatedly. Men will come to be known as regular, even daily, participants, stopping off at the same tearoom on the way to or from work. One physician in his late fifties was so punctual in his appearance at a particular restroom that I began to look forward to our daily chats. This robust, affable respondent said he had stopped at this tearoom every evening of the week (except Wednesday, his day off) for years "for a blow-job." Another respondent, a salesman whose schedule is flexible, may "make the scene" more than once a day—usually at his favorite men's room. At the time of our formal interview, this man claimed to have had four orgasms in the past twenty-four hours.

According to participants I have interviewed, those who are looking for impersonal sex in tearooms are relatively certain of finding the sort of partner they want. . . .

> You go into the tearoom. You can pick some really nice things in there. Again, it is a matter of sex real quick; and, if like this kind, fine—you've got it. You get one and he is done and before long, you've got another one.

. . . and when they want it:

> Well, I go there; and you can always find someone to suck your cock, morning, noon, or night. I know lots of guys who stop by there on their way to work—and all during the day.

It is this sort of volume and variety that keeps the tearooms viable as market places of the one-night-stand variety.

Of the bar crowd in gay (homosexual) society, only a small percentage would be found in park restrooms. But this more overt, gay bar clientele constitutes a minor part of those in any American city who follow a predominantly homosexual pattern. The so-called closet queens and other types of covert deviants make up the vast majority of those who engage in homosexual acts—and these are the persons most attracted to tearoom encounters.

Tearooms are popular, not because they serve as gathering places for homosexuals but because they attract a variety of men, a *minority* of whom are active in the homosexual subculture. When we consider the types of participants, it will be seen that a large group of them have no homosexual self-identity. For various reasons, they do not want to be seen with those who might be identified as such or to become involved with them on a "social" basis.

Privacy in Public

I have mentioned that one of the distinguishing traits of an active tearoom is its isolation from other facilities in a park. The addition of four picnic tables close to a once popular restroom all but eliminated that facility for research purposes. This portion of a tape, made as I toured the parks in search of action one April Sunday, is indicative of this ecological pattern:

> This [park] is really dead! The tremendous volume of picnickers in all of the parks. . . . It seems like every family in the city is out today. It is a beautiful day, very warm, very pleasant. And everyone is out with their children. . . . The one facility in this park, which is most active consistently, is just completely surrounded by picnickers, and this would kill any gay activity. . . .

At this stage in the development of American culture, at least, some sort of privacy is requisite for sex. Whether deviant or "normal," sexual activity demands a degree of seclusion. Even orgies, I am told, require darkness or a minimum of light. When, as is the case with fellatio, the form of sexual engagement is prohibited, privacy decreases risk and is even more valued.

This constitutes a dilemma for those who would engage in impersonal sex of this type: how to find a setting that is accessible and identifiable, that will provide the necessary volume and variety of participants, while preserving at least a minimum of privacy? The trysting place must not be too available for the undesired. It must not be identifiable by the uninitiated. The potential participant passing by should be able to perceive what is taking place inside, while those playing baseball across the way should remain ignorant of the sexual game behind tearoom walls.

Ecological factors, the tearoom purlieu, that separate these facilities from other activity in the public park, have already been discussed. The presence of walls and stalls and opaque windows also help preserve the needed privacy. But there is another aspect of the tearoom encounters that is crucial to the maintenance of privacy in public settings. I refer to the silence of the interaction.

Throughout most homosexual encounters in public restrooms, nothing is spoken. One may spend many hours in these buildings and witness dozens of sexual acts without hearing a word. Of fifty encounters on which I made extensive notes,[6] only fifteen included vocal utterances. The fifteen instances of speech break down as follows: Two were encounters in which I sought to ease the strain of legitimizing myself as lookout by saying, "You go ahead—I'll watch." Four were whispered remarks between sexual partners, such as, "Not so hard!" or "Thanks." One was an exchange of greetings between friends. The other eight verbal exchanges were in full voice and more extensive, but they reflected an attendant circumstances that was exceptional. When a group of us were locked in a restroom and attacked by several youths, we spoke for defense and out of fear. . . . This event ruptured the reserve among us and resulted in a series of conversations among those who shared this adventure for several days afterward. Gradually, this sudden unity subsided, and the encounters drifted back into silence.

Barring such unusual events, an occasionally whispered "thanks" at the conclusion of the act constitutes the bulk of even whispered communication. At first, I presumed that speech was avoided for fear of incrimination. The excuse that intentions have been misunderstood is much weaker when those proposals are expressed in words rather than signaled by body movements. As research progressed, however, it became evident that the privacy of silent interaction accomplishes much more than mere defense against exposure to a hostile world. Even when a careful lookout is maintaining the boundaries of an encounter against intrusion, the sexual participants tend to be silent. The mechanism of silence goes beyond satisfying the demand for privacy. Like all other characteristics of the tearoom setting, it serves to guarantee anonymity, to assure the impersonality of the sexual liaison.

Tearoom sex is distinctly less personal than any other form of sexual activity, with the single exception of solitary masturbation. . . . For now, let me indicate only what I mean by "less personal" is simply that there is less emotional and physical involvement in restroom fellatio—less, even, than in the furtive action that takes place in autos and behind bushes. In those instances, at least, there is generally some verbal involvement. Often, in tearoom stalls, the only portions of the players' bodies that touch are the mouth of the insertee and the penis of the inserter; and the mouths of these partners seldom open for speech.

Only a public place, such as a park restroom, could provide the lack of personal involvement in sex that certain men desire. The setting fosters the necessary turnover in participants by its accessibility and visibility to the "right" men. In these public settings, too, there exists a sort of democracy that is endemic to impersonal sex. Men of all racial, social, educational, and physical characteristics meet in these places for sexual union. With the lack of involvement, personal preferences tend to be minimized.

If a person is going to entangle his body with another's in bed—or allow his mind to become involved with another mind—he will have certain standards of appearance, cleanliness, personality, or age that the prospective partner must meet. Age, looks, and other external variables are germane to the sexual action. As the amount of anticipated contact of body and mind in the sex act decreases, so do the standards expected of the partner. As one respondent told me:

> I got to bed with gay people, too. But if I am going to bed with a gay person, I have certain standards that I prefer them to meet. And, in the tearooms, you don't have to worry about these things—because it is just a purely one-sided affair.

Participants may develop strong attachments to the settings of their adventures in impersonal sex. I have noted more than once that these men seem to acquire stronger sentimental attachments to the buildings in which they meet for sex than to the persons with whom they engage in it. One respondent tells the following story of his roommate's devotion to a particular restroom:

> We had been discussing the relative merits of various facilities, when I asked him: "Do you remember that old tearoom across from the park garage—the one they tore down last winter?"
>
> Do I ever! That was the greatest place in the park. Do you know what my roommate did last Christmas, after they tore the place down? He took a wreath, sprayed it with black paint, and laid it on top of the snow—right where that corner stall had stood. . . . He was really broken up!

The walls and fixtures of these public facilities are provided by society at large, but much remains for the participants to provide for themselves. Silence in these settings is the product of years of interaction. It is a normative response to the demand for privacy without involvement, a rule that has been developed and taught. Except for solitary masturbation, sex necessitates joint action; and impersonal sex requires that this interaction be as unrevealing as possible. In a number of ways, the structure of tearoom encounters has been developed, refined, and communicated. The primary task of this book is to describe for the reader the social structure of impersonal sex, the mechanisms that make it possible.

How, then, does such an operation work? What rules govern it? What roles may people play in it? What sort of ritual sustains the action? What are the risks—to players and others—of such activity? What kinds of people find the tearooms inviting for sexual experience, and how do they relate this behavior to the rest of their lives? These questions remain to be answered; but, before I can reply to them, it is important for the reader to know how I found these answers. Answers become clear only when we are aware what questions were asked and how conclusions were reached.

NOTES

1. Evelyn Hooker, "Male Homosexuals and Their 'Worlds'," in Judd Marmor, ed., *Sexual Inversion* (New York: Basic Books, 1965), p. 97.
2. Like most other words in the homosexual vocabulary, the origin of *tearoom* is unknown. British slang has used "tea" to denote "urine." Another British usage is as a verb, meaning "to engage with, encounter, go in against." See John S. Farmer and W. E. Henley, *A Dictionary of Slang and Colloquial English* (London: George Rutledge & Sons, 1921).
3. It is not possible to know how many sexual acts are performed in the various types of settings. Writers on the homosexual subculture agree, in general, on the relative popularity of these locales. For general surveys of the homosexual scene, see especially Evelyn Hooker, "The Homosexual Community," in *Personality Research* (Copenhagen: Monksgaard, 1962), pp. 40–59; and Maurice Leznoff and William A. Westley, "The Homosexual Community," *Social Problems,* Vol. 3, No. 4 (April, 1965), pp. 257–263.
4. By estimating (a) the average daily frequency of sex acts in each of twenty restrooms observed and (b) the average number of automobiles suspected of having been parked by participants near restrooms in five different parks, I have concluded that approximately 5 percent of the adult male population of the metropolitan area under study are involved in these encounters in a year's time. The imprecision of the methods used in obtaining this "guesstimate" does not warrant elaboration.
5. Alfred C. Kinsey and others, *Sexual Behavior in the Human Male* (Philadelphia: Saunders, 1948), pp. 650–651. See also William Simon and John H. Gagnon, "Homosexuality: The Formulation of a Sociological Perspective," *Journal of Health and Social Behavior,* Vol. 8, No. 3 (September, 1967), p. 180: "About one half [of the male homosexuals studied] reported that sixty percent or more of their sexual partners were persons with whom they had sex only one time. Between ten and twenty percent report that they often picked up their sexual partners in public terminals, and an even larger proportion reported similar contacts in other public or semipublic locations."
6. Although I made fifty systematic observations of tearoom encounters, fifty-three acts of fellatio were observed at those times. The sexual acts sometimes occur in such rapid succession that it is impossible to report them as involving separate encounters.

Application Exercise 2.1

Name of Student:______________

Student ID No.:______________

Course/Section No.:______________

Date:______________

1. *Tearoom Trade* (1970) is one of the most notorious studies in deviance, and it is widely read by scholars in the fields of sociology and criminology. Why do you think this article has garnered so much sustained attention in the near 40 years since Humphreys's published his work?

2. What is the most egregious ethical violation in this work? Justify your answer.

3. What are the potential social benefits of this study, if any?

4. Are the ethical breaches in this study worth the potential benefits of the findings? Justify your answer.

5. If you were charged with revising Humphreys's protocol such that it met with IRB approval, what three changes would you make?

Exercise 2.2 Informed Consent

Institutional Review Boards: Virtue Machines or Villains?

Bruce L. Berg, W. Timothy Austin, and Glenn A. Zuern

CRIMINAL JUSTICE POLICY REVIEW
VOL. 6, NO. 2, PP. 87–102, JUNE 1992

INTRODUCTION

One hundred years from now the advances in contemporary social science will be history. The most controversial chapters in written accounts of this history, no doubt, will be those that describe ethical, methodological, and political issues surrounding the research enterprise. As controversial as these chapters may continue to be in the future, they hold a singular advantage over writing on these subjects today: they will be in the past not the present and consequently dispassionate. Issues such as ethical conduct, methodological deceptions, and the politics of research currently invoke extreme passion from social scientists. Interestingly, these passions run equally high among politicians who would see social scientific research regulated as strenuously as the Food and Drug Administration regulates new medicines.

This article examines the history of institutional review boards (IRBs), and the way present day IRBs may be impacting the nature and quality of research in the social sciences.

RESEARCH REGULATIONS

The history of regulations, statutes, and research guidelines is largely of recent origin. They have been primarily invoked by biomedical and psycho-experimental research, and only secondarily understood through the natural history of the social sciences (Olesen, 1979; Chambers, 1980). This statement is not by any means suggesting that social sciences are exempt from their share of exploitive studies. For example, Stanley Milgram's (1963) experiment on authority and following orders, and Laud Humphreys's (1970) study of public sexuality, may also exemplify social scientific indiscretions.

Milgram (1963) was interested in learning about human tendencies to obey authority figures. In order to observe this phenomenon, he told voluntary subjects that they were going to assist in teaching another volunteer a simple word association task. This explanation, however, was a deception, and the "other volunteer" was really one of Millgram's confederates. The subject/teacher was instructed by Milgram to administer an electric shock to the learner (the research confederate) whenever the learner made a mistake. The subject/teacher was told that this electric shock was intended to facilitate learning and should be increased in intensity progressively with each error. Many of the subjects obediently advanced the shock levels to potentially lethal levels.

Actually, the supposed learner felt no electricity at all. Instead, each time the subject/teacher administered a shock, a signal indicated that the learner should react as if shocked. The performance by the learner was sufficient to convince the subject/teachers that they were being electronically shocked and aroused considerable emotional anguish in these subjects.

The other example, Laud Humphreys's (1970) study of casual sexual encounters in public places, has been the focus of considerable ethical debate since its publication. Humphreys was interested in gaining an understanding not only about practicing homosexuals, but also about non-homosexuals who briefly engaged in intimate same gender sexual encounters. In addition to observing encounters in public toilets (tearooms), Humphreys developed a way to gain access to detailed information about subjects he had covertly observed.

While serving as a "watch queen" (a voyeuristic lookout), Humphreys was able both to observe the various encounters and to also catch a glimpse of participants' car licenses. Once Humphreys had license plate numbers, he could locate home addresses of the tearoom participants through the Department of Motor Vehicles. Next, he disguised himself and deceived these men into believing that he was conducting a survey in the neighborhood. The result was that Humphreys was able to collect considerable amounts of information on each of the participants he had observed engaging in public sexual encounters.

Shortly after publication of Humphreys's work in 1970, there was considerable outcry against invasions of privacy, misrepresentation of researcher identities, and deception commonly being practiced during the course of research. Many issues arising out of Humphreys's research continue to serve as fodder for ethical debate. Especially critical among these are the justifications that the subject matter was of significant importance to the scientific community, and that it could not have been investigated in any other manner but through covert strategies.

The blurring of distinctions between biomedical research and that of social scientific inquiry has resulted in official regulations being tilted toward an image of experimental research. In part, this results from the origins of official regulations. For example, it is fairly well established that the context in which federal regulations originated was significantly influenced by the Nuremberg Code (Bower and de Gasparis, 1978; Olesen, 1979). This code emerged after the infamous Nuremberg trials where Nazi scientists were held to account for their inhumane behavior during World War II. The Nuremberg Code became the foundation for the "Declaration of Helsinki" adopted by the World Health Organization in 1964, and the "Ethical Guidelines for Clinical Investigation" adopted by the American Medical Association in 1966.

It was also in 1966 that the Surgeon General issued what may have been the first official rules concerning all Public Health Service research. This statement specified that any research financially supported by the Public Health Service was contingent upon an institutional review committee. The committee was charged with the responsibility of assuring that any research procedures would not harm human subjects and that subjects were informed of any potential risks (and benefits) from their participation. In essence, the institutional review board for research was born.

Several revisions of this general policy occurred throughout the late 1960s, and finally, in 1971 the Department of Health, Education, and Welfare (DHEW) published a booklet entitled "The Institutional Guide to DHEW Policy on Protection of Human Subjects." This booklet extended the review requirements to all DHEW grant and contract activities involving human subjects—including "non-medical" and "nonexperimental" studies. The booklet also spelled out the requirement of obtaining "informed consent" from subjects before including them in research projects.

In 1974, the National Research Act was passed by Congress, and the National Commission on Protection of Human Subjects of Biomedical and Behavioral Research was created by Title II of this law. The National Research Act directed all institutions that sponsored research to establish institutional review committees. Today, these committees are more commonly called Institutional Review Boards, or simply IRBs.

IRBs and Their Duties

Among the most important factors effected by the DHEW regulations are those regarding the establishment of locally appointed Institutional Review Boards and the requirements for obtaining written informed consent from research subjects. Both of these requirements have drawn heavy critical fire from social scientists (Meyer, 1977; Gray, 1977; Fields, 1978). Qualitative researchers, especially those involved in ethnographic research, have been particularly vocal. Their concerns often pertain to the way formal requirements for institutional review and written informed consent damages their special fieldworker/informant relationships (Wax, 1977; Cassell, 1978).

The National Commission for the Protection of Human Subjects, created by the National Research Act of 1974, has reviewed their own guidelines (DHEW, 1978) and offered revisions (*Federal Register,* 1978). These revisions are more specific about the role that the IRB should play. For example, the *Federal Register* points out that board members may be liable for legal action if they exceed their authority and interfere with the investigator's *right* to conduct research. These revised guidelines also recommend that the requirement for written informed consent could be waived for certain types of *low risk styles of research.* Unfortunately, the guidelines remained nonspecific in identifying the characteristics endemic to ethnographic research which might qualify for exceptions.

Because their research procedures are more formalized and require contacts with subjects, the more limited and predictable characteristics of quantitative methodologies are generally simpler to define. As a result, the specific exemptions or styles of research that can be expedited through IRBs largely are quantitative survey types, observation in public places, research involving educational tests (diagnostic, aptitude, or achievement), and archival research (*The Belmont Report,* 1978).

Clarifying the Role of IRBs

Initially, IRBs were charged with the responsibility of reviewing the adequacy of consent procedures for the protection of human subjects in research funded by the U.S. Department of Health, Education, and Welfare (DHEW). This mandate was soon broadened to include a review of all research conducted in an institution receiving any funds from DHEW—even when the study itself did not (Burstein, 1987; *Code of Federal Regulations, 45 CFR 46,* 1989).

As part of the IRB's review duties, they were to assure that subjects in research studies were advised both of their potential risks from participation, and possible benefits. This task seems to have evolved among some IRBs to become an assessment of risk to benefit ratios of proposed studies. In some cases, this is based upon the IRB's impression of the *worth* of the study. In other cases, this may be based upon the IRB's presumed greater knowledge of the subject and methodological strategies then potential subjects are likely to possess (Burnstein, 1987). Thus, in many cases, IRBs, and not subjects, predetermine whether the subject will even have the option of participating or declining participation in a study.

Today, many IRBs have further extended their purview to include evaluation of methodological strategies, not, as one might expect, as these methods pertain to human subject risks but in terms of the project's methodological adequacy. The justification for this apparently being that even where minimum risks exist, if a study is designed too poorly, it will not yield any scientific benefit.

Several problems immediately surface when one considers the original intent of IRBs and their current practices. These include the question of informed consent; the calculation of risk benefit; and what and who decides when a research design is *good* (Burstein, 1987). Further complicating issues is the fact that these actually are three overlapping questions, often weaved together as one.

Informed Consent

What proper informed consent involves according to Federal regulations, and how an IRB interprets this requirement, may differ. According to the *Code of Federal Regulations* (*45 CFR 46,* 1989), "General Requirements for Informed Consent" include the following:

> Except as provided elsewhere in this or other sub-parts, no investigator may involve a human being as a subject in research covered by these regulations unless the investigator has obtained the legally effective informed consent of the subject or the subject's legally authorized representative.

This general requirement specifies a number of recommended inclusions, such as a statement about what the study involves; a description of any reasonable and foreseeable risks or discomforts to the subject; a description of any benefits afforded to the subject; and disclosure of any possible alternative treatments, if any apply, that might be advantageous to the subject. Other suggested criteria include a statement addressing confidentiality of records identifying the subjects; explanations about any medical treatments that may be available if injury occurs in the course of the research; information about who the subject can contact in the event he or she is so injured; and a statement that the individual understands his or her participation is voluntary.

The general requirements, however, also provide for exceptions and alterations to some of these inclusions. Section C (*Code of Federal Regulations, 45 CFR 46*, 1989:10) reads:

> 6(c) An IRB may approve a consent procedure which does not include, or which alters, some or all of the elements of informed consent set forth above, or waive the requirement to obtain informed consent set forth above, or waive the requirement to obtain informed consent. . . .
>
> The policy outlines situations acceptable for waivers or alterations to usual requirements for informed consent (*Code of Federal Regulations, 45 CFR 46*, 1989:10):
>
> 1. The research involves no more than minimal risk to the subjects;
> 2. The waiver or alteration will not adversely affect the rights and welfare of the subjects;
> 3. The research could not practicably be carried out without the waiver or alteration; and
> 4. Whenever appropriate, the subjects will be provided with additional pertinent information after participation.

Thus, in many cases, researchers may entirely avoid the necessity for a signed written consent form. The decision rests largely in the hands of the IRB members and the ability of the researcher to convince these members that a waiver is warranted.

Risk/Benefit Concerns

The question of level of risk to participants is likewise vague and ambiguous. While the language of the federal regulations remains largely directed toward medical and biomedical risks to subjects, its auspice blankets the social sciences as well. In this regard, psychological risks often seem to loom large. Again, there are instances where this may be fairly clear-cut, but there are likely greater instances where this potential risk is simply unpredictable. Consider, for example, Philip Zimbardo's study of a mock prison (Zimbardo, 1972; Haney, Banks, and Zimbardo, 1973). Zimbardo hypothesized that the conditions of prison as a social setting—and not the personalities of the people involved—are the major cause of prison violence.

Zimbardo placed twenty-four male college student volunteers in a mock prison. The men had agreed to take part in this two-week-long experiment for a daily payment of $15.00. All twenty-four men had been screened to assure they were exceptionally physically and psychologically healthy. Half of these men were randomly assigned as guards, and half as prisoners.

Designated "prisoners" were arrested in their homes—without warning—by the Palo Alto police. After being fingerprinted and photographed at the police station, prisoners were taken in handcuffs to the Stanford County Prison on campus. Conversely, guards were given an orientation, where they were warned about the dangers of prison work. Guards were also admonished to keep the prison secure at all times. Zimbardo and his team of researchers now waited to see what would happen.

What happened next was entirely unforeseen by anyone. Within hours, the two groups had begun taking their *roles* very seriously. Both groups began to act much like stereotypical guards and inmates—both groups rapidly put aside all they had ever learned about appropriate behavior and human decency. Guards showed increasing hostility and even brutality toward prisoners, including forcing prisoners to engage in humiliating tasks such as cleaning toilet bowls with their bare hands.

Prisoners similarly began to act-out as inmates. Within the first five days of the experiment five prisoners had to be removed from the study because they began showing signs of "extreme emotional depression, crying, rage and acute anxiety" (Haney, Banks, and Zimbardo, 1973, p. 81). Before the end of the first week, and with the threat of a possible jailbreak, the experiment had to be canceled.

The Zimbardo study is often discussed regarding the ethical conduct of research. Yet, even had the regulations for informed consent been in place (the study predated the 1974 appearance of the National Research Act), and followed meticulously, problems still would have surfaced. No one ever suspected the magnitude of the effect this experience would have on subjects. It would have been impossible for an IRB to accurately predict the psychological risk and subsequent psychological and emotional harm to subjects.

Although speculative at this point, it is likely that most universities simply appoint a group of faculty to their IRBs for some unspecified time frame. The underlying assumption here is that, as university faculty, they should be automatically qualified to serve in such a capacity. Unfortunately, the assumption that because a faculty member has managed to secure work in a university setting he or she is the best choice for an IRB is unacceptable if not naive. IRB members are expected to serve as gatekeepers of virtuous research. At minimum, then, each member should have experience that includes serving as the principal investigator on a study involving human subjects. Ideally, universities should strive to have IRB membership reflect a diversity of researchers. Experience from physical and social science disciplines, and we would hope, given the relationships between subjects and investigators, ethnographers also would be represented. Furthermore, membership should require ratification by other members of the university community, and not merely reflect an administrative appointment. Finally, membership should be for a specified time period, to allow attitudes and prevailing viewpoints on the board to change over time.

References

The Belmont Report 1979 Department of Health Education and Welfare. Pub. no. (05) 78-0012.

Bower, R. T., and P. de Gasparis 1978 Ethics in Social Research. New York: Praeger.

Burstein, A. G. 1987 The virtue machine. American Psychologist. (February):199–202.

Cassell, J. 1978 Risk and benefit to subjects of fieldwork. American Sociologist. 13(August):134–143.

Chambers, E. 1980 Fieldwork and the law: New contexts for ethical decision making. Social Problems. 27(3):330–341.

Code of Federal Regulations (*45 CFR 46*) 1989 Protection Of Human Subjects. Washington, D.C.: Department of Health and Human Services, National Institute of Health, Office for Protection from Research Risks.

DHEW 1978a Report And Recommendations On Institutional Review Boards. Washington, D.C.: Department of Health Education and Welfare, Pub. no. (05) 78-0008.

Federal Register 1991 Federal policy for the protection of human subjects: Notices and rules (Part II). June 18 (FR Doc. 91-14257). 1978 Protection of human Subjects: Institutional review boards. November 3D (43 FR56174).

Fields, C. M. 1978 Universities fear impact of rules to protect research subjects. The Chronicle of Higher Education. (March 12):5–6.

Gray, B. G. 1977 The functions of human subjects review committees. American Journal of Psychiatry. 134:907–909.

Haney, C., C. Banks, and P. Zimbardo 1973 Interpersonal dynamics in a simulated prison. International Journal of Criminology and Penology. 1:69–97.

Humphreys, L. 1970 Tearoom Trade: Impersonal Sex in Public Places. Chicago: Aldine.

Meyer, R. E. 1977 Subjects' rights, freedom of inquiry, and the future of research in the addictions. American Journal of Psychiatry. 134(8):899–903.

Milgram, S. 1963 Behavioral study of obedience. Journal of Abnormal and Social Psychology. 67:371–378.

Olesen, V. 1979 Federal regulations, institutional review boards and qualitative social science research. In Murray L. Wax and Joan Cassell, Federal Regulations: Ethical Issues and Social Research. Boulder Colorado: Westview Press: 103–118.

Wax, M. L. 1977 On fieldworkers and those exposed to fieldwork: Federal regulations and moral issues. Human Organizations. 36(3):321–327.

Zimbardo, P. 1972 Pathology of imprisonment, Society. 9(April):4–8.

Application Exercise 2.2

Name of Student:______________

Student ID No.:______________

Course/Section No.:______________

Date:______________

1. You have been hired by a leading university to create guidelines for membership on their institutional review board (IRB). The university is particularly interested in directing your attention toward several areas. Please address the following questions with this in mind:
   a. What background should IRB members be required to have?

   ____
   ____
   ____
   ____
   ____
   ____

   b. Should IRB members be appointed by the university administration or elected by the faculty? Justify your answer.

   ____
   ____
   ____
   ____
   ____
   ____

   c. Should IRB membership be set as a specific term or duration? Should members be eligible for re-election or reappointment? Justify your answer.

   ____
   ____
   ____
   ____
   ____
   ____
   ____
   ____
   ____

   d. What sorts of research, if any, should be exempt from review? Justify your answer.

   ____
   ____
   ____
   ____
   ____
   ____

2. You are a member of an IRB at a leading university. The following study has been presented for your review:

   This research will involve a study of elementary aged children whose parent is incarcerated. The sample of children will be randomly assigned to two groups. One group will be instructed in a course designed to reinforce prosocial values (including both obedience of the law and love of parents); this instrument has been pilot tested and is deemed reliable and valid with regard to increasing student identification with prosocial norms. The other group will not receive any special training. The students who received training are expected to increase their identification with prosocial values by the end of the course, and the students who did not receive special instruction are not expected to improve in this regard.

   a. What are some of the ethical problems presented by this research plan?

   ____
   ____
   ____
   ____
   ____
   ____
   ____

b. How might each of these ethical problems be avoided or eliminated?

3. You are a researcher who has currently studied marijuana growers. As part of your study, you interviewed 50 large-scale marijuana farmers. Although you conducted these interviews in numerous locations, some of them contain various pieces of identifying information, such as the names of seed suppliers, other marijuana farmers, and various midlevel dealers. Somehow, the local police department has learned about your research and asked you to turn over your tapes of the interviews.
   a. Will you refuse to release this information and risk going to jail? Explain your answer.

   b. What could you have done to better ensure the confidentiality of your findings?

Exercise 2.3 Certificate of Confidentiality

NOTE: THIS GUIDANCE REPLACES THE 9/1998 OHRP GUIDANCE: "Privacy Protection for Human Research Subjects, Certificates of Confidentiality" CLICK HERE. **THIS GUIDANCE HAS BEEN UPDATED IN FORMAT, PROVIDES EMPHASIS ON LIMITATIONS OF THE CERTIFICATES OF CONFIDENTIALITY, AND PROVIDES LINKS TO RELEVANT MATERIALS ON THE NATIONAL INSTITUTES OF HEALTH (NIH) WEB SITE. Office for Human Research Protections (OHRP) Department of Health and Human Services (HHS)**

Guidance on Certificates of Confidentiality

Date: February 25, 2003

SCOPE

The purpose of this document is to provide guidance about Certificates of Confidentiality and assistance in locating resources for obtaining a Certificate of Confidentiality to protect the privacy of research subjects.

TARGET AUDIENCE

Institutions, institutional review boards (IRBs), and investigators.

BACKGROUND

The Public Health Service Act 301(d), 42 U.S.C. 241(d), "Protection of privacy of individuals who are research subjects," states:

> The Secretary may authorize persons engaged in biomedical, behavioral, clinical, or other research (including research on mental health, including research on the use and effect of alcohol and other psychoactive drugs) to protect the privacy of individuals who are the subject of such research by withholding from all persons not connected with the conduct of such research the names or other identifying characteristics of such individuals. Persons so authorized to protect the privacy of such individuals may not be compelled in any Federal, State, or local civil, criminal, administrative, legislative, or other proceedings to identify such individuals.

The privacy of the research subjects referred to in 301(d) is protected through the issuance of Certificates of Confidentiality. These Certificates of Confidentiality provide protection against compelled disclosure of identifying information about subjects enrolled in sensitive biomedical, behavioral, clinical, or other research. This protection is not limited to federally supported research.

GUIDANCE: OHRP DOES NOT ISSUE CERTIFICATES OF CONFIDENTIALITY

Certificates of Confidentiality are issued by the National Institutes of Health (NIH) and other HHS agencies to protect identifiable research information from forced or compelled disclosure. They allow the investigator and others who have access to research records to refuse to disclose identifying information on research participants in civil, criminal, administrative, legislative, or other proceedings, whether federal, state, or local. Certificates of Confidentiality may be granted for studies collecting information that, if disclosed, could have adverse consequences for subjects, such as damage to their financial standing, employability, insurability, or reputation. By protecting researchers and institutions from being compelled to disclose information that would identify research subjects, Certificates of Confidentiality help to minimize risks to subjects by adding an additional level of protection for maintaining confidentiality of private information.

Certificates of Confidentiality protect subjects from compelled disclosure of identifying information but do not prevent the voluntary disclosure of identifying characteristics of research subjects. Researchers, therefore, are not prevented from voluntarily disclosing certain information about research subjects, such as evidence of child abuse or a subject's threatened violence to self or others.

However, if a researcher intends to make such voluntary disclosures, the consent form should clearly indicate this. Furthermore, Certificates of Confidentiality do not prevent other types of intentional or unintentional breaches of confidentiality. As a result, investigators and IRBs must ensure that other appropriate mechanisms and procedures are in place to protect the confidentiality of the identifiable private information to be obtained in the proposed research.

For more information on Certificates of Confidentiality and their limitations, see http://grants.nih.gov/grants/policy/coc/index.htm.

For Certificate of Confidentiality contacts at the National Institutes of Health, see http://grants.nih.gov/grants/policy/coc/contacts.htm.

For information on obtaining a Certificate of Confidentiality for research supported by other HHS agencies, please contact the appropriate program official. ***Again, please note that the OHRP does not issue Certificates of Confidentiality.***

Certificates of Confidentiality constitute an important tool to protect the privacy of research study participants. Thus, NIH would like to encourage their appropriate use. NIH is making information widely available to investigators working on sensitive biomedical, behavioral, clinical or other types of research at this Certificate Kiosk. Information may get added to this site periodically. Readers are encouraged to check back periodically.

Certificates of Confidentiality are issued by the National Institutes of Health (NIH) to protect identifiable research information from forced disclosure. They allow the investigator and others who have access to research records to refuse to disclose identifying information on research participants in any civil, criminal, administrative, legislative, or other proceeding, whether at the federal, state, or local level. Certificates of Confidentiality may be granted for studies collecting information that, if disclosed, could have adverse consequences for subjects or damage their financial standing, employability, insurability, or reputation. By protecting researchers and institutions from being compelled to disclose information that would identify research subjects, Certificates of Confidentiality help achieve the research objectives and promote participation in studies by assuring confidentiality and privacy to participants.

U.S. Department of Health and Human Services

Office of Extramural Research

National Institutes of Health

Detailed Application Instructions for Certificate of Confidentiality: Extramural Research Projects

Updated: March 15, 2002

Applicants should read NIH's background information and instructions on Certificates of Confidentiality, which are available at http://grants.nih.gov/grants/policy/coc/background.htm. See also Frequently Asked Questions, which are available at http://grants.nih.gov/grants/policy/coc/faqs.htm.

The Food and Drug Administration handles requests for Certificate of Confidentiality protection for studies that obtain an Investigational New Drug (IND) authorization or other FDA authorization. Projects with INDs or IDEs should apply to the FDA (Leslie Vaccari, Project Management Officer, Division of Scientific Investigations, HFD-45 Office of Compliance Center for Drug Evaluation and Research, Leslie.vaccari@fda.hhs.gov, 301-796-3396 OR Patricia Holobaugh, Bioresearch Monitoring Branch, HFM-664, Center for Biologics Evaluation and Research, patricia.holobaugh@fda.hhs.gov, 301-827-6347).

The application should be written on the letterhead of the research applicant institution and submitted to the appropriate NIH Institute or Center (NIH IC). For a list of NIH Certificate contacts, see http://grants.nih.gov/grants/policy/coc/contacts.htm. The application letter should include the following information.

1. Name and address of applicant research institution. This is the institution with which the applicant is affiliated and the recipient of grant support for the research, if there is any.
2. Sites where the research will be conducted and a brief description of the facilities available for the conduct of the research. Please indicate if this is a multi-site project. The lead site of a multi-site project should apply for a single Certificate to protect participants enrolled at all sites. However, multi-site applicants must list each participating unit, its address, and project director. If any new sites are added after the certificate is issued, the lead site should provide NIH with an updated list and the cover letter should include a statement by the lead site that IRB approval has been given at the new site and that the lead site is maintaining a copy of that approval (see item 5(b) below.)
3. Title of the research project. If the project title on the IRB form (see item 5 below) is different from the title given here, the applicant must document that the IRB approval pertains to this project.
4. Source and number of the supporting grant, if applicable (e.g., National Institute of XYZ, NIH, 1 R01 XY 12345-01; ABC Foundation, Grant No. 123). If the NIH funds the project, please provide the name and telephone number of the Project Officer at the funding IC. If there is no support, type "None."
5. (a). Requirement—A Certificate of Confidentiality will not be issued to an applicant conducting research involving human subjects unless the project has IRB approval. The approving IRB must be in compliance with applicable Federal requirements. If the applicant institution is receiving DHHS funding for research involving human subjects, an OHRP-approved IRB for that institution must approve the project for which a Certificate of Confidentiality is sought. For additional information on OHRP and IRB assurances, see http://www.hhs.gov/ohrp/assurances/assurances_index.html

   If the applicant institution does not receive DHHS funding for this research involving human subjects but has an IRB that complies with the requirements for IRBs imposed by another Federal agency, that IRB must approve the research. If the applicant institution does not have an IRB, the project should be reviewed by an IRB in accordance with 45 CFR Part 46.

(b). Documentation of IRB approval: Attach letter or form signed by an authorized IRB representative. Approval must be current and unconditional, or conditioned only upon the issuance of a Certificate of Confidentiality and documented by a letter or form signed by an authorized IRB representative. If this is a multi-site project, the lead site must maintain a copy of the IRB approval from each site, which must be made available to the NIH upon request.

(c). Documentation of IRB qualifications: For all projects, submit for the IRB that reviewed the project the assurance number assigned by OHRP or documentation that the IRB complies with the applicable Federal regulations governing research involving human subjects. If this is a multi-site project, the lead site must maintain the OHRP assurance number for the reviewing IRB at each site, which must be made available to the NIH upon request.

6. Name, title, mailing and email addresses, telephone and fax numbers of the Applicant as well as name and title of other key personnel. Also include a brief summary of the scientific training of the Applicant and key personnel. If this is a multi-site project, only information from the lead site should be submitted to the NIH. However, the lead site must collect and maintain this information for each site and make it available to the NIH upon request.

7. Beginning date and expected end date of the project. The Certificate will state the date upon which it becomes effective and the date upon which it expires. A Certificate of Confidentiality protects all information identifiable to any individual who participates as a research subject (i.e., about whom the investigator maintains identifying information) during any time the Certificate is in effect. The protection afforded by the Certificate is permanent. If this project is not completed by the expiration date, the Applicant must submit a written request for an extension three months prior to the expiration date. Any such request must include a brief description of the reason for the extension, documentation of the most recent IRB approval, and the expected date for completion of the research project.

8. Concise description of project aims and research methods (1–2 paragraphs, omit background). This section should include a brief description of procedures for the collection and storage of identifying information as well as the number of subjects to be included in the study, the source from which they will be recruited, and a description of the study population (e.g., gender, age, race, etc.) If significant changes are made to the project aims or methods during the course of the study, the Applicant should contact the Certificate Coordinator who issued the Certificate. That person will determine if the Certificate can be modified or if the Applicant will need to submit an amended application.

9. A description of means used to protect subjects' identities (i.e., subjects are coded by numbers not names, linking information is kept in locked files, identifiers will be destroyed when the study is completed, etc.)

10. Reasons for requesting a Certificate of Confidentiality (e.g., will collect sensitive information, identifying information on subjects, etc.); include brief description of sensitive and identifying information to be collected.

11. Informed consent forms for human subjects, as approved by the IRB (attach copy). The informed consent form must include a description of the protections and limitations of the Certificate of Confidentiality, including the circumstances in which the investigators plan to disclose voluntarily identifying information about research participants (e.g., child abuse, harm to self or others, etc.). Sample language is provided below. If significant changes are made to the informed consent form, the Applicant should contact the Certificate Coordinator who issued the Certificate and submit a copy of the revised consent form. If this is a multi-site project, the lead site must indicate that it has on file a copy of the consent form as approved by the IRB from each site, which will be made available to the NIH upon request.

12. Research not funded by NIH in which drugs will be administered to human subjects must provide the following additional information:

- Identification of drugs to be administered;
- Description of methods for administration of these drugs, including a statement of dosages;
- Evidence that individuals who will receive the drugs are authorized to do so under applicable Federal and State law.

13. All research in which a controlled drug or drugs will be administered must submit a copy of the Drug Enforcement Administration Certificate of Registration (BND Form 223) under which the research project will be conducted.

14. If the research project is testing for reportable communicable diseases, the applicant must submit information relating to its compliance with State reporting laws as specified in the August 9, 1991 memorandum from the Assistant Secretary for Health (http://grants.nih.gov/grants/policy/coc/cd_policy.htm).

ASSURANCES

The following assurances are required and the following information should be inserted verbatim into the Certificate application letter. Both the PI and the Institutional Official must sign this letter. The name and title of the Institutional Official should be typed below the signature.

> This institution agrees to use the Certificate of Confidentiality to protect against the compelled disclosure of personally identifiable information and to support and defend the authority of the Certificate against legal challenges.
>
> The institution and personnel involved in the conduct of the research will comply with the applicable Federal regulation for the protection of human subjects or, if no such Federal regulation is otherwise applicable, they will comply with 45 CFR Part 46.
>
> This Certificate of Confidentiality will not be represented as an endorsement of the project by the DHHS or NIH or used to coerce individuals to participate in the research project.
>
> All subjects will be informed that a Certificate has been issued, and they will be given a description of the protection provided by the Certificate.
>
> Any research participant entering the project after expiration or termination of the Certificate will be informed that the protection afforded by the Certificate does not apply to them.

____________________________ ____________________________

Signature of Principal Investigator Signature of Institutional Official

____

Name and Title of Institutional Official

INFORMED CONSENT

When a researcher obtains a Certificate of Confidentiality, the research subjects must be told about the protections afforded by the certificate and any exceptions to that protection. That information should be included in the informed consent form. Examples of appropriate language follow. Researchers may adapt the language to the needs of the research participants and to the subject matter of the study. However, the language used must cover the basic points.

Researchers should also review the language about confidentiality and data security that is routinely included in consent forms to be certain that it is consistent with the protections of the Certificate of Confidentiality.

Example:

To help us protect your privacy, we have obtained a Certificate of Confidentiality from the National Institutes of Health. With this Certificate, the researchers cannot be forced to disclose information that may identify you, even by a court subpoena, in any federal, state, or local civil, criminal, administrative, legislative, or other proceedings. The researchers will use the Certificate to resist any demands for information that would identify you, except as explained below.

The Certificate cannot be used to resist a demand for information from personnel of the United States Government that is used for auditing or evaluation of Federally funded projects or for information that must be disclosed in order to meet the requirements of the federal Food and Drug Administration (FDA).

You should understand that a Certificate of Confidentiality does not prevent you or a member of your family from voluntarily releasing information about yourself or your involvement in this research. If an insurer, employer, or other person obtains your written consent to receive research information, then the researchers may not use the Certificate to withhold that information.

[The researchers should include language such as the following if they intend to make voluntary disclosure about things such as child abuse, intent to hurt self or others, or other voluntary disclosures.] The Certificate of Confidentiality does not prevent the researchers from disclosing voluntarily, without your consent, information that would identify you as a participant in the research project under the following circumstances. [The researchers should state here the conditions under which voluntary disclosure would be made. If no voluntary disclosures will be made, the researchers should so state.]

Application Exercise 2.3

Name of Student:_______________

Student ID No.:_______________

Course/Section No.:_______________

Date:_______________

1. You are about to continue your research on 50 large-scale marijuana growers. You know that your research subjects are violating the law, and thus, they are in potential jeopardy of criminal prosecution by disclosing information to you. How will you address this in your research protocol?

2. Assume that you will file for a federal certificate of confidentiality to provide subpoena protection for yourself and research staff. Item 2 in the *application* for a Certificate of Confidentiality above (which is submitted before you have the subpoena protection) asks you to provide:

   Sites where the research will be conducted and a brief description of the facilities available for the conduct of the research. Please indicate if this is a multi-site project. The lead site of a multi-site project should apply for a single Certificate to protect participants enrolled at all sites. However, multi-site applicants must list each participating unit, its address, and project director. If any new sites are added after the certificate is issued, the lead site should provide NIH with an updated list and the cover letter should include a statement by the lead site that IRB approval has been given at the new site and that the lead site is maintaining a copy of that approval (see item 5(b) below.)

   a. Are you concerned that this application itself could put your subjects in jeopardy? Why or why not?

   b. How will you complete this section?

3. How will you ensure the protection of subjects' identities required in item 9, in the Certificate of Confidentiality, above? It reads:

   A description of means used to protect subjects' identities (i.e., subjects are coded by numbers not names, linking information is kept in locked files, identifiers will be destroyed when the study is completed, etc.)

   ____
   ____
   ____
   ____
   ____
   ____
   ____
   ____

CHAPTER 3

Issues of Measurement

In this chapter, we will consider the issue of measurement. Measurement is defined as the process by which concepts are transformed into variables through operationalization. We will illustrate various types of measurement strategies and provide opportunities to practice many of these techniques. First, however, we need to introduce a number of terms and concepts and explain the importance of measurement.

A research study usually begins with a fairly simple idea. A researcher poses a question to himself or herself, for example, "Does marijuana use affect adolescents' later delinquency?" Next, the researcher may start thinking about hypotheses or may ask other tentative questions about the topic or offer a personal theory. As the researcher continues to read about the subject matter, he or she will refine propositions and eventually develop a formal theory.

Theories are composed of sets of logically linked concepts. However, since theories are neither directly observable nor testable, these concepts must be transformed into variables. In many ways, measurement is the process by which this transformation takes place.

The task of transforming elements of theory into measurable indices—variables—is one of the toughest challenges facing social scientists. Some of the concepts that arise during a given research project are relatively easy to measure, because there is a broad consensus on how to evaluate their underlying properties. For example, an individual's "age," "educational level," and "income" are concepts that are relatively straightforward and easy to measure; these concepts have properties that are clear, objective, concrete, and easy to assess. However, many concepts have more elusive properties. For example, "friendship," "involvement," "socialization," "social status," "value," and "social class" are among the many thousands of concepts that are regularly measured in criminological research but have vague properties.

Consider, for example, "delinquency"—an important concept in many criminological studies but quite a difficult one to measure. One way to consider the variable "delinquency" is to think about the various ways in which youth can be identified as being delinquent. Initially, we may consider various behavioral issues, such as runaway, truancy, and other "status offenses." We may also consider official sanctions, such as suspension, arrest, or adjudication, as demarcating delinquency. Alternately, we might consider a youth's primary identification with certain organizations such as gangs, or his or her commitment to antisocial norms. We might also survey the youth and ask for his or her self-reported behaviors to assess "delinquency." Each of these, then, represents a kind of subcategory of delinquency, and each can be transformed into a measurable index.

Measurement provides researchers with a means by which to make evaluations, assessments, and comparisons of various kinds. These analytic activities, in turn, give meaning to our everyday reality. For example, we might want to know whether the crime rate in a given community has gone up or down, whether the individuals' religious attitudes have anything to do with their involvement in certain kinds of crime, and whether alcohol use impacts the commission of predatory crime, and so forth. To answer any of these questions, the researcher must find a way to measure the variables of interest.

As several of the abstracts reprinted in this book demonstrate, measurement in the research context is not always clear cut or strictly numerical. When someone asks, "How dangerous is it to walk through this neighborhood?" a response is not immediately quantifiable. Thus, research on the subject "fear of crime" requires the researcher to consider what measures of danger can be identified and used to represent various degrees of perceived danger.

WHY DO SOCIAL SCIENTISTS MEASURE VARIABLES?

Sometimes, a numerical representation of the frequency of occurrence or the magnitude of some event or phenomenon is considered to be sufficient measurement for a study. In other cases, more specific measures may be required.

Social scientists often devise measures to describe properties associated with various social ideas and phenomena. For example, the ideas "social class" and "social status" conjure images in our minds, yet those images may be slightly different for each of us. For some, "social class" may bring to mind images of income levels, relative levels of education, certain patterns of consumer buying, and various kinds of lifestyles or economic strata in our society. For others, "social status" may evoke images of certain careers, access to restricted social organizations, specific categories of occupations, or even rankings of certain occupations in a given society. The concept of "robbery" is equally vague at first glance. Many people consider the following acts examples of robbery: stealing from a purse left in a car; coming home to find the house ransacked and jewelry stolen; taking makeup from a cosmetic counter without paying for it. While none of these examples meets the legal definition of robbery (which is defined in most states as taking of property by force or fear), few people consider "robbery" to be defined by the elements specified in the state penal code. Consider the example of "burglary," which most criminal justice students would articulate as unauthorized entry into some location with the intent to commit a felony. However, "burglary" is not so straightforward. In many states, it is a wobbler. This means that the same behavior might be prosecuted as a misdemeanor (trespassing, petty theft, vandalism) or felony (burglary) based on the criminal history of the accused. Some research further documents that changes in official crime rates for a given category are not generally driven by an onslaught of criminal behavior; rather, these changes in official crime data represent a change in legal definitions, the availability of diversion programs (Bechard, 2006), and so on.

Many of the ideas and events we value are constructed in terms of an essentially arbitrary system of measurement. In order for more than a single individual to appreciate the meanings of these concepts, the researcher must declare some form of systematic measurement. The process of formally defining how a concept will be measured is called *operationalization.*

Operationalization is perhaps the most difficult task a researcher has to undertake. The reason for this is that operationalization involves moving from the abstract, namely, a concept, to something concrete, like a variable. Throughout most of socialization in American educational settings, we have been trained to take concrete items and make them abstract. If asked to write about the topic "A Day in the Life of a Police Officer," most criminal justice students would have little trouble moving from the concrete prompt to the abstract. However, when asked to take an abstract concept such as "social class," many of us would find it difficult to derive concrete measures of this term. We might decide that "social class" is made up of several elements for which we can identify concrete measures. For example, certain levels of income and education may be thought to represent different social class strata. By identifying people who fit into different income and educational groups, we can establish a hierarchy intended to represent the social class rankings of a given population. Doing so would provide us with an operationalized definition of "social class": Social class is an individual's placement in one of the hierarchy of categories representing income and class.

RELATIONSHIPS BETWEEN VARIABLES

Measurement also permits examination of and comparison between variables. Analysis of such comparisons permits researchers to make predictions and assessments about relationships between variables. For example, "Does an adolescent's marijuana use predict his or her likelihood of becoming delinquent?"; "Does a baccalaureate degree increase the likelihood that a police officer will perform his or her duties more professionally than officers with a high school equivalent?"; and "Do minority officers with baccalaureate degrees have the same career success as similarly educated Caucasian officers?" By carefully operationalizing "delinquent," "professionally," "minorities," and categories of "career success," we could potentially assess these questions.

Now that we have established what measurement is and suggested how it works in criminological research, we must consider various kinds of measurement. Typically, measurement is classified into four groups or levels of data: nominal, ordinal, interval, and ratio. These categories are conceived in terms of their increasing and cumulative mathematical properties (discussed below).

LEVELS OF MEASUREMENT

Nominal Level

The nominal level of measurement involves sorting elements to be measured into discrete categories. For example, we could measure people's hair color by categorizing it as "brown," "blond," "red," and "black." In terms of the mathematical properties associated with nominal-level data, we can use only operations related to relationships that are equal or not equal. Stated simply, nominal-level data involve assigning names or numbers to categories. These names and numbers have no literal mathematical meanings.

Many of the variables that criminologists find interesting are of the nominal type. Gender, race, marital status, education/literacy level, drug of choice, and religious preference are typical examples. Gender is usually depicted as involving two categories—"male" and "female"—but no underlying mathematical meaning is imputed to these categories. We can neither order them nor can we add them in the same way we add a quarter and a nickel and derive the sum 30 cents. Even if we assign numbers to these categories ("male" = 1, "female" = 2), adding the numbers makes no sense. Certainly, "male" + "female" does not equal 3.

The categories in any nominal set must meet two criteria:

1. They must be mutually exclusive, so that each case is counted in only one category.
2. They must be logically exhaustive, so that every case belongs in one category.

The fact that nominal-level measures have no mathematical properties does not mean that mathematical operations are inappropriate in every case. We may not be able to order or average the categories, but mathematical functions can be performed and used to compare between and across categories. The mathematical operations most frequently used on nominal-level measures are the calculations of frequencies (e.g., number of males = 15, number of females = 10), simple proportions (males = 15/25, females = 10/25), and percentages (males = 32%, females = 68%).

Ordinal Level

Unlike nominal-level measures, ordinal-level measures do possess basic mathematical properties. Ordinal-level data are ordered or ranked, usually involving a rising order of inequality between categories from the lowest rank to the highest. For example, we could take the sentence type from a group of inmates and order them from the lowest to the highest scores (detention, jail sentence, prison sentence). This would provide us with a means for ranking each inmate. Similarly, we could rank order the positions in a police agency: cadet, patrol officer, sergeant, lieutenant, captain, and chief. However, this simple ranking would not tell us how far apart the officers are in professional training, years on the force, or job performance.

We can consider another example from the world of horse racing. When a horse "places" in a race, we immediately know it has come in second. However, we do not know whether the second-place horse has edged out the "show" horse (the third-place horse) or has beaten it by several lengths, nor do we know whether the "place" horse has followed the winning horse (the first-place horse) by inches or meters. We do know, however, the first-, second-, and third-place rankings of the horses. All ordinal-level measures incorporate this mathematical property of order or rank.

All ordinal-level measures incorporate this mathematical property of order or rank. Here are several other examples of ordinal measures.

Levels of criminal justice supervision

Informal probation
Formal probation
Jail sentence
Prison sentence

Police officer discretion

Advise
Infraction citation
Criminal citation/release
Arrest

For such measures, rank is assigned (1) according to the number of categories and (2) in ordered sequence (from less to more of a property). Ordinal variables must meet three criteria:

1. They must be mutually exclusive, so that each case is counted in only one category.
2. They must be logically exhaustive, so that every case belongs in one category.
3. They must be rank ordered.

Interval Level

The third level of data is interval measurement. In addition to possessing the mathematical property of order, interval-level scales assume an equal distance between points representing order. In an interval scale, the distance between the points on a measuring instrument is known, and this value is equal throughout the scale. For example, the difference between a score of 40 and a score of 50 on an addiction severity scale is the same as the difference between 70 and 80 on the same scale. Thus, the ratio of measured intervals is meaningful. In other words, any given interval is exactly equal to every other interval in the scale, regardless of its position in the series of units.

However, we would not be accurate in saying that an individual with a score of 80 is twice as addicted as someone with a score of 40 on the same addiction severity scale. The reason for this is that in interval measures, we operate with an arbitrary zero point. The placement of zero on this scale is arbitrary, since the best we can do is operationally define the absence of the property being measured; however, the true "absence" of the variable may not be measurable. For example, if an individual received a score of zero on an addiction severity scale, this would not mean that he or she had absolutely no addiction. As another example, consider an ambient temperature of 70°F, a comfortable temperature. We know that 80°F is 10°F warmer than 70°F, and 60°F is 10°F cooler. However, a temperature of 0°F, albeit very cold, does not reflect the absence of temperature. We arbitrarily set a temperature of 0°F. While the Celsius scale is somewhat more deliberate—0°C is the point at which water freezes—0°C is still not the absence of temperature.

Mathematically, interval measures possess several basic properties. Operations of addition, subtraction, multiplication, and division normally can be performed on interval scales. When measuring various cognitive, perceptual, and behavioral phenomena, social scientists frequently employ the use of an arbitrary zero.

If we were to measure student perspectives about the death penalty, for example, we could assume that the difference between scores of 2 and 3 is the same as that between scores of 6 and 7. However, accounting for individuals who have no feelings about the death penalty (neutrality) still requires an arbitrary placement of zero.

Interval variables must meet four criteria:

1. They must be mutually exclusive, so that each case is counted in only one category.
2. They must be logically exhaustive, so that every case belongs in one category.
3. They must be rank ordered.
4. There is equal distance between units on the scale.

Ratio Level

Ratio measures incorporate both the mathematical properties already mentioned (order and equal intervals) and one additional property: The presence of a natural or absolute zero. The ratio level of measurement is based on an ordered series of equal intervals, beginning with an absolute or natural zero. In situations where the zero on the ratio scale is absolute, it represents a condition where the absence of a property is measured: "None of something."

Ratio variables must meet five criteria:

1. They must be mutually exclusive, so that each case is counted in only one category.
2. They must be logically exhaustive, so that every case belongs in one category.
3. They must be rank ordered.
4. There is equal distance between units on the scale.
5. The scale has a true, or absolute, zero.

For example, if you withdraw all your savings from a bank account, you reach the natural origin of zero. If you replace $25, you increase the balance to a positive $25. If you add a second deposit of $50, your balance increases to $75 (assuming no other deposits or withdrawals have occurred). At this point, the balance is three times as large as it was following your first deposit.

This example demonstrates that when we work with a natural zero, the numbers on the scale represent the actual amount of a property following the first deposit. Because the actual amount of property is scaled, mathematical operations are possible with ratios. The ratio of $75 to $25 is 75:25, or 3:1. In other words, we can legitimately claim that $75 is three times as much as $25.

Another commonly employed example of a ratio-level measure is age, where the moment of birth (in most Western cultures) represents a natural zero. Accepting this natural zero point allows the social scientist to suggest that a person who has lived 50 years has lived twice as long as someone who is 25.

OVERVIEW OF LEVELS OF MEASUREMENT

For most concepts, there is no single correct measure. In fact, most concepts can be transformed into variables in many different ways. As long as you start with a higher-order level of measurement, such as ratio, you can collapse down into lesser levels of measurement. For example, consider the variable age, a ratio-level variable. Given a data set listing age for a given prison population, one could collapse it into an ordinal-level variable—young (18–29), middle (30–49), and old (50+) inmates—to help plan institutional staffing and programming. One could then take this ordinal data and collapse it further into a nominal scale to track geriatric inmates along a dichotomous variable: geriatric and nongeriatric. With this data, state-level administrators could plan geriatric programs at institutions with the highest percentage of geriatric inmates. However, once collapsed, lower levels of measurement cannot be expanded to higher levels of measurement. Consider, for example, a data set that tracks addiction status for a group of criminal defendants (addicted and not addicted); one could not extrapolate to determine the length of addiction or drug of choice for any individual in the sample.

It is quite possible to have different measures of a given concept represented at different levels. Which measure the researcher chooses for a given concept will depend on what measures are selected, what measures were used previously in similar research, and which measures are proven effective. At least two major techniques are used in the social sciences for constructing measures: single-measure indicators and scales.

Single-Measure Indicators

A single-measure indicator can be constructed in just two steps: The researcher decides (1) what observations to use as measures of a concept and (2) what procedure to use for combining these observations operationally. For example, we might decide to use the number of law violations reported to the police as an approximate indicator of the annual crime rate in a given city. Although operationally possible, such an indicator would be limited, since as many as half of all violations (e.g., tax and insurance fraud, petty theft) may never be discovered, let alone reported.

Social scientists, then, must make decisions about how helpful a selected indicator will be toward measuring a given concept. Also, the researcher must decide whether a single limited indicator will be sufficient or whether several indicators might yield more satisfactory results. One way to use several indicators of a concept and to measure these together operationally is through scaling.

SCALES OF MEASURES

The term *scale* refers to a special type of measurement in which numbers are assigned to positions, indicating varying degrees of the property under consideration. When a concept is measured using a scale, the result is usually a single score for an individual, representing the degree to which that individual possesses the property being measured. Many different types of scales are used in social science research. We will discuss only two major types: rating scales and questionnaire-based scales.

Rating Scales

In general, all rating scales have one feature in common: The person or object being rated is placed in one category within an ordered set, in which numerical values are assigned to categories. Rating scales can be used to secure individuals' ratings of themselves or others. If we want to transpose this type of categorical scaling strategy to a more qualitative mode, this, too, is possible. By assessing either self-perceptions or perceptions of others, we can create various types of categorical or typological schemes. Three of the most commonly used rating scales are the graphic rating scale, the itemized rating scale, and the comparative rating scale.

An alternative scaling technique uses a measured line, usually 10 centimeters in length. At one end, the researcher places a zero or a term such as "Low," "Disagree," or "Never." At the other end, the researcher places a 10 or a term such as "High," "Agree," or "Always." In response to a question or statement, the subject places a mark on the line in relation to how he or she rates something—for example, high or low. Because the questionnaires are identical (e.g., each line is exactly 10 cm long), each subject's rating can be determined and scaled.

GRAPHIC RATING SCALES Graphic rating scales are those constructed with (1) designated number-ordered scale points and (2) a written description for every other scale point. It may help to think of a graphic rating scale as analogous to a ruler. Unlike the 10 cm line, which shows starting and ending points, graphic rating scales show points positioned at equal intervals, and written descriptions are supplied for most or all points. The subject is told to select one written description (and hence the corresponding scale point) that most closely approximates his or her position. For example, consider the following scale:

Confidence in personal security

1	2	3	4	5	6
Low confidence in personal security. Men and women restrict all movements at night to predetermined precautions. Extensive use of locks, dogs, and guards is made.		Moderate confidence in personal security. Men may be confident of personal safety, but women are warned to take precautions. Women's movements are restricted to daytime.		High confidence in personal security. Free movement night and day, for both sexes. Locking homes is optional.	

ITEMIZED RATING SCALES Itemized rating scales are composed of series of ordered statements to which point values have been assigned. In some scales, subjects are instructed to read statements and select all those statements with which they agree. In other cases, subjects may be asked to read statements and select only one statement that best describes their view. Usually, the statements vary in terms of intensity, with the middle statement expressing a relatively neutral position. Statements also may vary in length, from a single sentence to several sentences or illustrations. The clearer the distinction between statements, the more vivid the scale positions and the more reliable the scale. For example, consider the following statements in the order presented:

1. The state criminal code is an objective document that reflects public consensus about crimes, their severity, and appropriate punishment.
2. The state criminal code generally reflects public consensus about crimes, but it is subject to some human error.
3. The state criminal code is the best mechanism by which we can enforce laws, but it is deeply flawed and rarely objective.
4. The state criminal code was written by powerful White men who have assured that the criminal code serves their vested interests.

COMPARATIVE RATING SCALES Comparative rating scales ask subjects to position themselves or others on scales where the positions are judged relative to other individuals or groups. This type of scale differs from an itemized scale, since it does not require that subjects rate some objects or people in reference to others. In effect, subjects are asked to respond on the basis of their knowledge about something or someone. For example, felony sentencing is often driven by statute, which specifies an appropriate sentence based on the judge's assessment of the current case in relation to other examples of the same penal code violation. An assessment of aggravating and mitigating circumstances is generally used to help determine the appropriate sentence: low, middle, or high terms. If the current case is more severe than typical instances of the same law violation, a high term is generally imposed. If the current case is less severe, a low term is generally imposed. To administer equitable sentences, the judge must have a clear picture of this defendant in relation to other defendants charged with the same crime.

Likewise, when a professor is asked to evaluate a student seeking entrance into a graduate, law, or medical program, he or she is frequently asked to rate the student's performance in comparison with the performances of other students. A typical question might look like the following:

Of the students you have known, is the student in the top

1. 5%?
2. 10%?
3. 25%?
4. 50%?

Questionnaire-Based Scales

Questionnaire-based scales are scales in which series of statements are tallied in order to create single composite scores or indexes. The use of the phrase *questionnaire based* is not meant to imply that rating scales are not included on these questionnaires. The phrase is only meant to suggest that questionnaire-based scales are formatted much like questionnaires, since they contain series of questions or statements.

The usual format for a questionnaire-based scale asks the subject to respond to every statement. Several questionnaire-based scales have received general acceptance in social science research, including the Thurstone, Likert, and Guttman scales.

THURSTONE SCALES The Thurstone scaling technique, named after its originator, L. L. Thurstone (1930), is generally held to be the most elaborate version of a questionnaire-based scale. Thurstone scales are one means of measuring attitudes. In the original Thurstone scale, a set of statements is arranged on a continuum, on which the scale points vary from 1 to 11, ranging from the least favorable ones to the most favorable ones; the midpoint, the 6 position, represents a neutral response. The locations of the statements along the continuum are decided by a panel of judges who are knowledgeable about the topic area. The judges respond to each statement in terms of its meaning, not in terms of their personal views. A final Thurstone scale typically consists of about 24 statements, allowing approximately 2 statements for each scale point. These reflect the positions on the scale to which all the judges have agreed.

Stated in general terms, the steps for creating a Thurstone scale are as follows:

1. A concept is selected for measurement. For example, we might be interested in measuring attitudes toward homosexuality, the death penalty, or victimization issues.
2. Next, the concept is transformed into measurable variables.
3. To measure the concept, the researcher collects or constructs a wide variety of statements about it. These statements may be collected from newspapers, magazines, books, individuals, broadcasters, or oneself and should represent a wide variety of opinions about the concept, since the end result is to identify statements that can be positioned at 11 different positions on the scale. For example, if we were interested in attitudes about victimization, some of the statements might be:
   - People who talk in poorly lit places are looking for trouble.
   - It is dangerous to go into certain neighborhoods at night.
   - Most muggings are entirely avoidable.
   - Locked doors are important for safety in the home.

   The researcher assembles about 100 different statements, recording them on file cards for convenience, a single statement per card.
4. In the next phase of development, the researcher identifies a panel of 200 to 300 judges, each knowledgeable on the subject "victimization," in our example. Each judge is asked to sort the statement cards into 11 piles, labeled "A" through "K," with "A" representing the most negative statements, "K" the most positive, and "F" neutral. In order for this procedure to work, the researcher must accept the assumption that the statements placed in each pile are at an equal distance from statements placed in every other successive pile, as assigned by the judges. In other words, those statements placed in pile A are assumed to be at an equal distance from those statements placed in pile B, which are assumed to be at an equal distance from those in pile C, and so on.
5. If the sortings of several judges are drastically different from those of the other judges, those few judges' piles are eliminated and the assumption is made that they were careless

in paneling statements. Once this cross-checking has been completed, scale values for each statement are calculated by computing the median scale values of each pile. The spread of judgments about the median is also computed. Some researchers prefer to use the mean and the spread of scores about the mean. The general rule is to use both measures when the size of the panel of judges is large. In this case, the two measures should give approximately equivalent results. When the panel of judges is small, the median measure is usually considered the most appropriate. Calculation of either the mean or the median assumes conversion of the scale to a number continuum, where A = 1, B = 2, and C = 3, and so on.

6. Final selection for the scale is made from those statements that have been calculated as having the smallest spread and that are equally spaced along this scale. Each of the numbered intervals is assigned 2 statements, so that the final scale contains 22 statements. When each pile contains many statements to choose from, the general rule is to select those statements that are the most clearly and concisely worded.

The scale is administered by having respondents check only those statements with which they agree, and each respondent's score is the mean scale value for all the statements he or she has endorsed.

LIKERT SCALES Shortly after the development of the Thurstone scale, Renis Likert (1932) offered a less time-consuming and complicated alternative. Like Thurstone, Likert began by compiling a large number of questions, usually 30 or more, all of which focused on the interest area (e.g., "victimization"). In practice, however, Likert scales frequently are employed using far fewer statements than 30.

We begin construction of a Likert scale with the assumption that each individual statement involves at least an ordinal level of measurement. This represents a major difference between Thurstone and Likert scales. In the case of Thurstone scales, no scale weights are given with the statements, and respondents are asked to check only those statements with which they agree. In Likert scales, respondents are asked to indicate the degree of agreement or disagreement for each statement on the instrument using a five-point scale. In other words, five response categories are provided for each statement: "Strongly Agree," "Agree," "Neutral," "Disagree," and "Strongly Disagree."

Next, a numerical value is assigned to each response category for scoring: For example, "Strongly Agree" (SA) = 5, "Agree" (A) = 4, and so on. The statements used may be either favorable or unfavorable, provided there is consistency in the researcher's weighting.

	SA	A	N	D	SD
Favorable Statements	1	2	3	4	5
Unfavorable Statements	5	4	3	2	1

The respondent will be assigned a total score, which is the sum of the numerical values of his or her responses to all questions.

It is a good idea to have both positively and negatively worded statements. Sometimes, when all the statements are worded in only one direction, a response set develops (sometimes called an acquiescent response set), which represents a tendency to answer all statements the same. If all the statements were positively worded, for example, a respondent might mark "Agree" for each statement without reading any of the statements carefully.

A second difference between the Likert and Thurstone scales is in the scoring. Whereas Thurstone scales are scored by computing the mean (or median) value of those statements endorsed, Likert scales are scored by simply summing the weights for all statements. For example, with a 20-statement Likert scale, we would expect a minimum score of 20 and a maximum score of 100. (Both these values assume that all 20 statements were answered.)

GUTTMAN SCALES A third prominent measurement technique, developed by Louis Guttman (1947) and his associates and introduced in the 1940s, is Guttman scaling. This technique, sometimes referred to as *cumulative scaling,* is a scoring technique that assumes that indicators of a concept can be arranged along a unidimensional continuum and that each indicator differs from the others in intensity. In other words, knowledge of a total score allows us to predict a subject's responses to individual statements. The statements assume an a priori order, such that agreement with any particular statement assumes agreement with the statements preceding it.

In his classic work, Reiss (1967), for example, used the concept "premarital sex" to develop a Guttman scale. In this scale, indicators ranged from "kissing" to "sexual intercourse." Reiss reasoned that anyone who approved of heavy petting also would approve of light petting and kissing. Conversely, anyone who disapproved of light petting also would disapprove of heavy petting, oral contact, and full sexual intercourse. This type of questions series might be expressed as follows:

1. Do you approve of kissing someone you are dating?
2. Do you approve of light petting with someone you are dating?
3. Do you approve of oral/genital contact with someone you are dating?
4. Do you approve of heavy petting with someone you are dating?
5. Do you believe in having sexual intercourse with someone you are dating?

If these five statements were given to a subject, treated as having ordinal properties, and one point was scored for each statement the subject approved of, we could predict the subject's degree of premarital sexual permissiveness. For example, if the subject scored 5, we would know that he or she approved of having intercourse with someone he or she was dating. If the subject scored four, we would know that he or she approved of a number of sexual activities while dating, but not intercourse. If the subject scored zero, we would know that the subject did not approve of any of the sexual activities indicated in the statements. The ability to predict accurately, of course, lies in the assumption that the statements represent a cumulative character along the same continuum (in this case, along the continuum of attitudes about premarital sexual behavior).

References

Bechard, S. (2006). The effects of net widening in a youth diversion program. *Dissertation Abstracts International, 45*(05). (UMI No. 1442646)

Guttman, L. (1947). The Cornell technique for scale and intensity analysis. *Educational and Psychological Measurement, 7*, 247–279.

Likert, R. (1932). A technique for the measurement of attitudes. *Archives of Psychology, 140*, 5–55.

Reiss, I. L. (1967). *The social context of premarital sexual permissiveness.* New York: Holt, Rinehart & Winston.

Thurstone, L. L. (1930). A scale for measuring attitude toward the movies. *Journal of Educational Research, 22*, 89–94.

Exercise 3.1 Texas Christian University (CEST Scales)

Special Report[1] August 2006

An Integrated Approach to Treatment for Addiction

D. Dwayne Simpson, Ph.D.

IBR Director & S.B. Sells Professor of Psychology

The "TCU Treatment System" refers to a collection of resources for planning, implementing, and assessing progress in using evidence-based treatment innovations for substance use problems. The system includes (1) manual-guided psychosocial interventions and related life skills counseling strategies, (2) integrated assessment instruments for measuring client needs and performance, and (3) program management tools to address organizational needs, functioning, and change. Scientific evidence and conceptual models that guide the use of these materials have been presented in relation to treatment process and program change in several hundred publications by the TCU research team.

Real-world partnerships with the national and regional offices of the *Addiction Technology Transfer Centers* (ATTC) network funded by the Substance Abuse and Mental Health Services Administration (SAMHSA), the federal *Bureau of Prisons,* numerous state agencies that oversee treatment services for community and correctional populations, and professional treatment associations—along with several international collaborations—have provided a wealth of opportunities and experience in transferring these resources into applied settings.

TCU interventions and assessments have many commonalities with others in the addiction treatment field. The interventions are unique in regard to their strategic integration using a *general conceptual framework* and uniform inclusion of *cognitive-based graphic tools* (i.e., TCU nodelink mapping) to enhance communications and treatment planning. The assessments target both *client-level progress* and *treatment satisfaction*, as well as *organizational factors* related to program effectiveness and adaptability.

A specialized series of short companion reports are available from our Web site which summarize the conceptual models, interventions, assessments, and treatment monitoring tools included in the *TCU Treatment System*. These reports explain applications of the resources and list citations for the most pertinent scientific publications on which they are based.

HOW TREATMENT WORKS

Treatment for drug addiction is sometimes viewed as a singular event for correcting an acute problem. In fact, it is much more complicated. Evidence shows there is a structured therapeutic process typically related to client recovery, and that different types of interventions serve to initiate or sustain client progress through stages of change. Medications may assist in this process but are not the "active ingredients" of psychosocial recovery foundations common to virtually all forms of drug addiction treatments.

The *TCU Treatment Model* (Simpson, 2004) is based on research from the addiction and mental health treatment fields that emphasize sequential relationships between needs and motivation for treatment, early engagement, early recovery, length of stay in treatment, and posttreatment outcomes. Findings demonstrate that a multidimensional index of client problem severity at intake (calculated from drug history and psychosocial functioning indicators) is related to during-treatment performance and follow-up outcomes (Joe, Simpson, Greener, & Rowan-Szal, 2004).

More importantly, repeated assessments throughout treatment show that more favorable scores at each stage increase by at least two-fold the chances of progressing successfully through the subsequent stage (Joe, Simpson, & Broome, 1999; Simpson & Joe, 2004). Findings supporting this model of treatment process come from diverse settings, including those for correctional populations (Simpson, Knight, & Dansereau, 2004).

The driving force for client progress towards recovery is a strategic series of interventions, as demonstrated in research that has programmatically tested this model using TCU treatment assessments and interventions. Because of the high frequency of early dropouts and associated costs, greater vigilance for "front end" stages of treatment is crucial. For instance, a few of our most recent experimental studies reaffirm that treatment induction and readiness training improves motivation and early engagement (Czuchry & Dansereau, 2005). Behavioral interventions (e.g., contingency management, see Rowan-Szal, Bartholomew, Chatham, & Simpson, 2005) and cognitive techniques (e.g., node-link mapping, see Newbern, Dansereau, Czuchry, & Simpson, 2005) improve treatment engagement indicators—participation and therapeutic relationship—as well as retention.

In programs without effective induction, planning, or early engagement strategies, many clients never receive what might be *superior* interventions tentatively scheduled for later. Like links in a chain, the

---

[1]*TCU Treatment System. Overview of Background and Structure: An Integrated Approach to Addiction Treatment* is published by the Institute of Behavioral Research, Texas Christian University, TCU Box 298740, Fort Worth, TX 76129. Phone: (817) 257-7226. FAX: (817) 257-7290. E-mail: ibr@tcu.edu. Web site: www.ibr.tcu.edu. Prepared by Dwayne Simpson and Charlotte Pevoto.

quality of all elements of treatment delivery must be insured to maintain its overall integrity. Within this stage-based framework, it can be argued that effectiveness of discrete interventions is most properly evaluated on the basis of their *interim* impact on client performance rather than judging them only by examining long-range outcomes (also see McLellan, McKay, Forman, Cacciola, & Kemp, 2005).

Deliberate planning, monitoring, and "on-time" delivery of specific program interventions is fundamental to improving treatment effectiveness. In addition to the evidence for stage-specific interventions as noted above, we have found their aggregated or collective use proportionately increases posttreatment outcome performance (Rowan-Szal, Chatham, Greener, Joe, Payte, & Simpson, 2004).

HOW TREATMENT AND ASSESSMENTS WORK TOGETHER

For too long at too many programs, assessments and interventions have been functionally detached. Formal assessments tend to be completed and filed away (or used mainly for research). Interventions tend to be delivered within a uniform schedule instead of responding to particular needs. Pieces of this process operate independently and do not inform each other about impact or deficiencies. Computer-based technologies offer a chance to change the system, but it is like putting together a complicated and expensive puzzle.

Ideally, treatment planning should occur at both the client and program levels. Program directors and clinical supervisors have responsibility for monitoring progress and managing resources for the services system, while individual counselors have responsibility for personalized planning and effective delivery of services. That means that at the program management level, aggregated client records are needed for tracking clinical needs and response patterns (including dynamic changes over time) by using indicators such as client attributes and severity levels, during-treatment functioning, treatment engagement, and retention.

Diagnostic indicators for a program might detect significant shifts in primary drug use, demographic profiles (e.g., gender or age), or referral sources at intake. Likewise, in-treatment functioning of clients might signal needs for new clinical tools that address low readiness for treatment, high levels of client anger or hostility, poor session attendance and counseling rapport, high rates of early dropout, etc. Assuming appropriate levels of skills and responsibility, counselors need ready access to an array of "plug-n-play" interventions shown to be effective (i.e., evidence-based) in addressing these issues.

A systems approach therefore suggests that targeted and relevant assessments be obtained and made available for *client-level* treatment planning and monitoring—and that they be used at the *aggregated* level for program planning and monitoring. In principle, innovations needed to address client needs and performance should be identified and selected based on scientific support, training requirement, and access (including via the internet) to user-friendly intervention tools. Tracking client and program level responses (using the on-going assessments) should inform decisions about clinical impact and organizational change following an iterative process.

But this is easier said than done. Architectural plans for the TCU Treatment System follow these blueprints. Assessments of client needs and severity at intake—along with a set of brief scales for motivation, psychological, and social functioning that are repeated during treatment—are tied into our treatment process framework, as are interventions shown to impact them. The *Client Evaluation of Self and Treatment* (CEST) is central to the monitoring of client functioning (individually and collectively), and it includes scales for therapeutic engagement and social support (Joe, Broome, Rowan-Szal, & Simpson, 2002). Information from approximately 10,000 clients provides comparative norms and functional thresholds for interpreting records at individual and program levels (see *Assessment FACT Sheets* on the IBR Web site). Program-wide assessment of client samples using the CEST can generate diagnostic profiles on client functioning. Interventions are then identified from TCU resources or elsewhere that are shown to be effective in addressing prominent needs or deficiencies.

HOW PROGRAMS MANAGE TREATMENT QUALITY AND CHANGE

Treatment effectiveness can best be viewed using both a micro and macro perspective—that is, at the client and program levels. Not only is the quality of client treatment planning and care important, as already discussed, but so is the proper placement of clients into the most appropriate level of care. Posttreatment outcomes of clients with low overall problem severity are comparable when treated either in high or low intensity settings (including outpatient and residential options). However, clients with high-severity problems at intake have been shown to have outcomes up to three times better if they received more highly structured residential care (versus low-structure outpatient care) for at least 3 months (Simpson, Joe, Fletcher, Hubbard, & Anglin, 1999).

The importance of retention on treatment outcomes is well established (Gossop, Marsden, Stewart, & Rolf, 1997; Simpson, Joe, & Brown, 1997), but there are large program variations in overall client engagement and retention levels (Broome, Simpson, & Joe, 1999; Simpson, Joe, Broome, Hiller, Knight, & Rowan-Szal, 1997). Not only are these differences related to quality of clinical planning and delivery, it is becoming more widely acknowledged that organizational climate and functioning are significant factors to consider. Programs with better staff communications, cohesion, and resources have records of better clinical care (Lehman, Greener, & Simpson, 2002).

The *TCU Program Change Model* (Simpson, 2002) uses findings from the literature on technology transfer to summarize major organizational influences on program quality and how these are related to institutional change. Evidence clearly points out that dissemination alone for transferring new innovations into practice is seldom effective. Organizations go through stages of change before new ways of doing things become "normal." Like clients moving towards recovery in treatment, program readiness for change and resource levels influence this process for adopting new innovations. On-going decisions about their implementation are guided by perceived needs for and satisfaction with the new resources and related training for using them. Reaching the level of full-scale practice with new procedures depends heavily on organizational functioning, tolerance, and active support.

TCU assessments include the *Organizational Readiness for Change* (ORC), which has been developed and tested (see Lehman Greener, & Simpson, 2002) for measuring organizational functioning. It focuses on staff perceptions about the adequacy of program resources, counselor attributes, work climate (e.g., mission, communication, cohesion, stress), and motivation or pressures for program changes. By combining information obtained using both the ORC (from staff) and the CEST (from clients), a *performance and needs report* on unit functioning is useful for diagnosing programmatic strengths, needs, and barriers to change. Repeating this assessment process over time can be used to evaluate progress.

Stage-based evaluations of how innovations get translated into practice have become a central focus of the TCU research team. A related aspect of this process are new efforts to find practical approaches to computing costs for services and studying how these financial considerations are related to the effectiveness of clinical services and organizational functioning.

References

Broome, K. M., Simpson, D. D., & Joe, G. W. (1999). Patient and program attributes related to treatment process indicators in DATOS. *Drug and Alcohol Dependence, 57* (2), 127–135.

Czuchry, M., & Dansereau, D. F. (2005). Using motivational activities to facilitate treatment involvement and reduce risk. *Journal of Psychoactive Drugs, 37* (1), 7–13.

Gossop, M., Marsden, J., Stewart, D., & Rolfe, A. (1999). Treatment retention and 1 year outcomes for residential programmes in England. *Drug and Alcohol Dependence, 57* (2), 89–98.

Joe, G. W., Broome, K. M., Rowan-Szal, G. A., & Simpson, D. D. (2002). Measuring patient attributes and engagement in treatment. *Journal of Substance Abuse Treatment, 22*(4), 183–196.

Joe, G. W., Simpson, D. D., & Broome, K. M. (1999). Retention and patient engagement models for different treatment modalities in DATOS. *Drug and Alcohol Dependence, 57* (2), 113–125.

Joe, G. W., Simpson, D. D., Greener, J. M., & Rowan-Szal, G. A. (2004). Development and validation of a client problem profile index for drug treatment. *Psychological Reports, 95*, 215–234.

Lehman, W. E. K., Greener, J. M., & Simpson, D. D. (2002). Assessing organizational readiness for change. *Journal of Substance Abuse Treatment, 22* (4), 197–209.

McLellan, A. T., McKay, J. R., Forman, R., Cacciola, J., & Kemp, J. (2005). Reconsidering the evaluation of addiction treatment: From retrospective follow-up to concurrent recovery monitoring. *Addiction, 100* (4), 447–458.

Newbern, D., Dansereau, D. F., Czuchry, M., & Simpson, D. D. (2005). Node-link mapping in individual counseling: Treatment impact on clients with ADHD-related behaviors. *Journal of Psychoactive Drugs, 37* (1), 93–103.

Rowan-Szal, G. A., Bartholomew, N. G., Chatham, L. R., & Simpson, D. D. (2005). A combined cognitive and behavioral intervention for cocaine-using methadone clients. *Journal of Psychoactive Drugs, 37* (1), 75–84.

Rowan-Szal, G. A., Chatham, L. R., Greener, J. M., Joe, G. W., Payte, J. T., & Simpson, D. D. (2004). Structure as a determinant of treatment dose. *Journal of Maintenance in the Addictions, 2* (4), 55–70.

Simpson, D. D. (2002). A conceptual framework for transferring research to practice. *Journal of Substance Abuse Treatment, 22* (4), 171–182.

Simpson, D. D. (2004). A conceptual framework for drug treatment process and outcomes. *Journal of Substance Abuse Treatment, 27* (2), 99–121.

Simpson, D. D. (August, 2006). A plan for planning treatment. *Counselor: A Magazine for Addiction Professionals, 7* (4), 20–28.

Simpson, D. D., & Joe, G. W. (2004). A longitudinal evaluation of treatment engagement, and recovery stages. *Journal of Substance Abuse Treatment, 27* (2), 89–97.

Simpson, D. D., Joe, G. W., Broome, K. M., Hiller, M. L., Knight, K., & Rowan-Szal, G. A. (1997). Program diversity and treatment retention rates in the Drug Abuse Treatment Outcome Study (DATOS). *Psychology of Addictive Behaviors, 11* (4), 279–293.

Simpson, D. D., Joe, G. W., & Brown, B. S. (1997). Treatment retention and follow-up outcomes in the Drug Abuse Treatment Outcome Study (DATOS). *Psychology of Addictive Behaviors, 11* (4), 294–307.

Simpson, D. D., Joe, G. W., Fletcher, B. W., Hubbard, R. L., & Anglin, M. D. (1999). A national evaluation of treatment outcomes for cocaine dependence. *Archives of General Psychiatry, 56*, 507–514.

Simpson, D. D., Knight, K., & Dansereau, D. F. (2004). Addiction treatment strategies for offenders. *Journal of Community Corrections, Summer*, 7–10, 27–32.

Application Exercise 3.1

Name of Student:______________

Student ID No.:______________

Course/Section No.:______________

Date:______________

1. After reading the Texas Christian University (TCU) synopsis, create Likert-type measures that could be used for the following variables they describe:
   a. Shifts in primary drug use

   ____
   ____
   ____
   ____
   ____
   ____

   b. Readiness for treatment

   ____
   ____
   ____
   ____
   ____
   ____

   c. Levels of client anger or hostility

   ____
   ____
   ____
   ____
   ____
   ____

   d. Session attendance and counseling rapport

   ____
   ____
   ____
   ____
   ____
   ____

For example:

Please Indicate Your Level of Agreement With the Following Statements:	**Disagree Strongly**	**Disagree**	**Not Sure**	**Agree**	**Agree Strongly**
"I am supportive of crime."	O	O	O	O	O
"I do not like to follow conventional attitudes, beliefs, and behaviors."	O	O	O	O	O
You get upset when you hear about someone who has lost everything in a natural disaster.	O	O	O	O	O
You deserve special consideration.	O	O	O	O	O
You were in prison because you had a run of bad luck.	O	O	O	O	O
The real reason you were in prison was because of your race.	O	O	O	O	O
When people tell you what to do, you become aggressive.	O	O	O	O	O
Anything can be fixed in court if you have the right connections.	O	O	O	O	O
Seeing someone cry makes you sad.	O	O	O	O	O
You rationalize your irresponsible actions with statements like "Everyone else is doing it, so why shouldn't I?"	O	O	O	O	O

(continued)

Please Indicate Your Level of Agreement With the Following Statements:	Disagree Strongly	Disagree	Not Sure	Agree	Agree Strongly
"I am supportive of crime."	O	O	O	O	O
Bankers, lawyers, and politicians get away with breaking the law every day.	O	O	O	O	O
You have paid your dues in life and are justified in taking what you want.	O	O	O	O	O
When not in control of a situation, you feel the need to exert power over others.	O	O	O	O	O
When questioned about the motives for engaging in crime, you justify your behavior by pointing out how hard your life has been.	O	O	O	O	O
You are sometimes so moved by an experience that you feel emotions that you cannot describe.	O	O	O	O	O
You argue with others over relatively trivial matters.	O	O	O	O	O
If someone disrespects you then you have to straighten them out, even if you have to get physical with them to do it.	O	O	O	O	O
You like to be in control.	O	O	O	O	O
You find yourself blaming the victims of some of your crimes.	O	O	O	O	O
You feel people are important to you.	O	O	O	O	O

Exercise 3.2 Self-Report Screening for Alcohol Problems among Adults

Self-Report Screening for Alcohol Problems among Adults

Gerard J. Connors, Ph.D., and Robert J. Volk, Ph.D.†*

*RESEARCH INSTITUTE ON ADDICTIONS, UNIVERSITY AT BUFFALO, BUFFALO, NY
†BAYLOR COLLEGE OF MEDICINE, HOUSTON, TX

Alcohol abuse and alcoholism are serious public health problems estimated to affect approximately 7 percent of the U.S. population (Grant et al. 1994), but many individuals with such problems remain undetected. Also undetected are many individuals who do not meet diagnostic criteria for alcohol abuse or alcohol dependence, but who nevertheless are experiencing negative consequences associated with their use of alcohol or are at risk for such consequences (Institute of Medicine, 1990). This is unfortunate for several reasons. First, their continued drinking holds significant potential for further alcohol-related negative consequences. Second, it is not possible to refer such drinkers for appropriate services until they are detected. As such, there is a need to develop and apply techniques to screen for alcohol use disorders. Fortunately, much work has occurred in this area, and this chapter focuses on a variety of issues and measures relevant to the identification of adults with alcohol-related problems.

OVERVIEW OF CHAPTER

The first section of this chapter provides a working definition of screening, identifies the goals of screening, discusses the distinction between screening and assessment, and comments on screening in relation to the treatment process. The topic of the validity of self-report data also is addressed. An overview of self-report screening measures is presented, followed by a discussion of guidelines for the selection and use of screening measures, a summary of studies that have compared measures, and some general suggestions regarding screening.

Definition of Screening

Definitions for the term *screening* are numerous, ranging from the narrowest to broadest breadth of focus or coverage. For the purposes of this chapter, the term will be used to represent the skillful use of empirically based procedures for identifying individuals with alcohol-related problems or consequences or those who are at risk for such difficulties. The definition of screening proposed here does not include diagnosis.

Distinguishing between Screening and Assessment

Screening is designed to identify persons experiencing an alcohol use problem. An abnormal or positive screening result may thus "raise suspicion" about the presence of an alcohol use problem, while a normal or negative result should suggest a low probability of an alcohol use problem. Screening measures are not designed (if for no other reason than because of their brevity) to explicate the nature and extent of such problems. By contrast, assessment procedures are designed to explore fully the nature and extent of a person's problems with alcohol. Such assessment information can be used to determine whether the person meets the criteria for a particular diagnostic category, such as alcohol abuse or alcohol dependence, depending on the nomenclature system being applied.

ASSESSING SCREENING MEASURES

Approaches to Evaluating Measures

There are a variety of dimensions along which one can determine the strengths of a particular screening measure. Because of their relevance to evaluating measures and making determinations regarding the utility of specific measures for particular purposes, settings, or populations, it is important to identify and describe these dimensions: sensitivity, specificity, predictive value, likelihood ratios, and receiver operating curves. The "gold standard" by which a screening test is evaluated (called the reference test or criterion) generally is a full diagnostic evaluation.

SENSITIVITY The sensitivity (or true positive rate) of a test concerns its ability to identify people with the disorder in question, in this case alcohol problems. Stated differently, sensitivity reflects the proportion of persons with alcohol use disorders correctly identified ("true positives") by the test. Consistent with this definition, a sensitive test is one that provides a minimum of false negatives (i.e., persons with alcohol problems who are not detected by the screening measure).

SPECIFICITY The specificity (or true negative rate) of a test refers to its ability to accurately identify people who do not have an alcohol use disorder. As such, specificity reflects the proportion of non-alcohol abusers correctly identified ("true negatives"). Accordingly, a specific test provides a minimum of false positives (i.e., non-alcohol abusers identified by the screening test as alcohol abusers). Specificity would be calculated by dividing the true negative cases by the total number of non-alcohol abusers (d/b + d). Similarly, the false positive rate, or 1 minus specificity, would be calculated by dividing the false positive cases by the total number of non-alcohol abusers (b/b + d).

PREDICTIVE VALUE In general, good screening tests when negative should "rule out" an alcohol use disorder, and when positive should "rule in" a disorder such that assessment is warranted. A useful statistic in evaluating screening tests is called positive predictive value. This refers to the proportion of persons identified as positive on the screening test who actually have the disorder.

SELF-REPORT VALIDITY AND SCREENING TESTS Although some researchers and clinicians have argued that information from self-reports on alcohol-related variables is suspect (e.g., alcohol abusers will deny they have problems), many others believe these reports can be valid and useful in the screening as well as assessment and treatment of alcohol abusers. This controversy over self-reports has been discussed in greater detail by Babor et al. (1987), Maisto et al. (1990), and Sobell and Sobell (1990).

OVERVIEW OF SCREENING MEASURES

There is no shortage of screening measures available for clinicians and researchers, and a culling of the available measures to a manageable number was performed for purposes of this chapter. Application of the inclusion criteria for this *Guide* (see Allen's "Introduction") yielded a core group of 14 screening measures. Tables 2A and 2B provide descriptive and administrative information on these measures, including examples of groups the measure has been used with, availability of normative data, format, number of items, and time needed to administer the measure. (Table 2A indicates whether norms are available generally as well as for particular subgroups.)

TABLE 2A. Self-report screening measures: sescriptive information

Measure	Target Population	Groups Used with	Norms Available?	Normed Groups	No. Items (No. of Subscales)
AAS	Adults		Yes	Normals; substance abusers; psychiatric patients	13
APS	Adults		Yes	Normals; alcohol/drug abusers; psychiatric patients	39
AUDIT[1]	Adults	Primary care, ER, surgery, psychiatric patients; DWI offenders; criminals in court, jail, and prison; enlisted men in Armed Forces; workers in EAPs and industrial settings	Yes	Heavy drinkers; alcoholics	10 (3)
CAGE	Adults and adolescents >16 yrs.	General medical population in a primary care setting	Yes		4
CLA	Adults and adolescents		Yes		350 (20)
DUSI-R	Adults and adolescents >16 yrs.; youth 10–16 yrs.	Known or suspected alcohol/drug users; matching specific treatments to specific problems	Yes		159 (11)
Five Shot Questionn-aire	Adults	Male early-phase heavy drinkers	Yes	Moderate/heavy drinkers; alcoholics	5
Mac	Adults	Alcoholics likely to deny problems with drinking when asked directly	Yes	Women; alcoholics with collateral drug problems	49

Measure	Target Population	Groups Used with	Norms Available?	Normed Groups	No. Items (No. of Subscales)
MAST[2]	Adults and adolescents	Alcoholics, medical patients, psychiatric patients	Yes		25
RAPS4	Adults	ER and primary care settings	No		4
SAAST	Adults	General medical patients	Yes	Gender; age	35 (2)
SASSI	Adults and adolescents	Adolescents (12–18 yrs.); inpatient and outpatient adults	Yes		Adults 93 (10); adolescents 100 (12)
T-ACE	Adults	Pregnant women	Yes	African American inner-city women attending antenatal clinic	4
TWEAK	Adults	Women	Yes	African American gravidas in inner-city clinic; M&F general population; M&F alcoholic patients; M&F outpatients	5

Note: The measures are listed in alphabetical order by full name; see the text for the full names. Information in the table is based primarily on material provided by the developers of the measures; see the appendix for more detail. DWI = driving while intoxicated; EAPs = employee assistance programs; ER = emergency room; M&F = male and female.
[1]Also available is a 3-item version called the AUDIT-C (see Piccinelli et al. 1997 and Gordon et al. 2001).
[2]Briefer versions of the MAST are available: the 10-item Brief MAST (Pokorny et al. 1972); the 13-item Short MAST (SMAST) (Selzer et al. 1975); and the 9-item modified version of the Brief MAST, called the Malmö modification (Mm-MAST) because it was first used in the city of Malmö (Kristenson and Trell. 1982). Also available is a geriatric version of the MAST, called the MAST-G (Mudd et al. 1993). Magruder-Habib et al. (1982) developed a MAST variant called the VAST, designed to distinguish between lifetime and current problems with alcohol.

All of the measures listed in Tables 2A and 2B are available for use with adults, and five of them were developed for use with adolescents as well. The measures range in length from very few items (such as the 4-item CAGE) to the 350-item Computerized Lifestyle Assessment (CLA). Six of the screening measures listed in the tables include 10 or fewer items (Alcohol Use Disorders Identification Test [AUDIT], CAGE, Five-Shot Questionnaire, Rapid Alcohol Problems Screen, T-ACE, and TWEAK). Several of the measures include two or more distinct scales, should such further information be of utility in a particular screening endeavor.

The majority of measures are available for use in a pencil-and-paper self-administered format, but other options are present. Several measures (e.g., AUDIT, CAGE, and MAST) can be used in an interview format, and several measures (e.g., Addiction Potential Scale, AUDIT, CAGE, Drug Use Screening Inventory, Self-Administered Alcoholism Screening Test [SAAST], Substance Abuse Subtle Screening Inventory, and TWEAK) have been adapted for computerized assessment. Regardless of format, most measures can be completed in under 15 minutes, and six can be completed in just 1 or 2 minutes. Scoring of the majority of the measures likewise requires relatively little time.

SELECTION OF MEASURES

It is not possible to make definitive statements on the selection of a screening measure because screening endeavors can vary dramatically along a number of dimensions, such as the population involved, the amount of time available for screening, the setting, and the goals of the screening. However, it is possible to provide guidelines and suggestions. This section provides guidelines for selecting and using a screening measure, summarizes studies that have compared screening measures, and makes some general suggestions regarding screening for alcohol problems. It is important to remember that these guidelines and suggestions need to be evaluated carefully in the context of the particular setting and context in which the screening will occur.

TABLE 2B. Self-report screening measures: Administrative information

Measure	Format Options[1]	Time to Administer (Minutes)	Computer Scoring Available?	Fee for Use?[2]
AAS	P&P SA; computer SA	5	Yes	Yes
APS	P&P SA; computer SA	10	Yes	Yes
AUDIT[3]	P&P SA; interview; computer SA	2	No	No
CAGE	P&P SA; interview; computer SA	<1	No	No
CLA	Computer SA	20–30	Yes	Yes
DUSI–R	P&P SA; interview; computer SA	20	Yes	Yes
Five Shot Questionnaire	P&P SA	1	No	Yes
Mac	P&P SA; computer SA	10	No	Yes
MAST[4]	P&P SA; interview	8	No	No
RAPS[4]	Interview	1	No	No
SAAST	P&P SA; computer SA	5	Yes	Unknown
SASSI	P&P SA; computer SA	10–15	Yes	Yes
T-ACE	P&P SA; interview	1	No	Unknown
TWEAK	P&P SA; interview; computer SA	<2	No	No

Note: The measures are listed in alphabetical order by full name; see the text for the full names. Information in the table is based primarily on material provided by the developers of the measures; see the appendix for more details. P&P = pencil and paper; SA = self-administered.
[1]Most of the self-administered tests can be supervised and scored by office or clinic staff in relatively brief periods of time.
[2]Information on fees was not always clear, so potential users should confirm whether there are fees before using any of these measures.
[3]Also available is a 3-item version called the AUDIT-C (see Piccinelli et al. 1997 and Gordon et al. 2001).
[4]Briefer versions of the MAST are available: the 10-item Brief MAST (Pokorny et al. 1972); the 13-item Short MAST (SMAST) (Selzer et al. 1975); and the 9-item modified version of the Brief MAST, called the Malmö modification (Mm-MAST) because it was first used in the city of Malmö (Kristenson and Trell 1982). Also available is a geriatric version of the MAST, called the MAST-G (Mudd et al. 1993). Magruder-Habib et al. (1982). developed a MAST variant called the VAST, designed to distinguish between lifetime and current problems with alcohol.

Guidelines for Selecting and Using Measures

There are four central questions that need to be addressed in selecting a screening measure:

- The goals of the screening
- The characteristics of the measure for the target population
- The time and resources available for conducting the screening
- The resources available for scoring the screening measure and providing feedback/referral for positive cases.

Identifying the goals of screening in a particular situation might appear straightforward. Indeed, all screening endeavors on some level are designed to detect alcohol problems among those tested. However, the degree of sensitivity and specificity desired will affect the selection of the measure. While one investigator may want to focus on maximizing sensitivity and thus identify as many true positives as possible, another investigator may want to key on specificity and thus maximize the likelihood that persons identified as positive are actually experiencing an alcohol problem.

The characteristics of the screening measure for use with the target population are also an important consideration in selecting a measure. Generally, a measure with high sensitivity is desirable, and ideally this has been demonstrated in screening populations similar to the target group. Measures with high likelihood ratios have the benefit of both high sensitivity and specificity, and may be effective in both ruling in and ruling out alcohol use problems. Similar information can be gained from the area under the characteristic receiver operating curve, although this estimate is only a global measure of a measure's characteristics, and it is desirable to consider sensitivity and specificity at a given cutoff point.

The amount of time available for performing the screening should not be a major impediment to its conduct. For measures that take more time to complete, one must weigh the relative benefits or advantages of the measures against the time factor. Finally, one must evaluate the resources available for scoring and interpreting the screening data collected and for acting on the results. Conveniently, a host of measures that can be scored and evaluated in just a few minutes are available.

Suggestions

Although, as has been emphasized throughout this chapter, it is important to consider the specific goals, setting, and other factors in selecting a screening measure, there are some general suggestions that can be made regarding screening for alcohol problems. These suggestions (see also Allen et al. 1995, and Maisto et al. 1995) have particular relevance to primary health care settings, where screening for alcohol problems is becoming more frequent.

Any screening endeavor requires responsive procedures regarding feedback to individuals screened and the making of appropriate referrals for further evaluation and assessment. The establishment of such procedures is a necessary component of the screening process that needs to be in place prior to the actual screening of individuals.

FUTURE DIRECTIONS AND NEEDS

Many screening measures have been developed for use in clinical settings, including primary health care settings. There have been some interesting historical trends in this research, which should be considered as future studies are planned. First, many screening tests share common roots with the CAGE questions and the MAST. There is a fairly extensive literature on the performance of these measures. A second trend has been to develop ever briefer measures, with several single-item measures now being touted. Whether these briefer measures will lead to increased screening, allow for feedback to patients, and provide for optimal management of patients with alcohol use problems has yet to be determined. A final trend has been to emphasize consumption indicators either alone or in combination with other consequence-based or dependence indicators.

Although these advances in screening measures are important, implementation appears to be lagging behind the development and evaluation of measures. Thus, more attention should be paid to strategies and approaches for increasing the use of screening measures in a variety of settings.

References

Aertgeerts, B.; Buntinx, F.; Ansoms, S.; and Fevery, J. Screening properties of questionnaires and laboratory tests for the detection of alcohol abuse or dependence in a general practice population. *Br J Gen Pract* 51:206–217, 2001.

Allen, J. P. The interrelationship of alcoholism assessment and treatment. *Alcohol Health Res World* 15:178–185, 1991.

Allen, J. P.; Maisto, S. A.; and Connors, G. J. Self-report screening tests for alcohol problems in primary care. *Arch Intern Med* 155:1726–1730, 1995.

Babor, T. F.; Stephens, R. S.; and Marlatt, G. A. Verbal report methods in clinical research on alcoholism: Response bias and its minimization. *J Stud Alcohol* 48:410–424, 1987.

Brown, R. L.; Leonard, T.; Saunders, L. A.; and Papasouliotis, O. A two-item conjoint screen for alcohol and other drug problems. *J Am Board Fam Pract* 14:95–106, 2001.

Cherpitel, C. J. Screening for problems in the emergency room: A rapid alcohol problems screen. *Drug Alcohol Depend* 40:133–137, 1995.

Cherpitel, C. J. Brief screening instruments for alcoholism. *Alcohol Health Res World* 21: 348–351, 1997.

Cherpitel, C. J. A brief screening instrument for problem drinking in the emergency room: The RAPS4. Rapid Alcohol Problems Screen. *J Stud Alcohol* 61:447–449, 2000.

Cherpitel, C. J., and Borges, G. Screening instruments for alcohol problems: A comparison of cut points between Mexican American and Mexican patients in the emergency room. *Subst Use Misuse* 35:1419–1430, 2000.

Clements, R. A critical evaluation of several alcohol screening instruments using the CIDI-SAM as a criterion measure. *Alcohol Clin Exp Res* 22:985–993, 1998.

Cyr, M., and Wartman, S. The effectiveness of routine screening questions in the detection of alcoholism. *JAMA* 259:51–54, 1988.

Daeppen, J-B.; Yersin, B.; Landry, U.; Pecoud, A.; and Decrey, H. Reliability and validity of the Alcohol Use Disorders Identification Test (AUDIT) imbedded within a general health risk screening questionnaire: Results of a survey in 332 primary care patients. *Alcohol Clin Exp Res* 24:659–665, 2000.

Dujardin, B.; Van den Ende, J.; Van Gompel, A.V.; Unger, J.; and Van der Stuyft, P. Likelihood ratios: A real improvement for clinical decision making? *Eur J Epidemiol* 10:29–36, 1994.

Fagan, T. J. Nomogram for Bayes's Theorem. *N Engl J Med* 293:257, 1975.

Feinstein, A. R. *Clinical Epidemiology: The Architecture of Clinical Research.* Philadelphia: W. B. Saunders, 1985.

Gordon, A. J.; Maisto, S. A.; McNeil, M.; Kraemer, K. L., Conigliaro, R. L.; Kelley, M. E., and Conigliaro, J. Three questions can detect hazardous drinkers. *J Fam Pract* 50:313–320. 2001.

Grant, B. F.; Harford, T. C.; Dawson, D. A.; Chou, P.; DuFour, M.; and Pickering, R. Prevalence of DSM-IV alcohol abuse and dependence: United States, 1992. *Alcohol Health Res World* 18:243–248. 1994.

Hermansson, U.; Helander, A.; Huss, A.; Brandt, L.; and Ronnberg, S. The Alcohol Use Disorders Identification Test (AUDIT) and carbohydrate-deficient transferring (CDT) in a routine workplace health examination. *Alcohol Clin Exp Res* 24:180–187. 2000.

Institute of Medicine. *Broadening the Base of Treatment for Alcohol Problems*. Washington, DC: National Academy Press, 1990.

Kristenson, H., and Trell, E. Indicators of alcohol consumption: Comparisons between a questionnaire (Mm-MAST), interviews and serum gamma-glutamyl transferase (GGT) in a health survey of middle-aged males. *Br J Addict* 77:297–304, 1982.

Leigh, G., and Skinner, H. A. Physiological assessment. In: Donovan, D. M., and Marlatt, G. A., eds. *Assessment of Addictive Behaviors*. New York: Guilford Press, 1988. pp. 112–136.

Magruder-Habib, K.; Harris, K. E.; and Fraker, G. G. Validation of the Veterans Alcoholism Screening Test. *J Stud Alcohol* 43:910–926, 1982.

Maisto, S. A.; McKay, J. R.; and Connors, G. J. Self-report issues in substance abuse: State of the art and future directions. *Behav Assess* 12:117–134, 1990.

Maisto, S. A.; Connors, G. J.; and Allen, J. P. Contrasting self-report screens for alcohol problems: A review. *Alcohol Clin Exp Res* 19:1510–1516, 1995.

Mudd, S. A.; Blow, F. C.; Hill, E. M.; Demo–Dananberg, L.; Young, J. P.; and Iacob, A. Differences in symptom reporting between older problem drinkers with and without a history of major depression. *Alcohol Clin Exp Res* 17:489, 1993.

Nochajski, T. H., and Wieczorek, W. F. Identifying potential drinking-driving recidivists: Do non-obvious indicators help? *Journal of Prevention and Intervention in the Community* 1:69–83, 1998.

Piccinelli, M.; Tessari, E.; Bortolomasi, M.; Piasere, O.; Semenzin, M.; Garzotto, N.; and Tansella, M. Efficacy of the Alcohol Use Disorders Identification Test as a screening tool for hazardous alcohol intake and related disorders in primary care: A validity study. *BMJ* 314:420–424, 1997.

Pokorny, A. D.; Miller, B. A.; and Kaplan, H. B. The brief MAST: A shortened version of the Michigan Alcoholism Screening Test (MAST). *Am J Psychiatry* 129:342–345, 1972.

Rosman, A. S., and Lieber, C. S. Biochemical markers of alcohol consumption. *Alcohol Health Res World* 14:210–218, 1990.

Russell, M.; Martier, S. S.; Sokol, R. J.; Mudar, P.; Bottoms, S.; Jacobson, S.; and Jacobson, J. Screening for pregnancy risk-drinking. *Alcohol Clin Exp Res* 18:1156–1161, 1994.

Sackett, D. L. The rational clinical examination. A primer on the precision and accuracy of the clinical examination. *JAMA* 267:2638–2644, 1992.

Selzer, M. L.; Vinokur, A.; and van Rooijen, L. A self-administered Short Michigan Alcoholism Screening Test (SMAST). *J Stud Alcohol* 36:117–126, 1975.

Seppa, K.; Lepisto, J.; and Sillanaukee, P. Five-shot questionnaire on heavy drinking. *Alcohol Clin Exp Res* 22:1788–1791, 1998.

Skinner, H. A. Assessing alcohol use by patients in treatment. In: Smart, R. G.; Cappell, H. D.; Glaser, F. B.; Israel, Y.; Kalant, H.; Popham, R. E.; Schmidt, W.; and Sellers, E. M., eds. *Research Advances in Alcohol and Drug Problems*. Vol. 8. New York: Plenum Press, 1984. pp. 183–207.

Sobell, L. C., and Sobell, M. B. Self-report issues in alcohol abuse: State of the art and future directions. *Behav Assess* 12:77–90, 1990.

Steinbauer, J. R.; Cantor, S. B.; Holzer, C. E.; and Volk, R. J. Ethnic and sex bias in primary care screening tests for alcohol use disorders. *Ann Intern Med* 129:353–362, 1998.

Taj, N.; Devera–Sales, A.; and Vinson, D. C. Screening for problem drinking: Does a single question work? *J Fam Pract* 46:328–335, 1998.

Williams, R., and Vinson, D. C. Validation of a single screening question for problem drinking. *J Fam Pract* 50:307–312, 2001.

Application Exercise 3.2

Name of Student:______________

Student ID No.:______________

Course/Section No.:______________

Date:______________

1. What is the main purpose of instruments such as the CAGE and TWEAK?

____

____

____

____

____

____

2. What information do the CAGE and TWEAK give us?

____

____

____

____

____

____

3. If you had to select one to use for your criminological research in addiction, which instrument would you select and why?

____

____

____

____

____

____

____

____

____

4. Look at the actual CAGE and TWEAK instruments below. Are these useful tools in criminal justice research? Why or why not?

____

____

____

____

____

____

____

____

CAGE:

Please check the one response to each item that best describes how you have felt and behaved over your whole life.

	Yes	No
1. Have you ever felt you should cut down on your drinking?	O	O
2. Have people *annoyed* you by criticizing your drinking?	O	O
3. Have you ever felt bad or *guilty* about your drinking?	O	O
4. Have you ever had a drink first thing in the morning to steady your nerves or get rid of a hangover (*eye-opener*)?	O	O

TWEAK:

1. How many drinks does it take to make you feel high?	O	O
2. Have close friends or relatives worried or complained about your drinking in the past year?	O	O
3. Do you sometimes take a drink in the morning when you first get up?	O	O
4. Has a friend or family member ever told you about things you said or did while you were drinking that you could not remember?	O	O
5. Do you sometimes feel the need to cut down on your drinking?	O	O

CHAPTER 4

Designing Research

TYPES OF RESEARCH DESIGN

If the authors of this book have learned anything in their varied career lives, it is that there is no *right* or *wrong* method or research design. The proper method and design, if one can actually use the term *proper* here, depends on what you are trying to achieve in your research. In turn, what you are trying to achieve depends heavily on your research idea. Thus, the starting point of any research study is the *research idea*. Your research idea then becomes the engine that pulls the rest of the research train. From one's research idea, one develops his or her design. The **research design** literally becomes the plan the researcher will use in undertaking the study. This will include identification of any theoretical framework that may bring together the overall orientation of the study, as well as identification and selection of the methodological technologies to be used in collecting data. Furthermore, the design will indicate how data, once collected, will be organized and analyzed.

Regardless of these truisms—that there are no right or wrong methods or designs—many inexperienced researchers (along with a fair number of so-called experienced ones) regularly use methodological designs and data collection strategies that are quite inappropriate for their particular research idea. What we mean by this, of course, is that when you want to simply examine what may be going on in some natural setting, undertaking some sort of *experimental design* will simply not work. Similarly, if you are interested in testing whether some action or variable seems to influence some other action or variable, undertaking a long involved *descriptive ethnographic* field–based study is not likely to yield appropriate data or results. Thus, it is useful for researchers to understand the distinctions between each of these types of general research design orientations. The following sections will undertake to offer a description of each of the major research designs, namely, experimental, inferential, descriptive, and exploratory designs.

Experimental Designs

Experimental designs typically seek to address questions having to do with cause and effect (Shadish, Cook, & Cambell, 2001). In scientific notation, this is often depicted in the following way:

$$X \longrightarrow Y$$

This phrase is usually read as "X causes Y." In causal relationships, the X variable is referred to as the independent variable, while the Y variable is referred to as the dependent variable. One way to remember this is that the Y variable is dependent on the X variable to occur. In other words, in the absence of the X, there would be no Y or changes in Y.

In order for a causal relationship to be accepted, three conditions have to be met. These conditions include that (1) X precedes Y in time (a temporal element), (2) changes in X result in changes in Y (a covariant relationship between the two variables X and Y), and (3) there are no other alternative variables that may be influencing the relationship so that it *appears* X causes Y. In other words, there is no alternative variable (usually depicted as Z) actually creating the appearance that X causes Y (what is usually referred to as a spurious effect). This spurious relationship also has a scientific notation as follows:

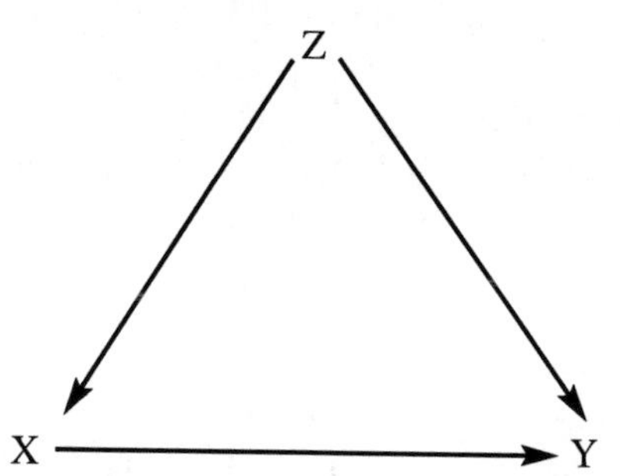

In order to accomplish an experiment, the researcher uses cases or people, typically referred to as *subjects*, whose features or characteristics—what may be labeled *variables*—are examined in terms of certain hypothesized relationships; namely, that some variable has a causal relationship with another variable (Ryan, 2007).

Ideally, experiments should have at least two groups drawn *randomly* from a research population: a control group and an experimental or treatment group (the distinctions between these two groups will be drawn out later). In what is sometimes referred to as a **classical experiment**, certain important conditions must be met in developing these two groups (Babbie, 2007). First, the research must identify the full research population in question, including the parameters of this population; in other words, all of the elements that make up this full working population. Let's say, for example, we hypothesize that when college students at the State University—eat Granny Smith apples, they develop stomachaches. Thus, our causal statement becomes Granny Smith apples [X] cause stomachaches in State University students [Y]. In this example, the full research population would be all students attending State University at a given point in time when the study was being conducted.

A second condition for our experiment is that subjects taken from our full population (all students attending State University) must be drawn **randomly**. This means that every student (potential subject) must have an equal opportunity or chance of being selected into one or the other of the two groups to be used in the experiment.

A third condition is that as subjects are selected from the full population, they must be randomly assigned to one or the other of the two groups (the control group or the experimental group).

At this point, many readers are probably asking, "What is the difference between the control and experimental groups?" Well, the control group will be used as a comparison to the experimental group. This means we will not do anything to the control group. On the other hand, the experimental group will have the variable in question, what may also be referred to as the *treatment* applied to it. In order for this to be an effective comparison, however, we need to create our two groups as *equivalent* to each other as we possibly can.

In an ideal world, we could clone one group to create the other, and we would have absolutely identical subjects in each group. Since this is not possible, we must settle on *similar* subject groupings, at least in terms of various demographic characteristics of subjects in each group. In this way, when the experimental group is given some treatment—that is, subjected to the experimental variable—any difference that appears among subjects in the experimental group, and not in the control group, may be attributed to the treatment (the independent variable). So, how do we create this equivalency between the two groups? There are essentially two major ways. First, we can create a *matched sample* in each group, where we will have *absolute equivalence* along certain limited demographic elements among subjects in each group, and second, we can create *approximate equivalence* in each group through randomization of selection.

In the first scenario, the **matched sample**, we would identify certain demographic factors that seem important or relevant to the study focus. This might include age, gender, educational level, family income, religious affiliation, and similar demographic factors (Rubin, 2006). Next, we seek to include subjects with specific aspects of each of these demographics in both the control and the experimental groups. In other words, if we identify a subject for our *control group* who is a 22-year-old man, a sophomore at State University, comes from a family whose annual income last year was $65,000.00, and who declares membership as a Lutheran; then, we would need another subject with these identical demographic factors to be placed into the experimental group. In a matched sample, the researcher can feel fairly confident that at least along the matched variables, the two groups are absolutely equivalent.

In the second scenario, **approximately equivalent** groups, the researcher relies on chance obtained through randomization to create approximate equivalence in the two groups. In other words, if each subject is selected from the full population and is then randomly assigned to one or the other of the two groups, the laws of probability suggest that approximately the same proportion of each demographic element among subjects in each group should be obtained. The experiment relies on this idea of group equivalence as a basis of making a comparison between groups after the experimental group has been subjected to whatever the treatment (the experimental variable) may be. Again, the notion is that since the groups are approximately equivalent, when the experimental group is exposed to the treatment variable and the control group is not, and a change occurs among the experimental group subjects, it can be attributed to their exposure to the experimental variable.

In our current example, that would mean that the experimental group would be given some Granny Smith apples to eat to see if subjects in this experimental group develop stomachaches, while the subjects in the control group would be given nothing (no apples). The initial basic logic to this experiment, then, would be to see if the State University students given Granny Smith apples to eat did develop stomachaches (our experimental group) while the other group (the control group) of State University students did not (since they did not eat the Granny Smith apples). In other words,

Eating Granny Smith apples [X] $\overrightarrow{\text{Stomachaches}}$ [Y]

The problem with this simple version of the experiment, as some readers may have noticed, is that we do not, from the current information offered, know if there may have been other alternative variables at play that are causing the stomachaches (a spurious relationship). So, what we need to do is to control a number of other conditions to ensure the only variable that may be causing the stomachaches is, in fact, the ingestion of the Granny Smith apples. This is usually referred to as *manipulating the independent* variable or *controlling external conditions*. How might we accomplish this in our current experiment? First, we would need to ensure that all subjects in the experiment (both in the control and in the experimental groups) are healthy and free from any flu or stomach illnesses. We might accomplish this by having each student examined by a physician. We might also want to ensure that none of the students are allergic to apples. Furthermore, we might want to ensure that, as much as possible, these students have not ingested anything else that might cause stomachaches. So, we might house both groups of students in a similar dormitory for 24 hours prior to the actual experiment (when we give the experimental group the Granny Smith apples to eat), thereby feeding them and controlling what all the students eat, thus guaranteeing that everyone eats exactly the same diet of foods for these 24 hours. By controlling these environmental elements, we effectively control the possibility of a spurious relationship creating the appearance of cause (Gravetter & Wallnau, 2004; Rubin, 2006).

When a researcher takes all of the precautions outlined above to create the two groups and undertake the experiment, the process is usually described as a *classical experiment*. However, there are many occasions when a researcher is unable to determine the parameters of a full population and thus cannot legitimately undertake a genuine random selection from a bounded full population when creating the two comparison groups (the control and experimental groups). In these cases, the research may be said to be undertaking a *quasi-experimental design*.

The necessary aspects of undertaking a classical experiment may be listed as follows:

1. Identify a research population, and determine its parameters.
2. Randomly select subjects to be placed into an experimental or control group.
3. Arbitrarily (randomly) assign subjects, as selected from the population, to one or the other of the two groups (the experimental or control group).
4. Manipulate the independent variable (to control for spuriousness).
5. Apply the treatment variable (the experimental variable).
6. Observe if a change occurs in the experimental group as compared with the control group.

Under many circumstances, it may be impossible to include all of the elements that go into the requirements of a classical experiment, but some sort of experimental design, often referred to as quasi-experimental, may still seem desirable.

QUASI-EXPERIMENTAL DESIGN A quasi-experimental design is one that looks a bit like an experimental design but lacks the key ingredient, namely, a completely randomly selected and assigned set of subjects into the two groups (Shadish et al., 2001). For example, let's say you are interested in studying asthma among Latino families in Madison, Wisconsin. It would be impossible to identify all of the Latino families residing in Madison, Wisconsin, let alone all those with a family member with asthma. On the other hand, you could create a research population containing these factors by advertising in local Latino-oriented newspapers and recruiting in local churches where the congregations are composed largely of Latino families. Once you created such a population, you could now employ randomization in your selection of subjects to be placed into the two study groups (control and experimental). Thus, the various demographic factors among those individuals who found themselves in your created research population should appear in approximately the same proportions in each of the two groups for which they have been randomly selected. In some situations, you may be unable to create two completely separate groups to use in comparison with one another during the course of an experiment. In such situations, the researcher may use the same group as both the control group and the experimental group. This is usually referred to as a *single group before and after comparison experimental design.*

Single Group Before and After Comparison Experimental Design Let's say you are an elementary school reading teacher interested in testing to see if a new experimental modular reading program was effective on sixth graders. One way to undertake this experiment is to create a list of all the six graders in the school, and then randomly assign half of the students to an experimental group and half to a control group. Next, you would administer a reading test to all subjects (both groups) to establish a baseline reading level of students. Following this, you would begin the modular reading program for only the experimental group. Let's say this program takes four months to complete. At the end of the program, all of the students will be administered the reading test again. If the students in the experimental group have higher reading scores than those in the control group, we might conclude that the modular reading program was effective. Success! Or is it? Actually, there are some serious ethical problems with the experimental design outlined above. Here is the problem: Reading is a very important skill in education, especially during elementary school years. Reading levels, in fact, are used to determine, for example, whether a student may be qualified for special advanced programs in science, math, and social studies. If the experiment allows the students in the experimental group to improve their reading skills appreciably, then they may have an advantage over the students in the control group when it comes to assignment into these various specialized types of classes. Conversely, if the program does not work well, and perhaps even slows the reading skill development of the students in the experimental group, then the experimental group students may be permanently disadvantaged as compared with the control group students. One possible and more ethical alternative would be to give all the students the reading test as a baseline measure, and then all of the students the reading module program. At the completion of the program, all the students would again be administered a reading test. By using the scores of the first rendering of the reading test as the control, and the second rendering of the examination as the experimental offering, one can measure whether the modular reading program was effective the same group has been used as both the control group and the experimental group (Creswell, 2008).

Inferential Research Designs

Inferential research designs use *inferential statistics* to draw out associations between variables and to reach conclusions that extend beyond the immediate data alone. For instance, we might use inferential statistics to try to infer from the sample data what the population might think about a given issue. Or, we might use inferential statistics to make judgments about the probability that an X variable will cause Y variable to change in a hypothesized causal relationship. Thus, as the term implies, we use inferential statistics to make *inferences* from our data to more general conditions; as will be indicated later, we use *descriptive statistics* simply to describe what's going on in our data.

Most of the major inferential statistics derive from a general family of statistical models known as the *general linear model*. This includes the *t* test, analysis of variance (ANOVA), analysis of covariance (ANCOVA), regression analysis, and many of the multivariate methods such as factor analysis, multidimensional scaling, cluster analysis, discriminant function analysis, and so on. Given the importance of the general linear model, it's a good idea for any fledgling social researcher to become familiar with its workings; however, there is neither time nor space in this text to fully elaborate on this model or the various inferential statistics associated with it. Suffice it to say that the logic of the general linear model would imply only consideration of a straight-line model. However, upon some investigation, the reader will learn that linear models may include curved lines as well, sometimes referred to as *curvilinear analysis* (Creswell & Plano-Clark, 2007).

Descriptive Research Designs

Descriptive research designs, as implied in the terminology, are intended to *describe* what is going on during some event or among some groups of people (Babbie, 2007). The general process involves the researcher carefully observing what is occurring in some setting, or during some event, and then detailing what he or she has witnessed. Because scientific observation is careful, systematic, and deliberate, descriptive research studies are typically more accurate than mere reminiscence from a casual observer who may also have been witness to some event. Furthermore, descriptions may derive from lengthy field explorations in which the researcher collects reams of detailed field notes or systematically collects form surveys during a single or series of administrations. The U.S. Census is often pointed to in textbooks as an excellent example of a study that uses a descriptive research design. The major goal of the U.S. Census is to describe a variety of characteristics of the U.S. population at the time of the data collections (the U.S. Census is administered every 10 years). Other examples of descriptive studies might include an examination of individuals who have been successful at long-term maintenance of a large weight loss, or a product-marketing survey that describes the kinds of people who wait in lines—sometimes for days at a time—in order to purchase new cutting-edge electronic devices, such as the latest telephone or video-game player. Or, a political researcher who assesses the voting patterns of state legislators may also be creating a descriptive study.

While many qualitative studies may be aimed at describing some condition or phenomenon, it should be obvious from the preceding examples that descriptive studies do not necessarily need to be qualitative in their orientation and that many quantitative studies are also constructed from descriptive research designs (Rubin & Babbie, 2007).

Exploratory Research Designs

Sometimes research is conducted in an effort to better understand exactly what is going on during an event or phenomenon, or to simply explore some topic where little empirical research may have previously been conducted (Marczyk, Dematteo, & Festinger, 2005). For example, when gas prices soared during the summer of 2008, rising to nearly $5.00 a gallon across the United States, what would have happened if many U.S. citizens had decided to boycott the gas pumps for one day a week for a month? Or perhaps a better question might be, what would need to occur to motivate people to undertake such a boycott? Either of these questions might have required an exploratory research design. One might be interested, for example, in considering how such a movement might be organized? Which types of people would be most likely to take part in such a boycott? An exploratory study would allow one to learn, at least approximately, what the answers are to these sorts of questions.

Exploratory designs are also useful for more pedestrian types of issues and phenomena. For example, let's say you are unhappy with having been refused admission into some professional school, such as a law school or medical school. You might study the history of admissions to such programs and those of the particular schools to which you have been unsuccessful in gaining admission. You may, as a consequence of this research, learn that your characteristics did not meet those of the schools you applied to, but may be better suited to some other school's program and admissions standards.

Like descriptive studies, sometimes the research design calls for various qualitative strategies; but in other situations, quantitative strategies such as surveys may be used. In the example above, one might research admissions requirements using a more qualitative archival strategy (locating admissions requirements in college bulletins either in libraries or on the Internet). Or, one might survey students who were successful at gaining admission in order to determine what characteristics they seem to share in common (e.g., GPA levels, collecting butterflies, extracurricular undergraduate college activities, certain scores on professional examinations such as the MCATS and LSATS).

There are three major reasons one might seek to undertake an exploratory study. These reasons are as follows: (1) to satisfy a researcher's curiosity about some situation, issue, or phenomenon, where little or no previous empirical research may exist; (2) to test the feasibility of a larger, more extensive study (perhaps a larger inferential study); and (3) to develop methods or hypotheses to be tested in some subsequent study.

Explanatory Research Designs

Whereas descriptive and exploratory research designs look at what, where, when, and how things occur during some situation, event, or phenomenon, explanatory research designs examine the *why* of things. Thus, the desire to explain the purpose of something, or some phenomenon, becomes the main objective in explanatory research designs (Creswell, 2008). Sometimes, explanatory research will build on descriptive and/or exploratory research studies by going further in identifying the reasons for something that occurred, or that occurred in a particular manner. Explanatory research looks for causes and reasons. For example, a descriptive research study may discover that 60% of juveniles officially identified as delinquents after adjudication from some crime were physically abused by their parents. An exploratory orientation, however, might seek to determine why having been physically abused by one's parents led the youth to commit a crime; or even why the parents of delinquents tended to abuse their children. In other words, it is one thing to determine crime rates for some juvenile category of crime; it is quite another to consider why these juveniles committed the crime. This latter effort becomes the principal focus of explanatory research.

There are a number of generally held goals in explanatory research designs. These include the following:

1. Explaining phenomena in an effort to enrich previous theories.
2. To ascertain which among a series of possible theories or explanations seems to be the best theory or explanation.
3. To further, enrich, or refine, current levels of understanding about some phenomenon, event, or situation.
4. To provide evidence to support or refute an explanation or prediction about something.

DEVELOPING RESEARCH IDEAS

As Berg (2007, p. 21) suggests, "Every research project has to start somewhere; typically, the starting point is an idea." The obvious next question, of course, is "How does one go about finding an idea that will serve as a good research topic?" For many new researchers, this can be a daunting task in itself. Ironically, many researchers arrive at their initial research idea simply by taking stock of their personal interests or by looking at what may be happening in their local community, the nation, or society. For example, listening to a new broadcast, you might hear a report indicating that there is an increase in juvenile crime, that several young girls had falsely reported that their gym teacher had fondled them in the locker room, or even that an orderly had been arrested for sexually assaulting several women in a maternity ward of some hospital. Any of these stories may spawn *ideas* for conducting research.

Similarly, many people have personal experiences that cause them to take interest in something that they would like to know more about, and this too may lead to their undertaking research. For example, while sitting in your Introduction to Criminal Justice class, you notice that the instructor seems to repeatedly call on students who are dressed in nice clothes and to ignore those wearing sloppy, torn, or very casual clothing. You might begin to wonder if what people wear has anything to do with teacher affinity, or even, perhaps grading. This too might lead to some sort of a research study. A person taking a ride along with a police officer might notice that the officer's interactions seem different depending on the age of the person whom he or she stops for a traffic citation—perhaps being more lenient about not issuing a ticket to adults and more often issuing tickets to young people. Again, this might lead to the ride-along passenger thinking about how a study of this deference might be undertaken. The long and short of it is that almost anything you see or do, learn about, hear about, or experience may be fodder for a research study. Ideas are all around us; the real trick is to select one of these ideas for which to undertake a study, without being continuously sidetracked by all the other possible research ideas. The next step in the research process is to take this potentially broad and even unstructured idea and turn it into a refined and sleek research topic or question to actually study. Toward this end, you need to consult the literature to uncover any theories that may inform you about this idea as it morphs into a research topic or question.

THEORY AND RESEARCH

Once you have identified the general idea for the study, the next thing you need to do is examine what other researchers have previously thought about and studied with regard to this topic. Say, as an example, you have an idea about preventing juveniles caught up in minor acts of delinquency from becoming further entangled in the juvenile or criminal justice system. You might begin by examining literature on previous research-related topics such as delinquency prevention, primary delinquency interventions, secondary delinquency interventions, alternative to adjudication programs, net widening, and similar related topics. The logical way to accomplish this is through a library search and a Web-based search on the Internet. Once you have identified literature on your topic and begin reading through it, you should notice that your research topic is becoming refined and starting to sound more like a traditional research problem or question.

So, using our current example, you may read various studies and theories offered as explanations in these studies, and become interested with the notion of net widening. In a nutshell, net widening involves placing juveniles who have committed minor infractions of the law under some form of observation or control of the justice system, or an agency working for the goals of the justice system (see Bechard, 2006; Macallair & Roche, 2001). Now you might reformulate your *idea* into a more viable research question, such as "Does net widening target appropriate juvenile populations?" Your direction and orientation, then, has been informed and shaped by the current theories and research on the topic found during your search and reading of the existing literature. In other words, your research question didn't just spring forth spontaneously but was influenced by the literature on delinquency prevention and net widening that you read about.

References

Babbie, E. (2007). *The practice of social research* (11th ed.). Belmont, CA: Thomson/Wadsworth.

Berg, B. L. (2007). *Qualitative research methods for the social sciences.* Boston, MA: Allyn & Bacon.

Bechard, S. (2006). The effects of net widening in a youth diversion program. *Dissertation Abstracts International, 45* (05). (UMI No. 1442646)

Creswell, J. W. (2008). *Research design: Qualitative, quantitative, and mixed methods approaches* (3rd ed.). Belmont, CA: Sage.

Creswell, J. W., & Plano-Clark, V. L. (2007). *Designing and conducting mixed method research.* Belmont, CA: Sage.

Gravetter, F. J., & Wallnau, L. B. (2004). *Statistics for the behavioral sciences* (6th ed.). Belmont, CA: Wadsworth.

Macallair, D., & Roche, T. (2001). *Widening the net in juvenile justice and the dangers of prevention and intervention.* National Criminal Justice Reference Service Abstracts. Retrieved June 8, 2007, from http://www.ncjrs.gov/

Marczyk, G. R., Dematteo, D., & Festinger, D. (2005). *Essentials of research design and methodology.* Malden, MA: John Wiley & Sons.

Rubin, A., & Babbie, E. (2007). *Research methods for social work* (6th ed.). Belmont, CA: Brooks/Cole.

Rubin, D. B. (2006). *Matched samples for causal effects.* New York: Cambridge University Press.

Ryan, T. (2007). *Modern experimental design.* San Francisco, CA: Wiley Interscience.

Shadish, W. R., Cook, T. D., & Cambell, D. T. (2001). *Experimental and quasi-experimental designs for generalized causal inference* (2nd ed.). Boston: Houghton Mifflin.

Exercise 4.1 Descriptive Research

ADVANCE FOR IMMEDIATE RELEASE **Bureau of Justice Statistics**

TUESDAY, APRIL 22, 2008 Contact: Stu Smith: 202-307-0784

www.ojp.usdoj.gov/bjs After hours: 301-983-9354

NUMBER OF HIV-POSITIVE STATE AND FEDERAL INMATES CONTINUES TO DECLINE

About 44 percent of state inmates and 39 percent of federal inmates have medical problems

WASHINGTON—Between 2005 and 2006 the number of state and federal prisoners who were HIV-positive decreased 3.1 percent—from 22,676 to 21,980 inmates, according to a report by the Justice Department's Bureau of Justice Statistics (BJS). Another BJS report estimated that 44 percent of state inmates and 39 percent of federal inmates reported a current medical problem other than a cold or a virus.

Sixteen states and the federal system reported a decrease in the number of HIV-infected prisoners and 25 states reported an increase from 2005 through 2006. Texas, with 293 more HIV-positive inmates, reported the largest increase. New York with 440 fewer HIV-positive prisoners reported the largest drop.

On December 31, 2006, an estimated 5,977 inmates had confirmed AIDS, up from 5,620 in 2005. Confirmed AIDS cases accounted for more than a quarter of inmates known to be HIV positive.

At yearend 2006, the rate of confirmed AIDS in state and federal prisoners was more than 2½; times higher than in the U.S. population. About 46 in 10,000 prison inmates were estimated to have confirmed AIDS, compared to 17 per 10,000 persons in the general population.

During 2006, the number of AIDS-related deaths in state and federal prisons totaled 167, down from 203 in 2005. In 2006, nearly 5 percent of state inmate deaths were attributable to AIDS, down from 34 percent in 1995.

At yearend 2006, 0.9 percent of federal inmates (1,530) were known to be HIV positive, down from 1,592 in 2005. Of the federal prisoners known to be HIV positive at year-end 2006, 656 had confirmed AIDS, up from 594 in 2005. During 2006, 12 federal inmates died from AIDS-related causes, down from 27 in 2005. During 2006, the rate of death due to AIDS-related causes among federal prisoners was 6 per 100,000 inmates.

Current medical problems among prisoners include arthritis, asthma, cancer, diabetes, heart problems, hypertension, kidney problems, liver problems, paralysis, problems due to a stroke, hepatitis, HIV, STDs, or tuberculosis. More than a half of female inmates and over a third of male inmates reported a current medical problem in a national inmate survey.

Among inmates admitted to state and federal prisons, about an eighth reported having surgery, and half reported having a dental problem. A third of state inmates and 28 percent of federal inmates reported either an accidental injury or a fight-related injury since admission to prison.

More than a third (36 percent) of state inmates and nearly a quarter (24 percent) of federal inmates reported having an impairment, including a learning, speech, hearing, vision, mobility, or mental impairment.

More than half of state (51 percent) and federal inmates (56 percent) who were homeless in the year prior to arrest reported a current medical problem compared to 43 percent of state and 38 percent of federal inmates who were not homeless. Sixty percent of state inmates and 58 percent of federal inmates who used a needle to inject drugs reported a current medical problem compared to 40 percent state and 36 percent of federal [inmates] who did not.

Among inmates who reported a medical problem, 70 percent of state inmates and 76 percent of federal inmates reported seeing a medical professional because of the problem. More than 8 in 10 inmates in state and federal prisons reported receiving a medical exam or a blood test since admission.

Among females in state prisons, 4 percent said they were pregnant at the time of admission; 3 percent of federal inmates were pregnant. Of those in state prisons who said they were pregnant at admission, 94 percent received an obstetric exam. More than half (54 percent) received some type of pregnancy care.

The reports, *HIV in Prisons, 2006* (NCJ-222179), and *Medical Problems of Prisoners* (NCJ-221740) were written by BJS Statistician Laura M. Maruschak. Following publication, the reports can be found at http://www.ojp.usdoj.gov/bjs/pub/html/hivp/2006/hivp06.htm and http://www.ojp.usdoj.gov/bjs/pub/html/mpp/mpp.htm. For additional information about the Bureau of Justice Statistics's statistical reports and programs, please visit the BJS Web site at http://www.ojp.usdoj.gov/bjs.

Application Exercise 4.1

Name of Student:________________

Student ID No.:________________

Course/Section No.:________________

Date:________________

1. The Bureau of Justice Statistics press release on inmate HIV status discusses several key findings. These are primarily descriptive, meaning that it describes a sample but makes no argument about causes or implications. Name three primary findings detailed in this report?

2. What empirical research questions might be sparked from this information?

3. What are the implications of these findings for prison administrators?

4. What implications do the findings have for public health?

5. What fiscal implications do the findings have?

Exercise 4.2 Exploratory Research

Sexual Assault During and After Separation/Divorce: An Exploratory Study

Walter S. DeKeseredy

MARCH 2007
U.S. DEPARTMENT OF JUSTICE

SUMMARY

Since the 1970s, social scientists have greatly enhanced an empirical and theoretical understanding of various types of woman abuse in ongoing heterosexual relationships. However, although we know that breaking up with a violent man greatly increases a woman's risk of experiencing lethal and non-lethal violence, relatively little empirical and theoretical attention has been paid to the victimization of women who want to leave, are in the process of leaving, or who have left their marital/cohabiting partners. Furthermore, the limited work that has been done on this topic focuses primarily on physical violence, such as beatings and homicide. Abuse, of course, is multidimensional in nature, and a few studies show that women are also at high risk of being sexually assaulted during and after separation/divorce. Still, almost all of the research on this problem, regardless of whether it is qualitative or quantitative, was conducted in urban areas. Thus, the main objective of this report is to help fill two major research gaps by presenting the results of a qualitative, exploratory study of separation/divorce sexual assault in rural Ohio.

PROJECT GOALS AND OBJECTIVES

This study was specifically designed to provide answers to the following questions:

1. Are survivors of separation/divorce sexual abuse also victims of physical and psychological abuse, or is sexual assault the only type of abuse they experience?
2. Is there evidence indicating that separation/divorce sexual assault is a major problem in rural communities?
3. Is sexual assault more frequent and severe during or after separation/divorce?
4. Is separation/divorce sexual assault multidimensional in nature? For example, do survivors of this abuse, like survivors of sexual assault in ongoing relationships, experience different types of forced sexual activity?
5. Based on survivors' point of view, what are the major characteristics of men who sexually assault their ex-partners?
6. What are the psychological, physical, and economic effects of separation/divorce sexual assault?
7. Based on survivors' perspectives, what types of social support and intervention strategies are most effective?
8. What new directions should be taken to develop and test explanatory models of separation/divorce sexual assault?
9. What are the implications for further qualitative and quantitative research on separation/divorce sexual assault?

In addition to trying to enhance a social scientific understanding of a problem that has garnered limited attention from the media, the scientific community, and the criminal justice system, the research team was equally concerned with generating policy-relevant data that can be used to tailor more effective prevention and social support services for a group of women who continue to suffer in silence. Too often, separation/divorce does not end abuse and thus it is necessary to develop policies and practices that meet the unique needs of women victimized by sexual violence during and after the process of leaving marital/cohabiting relationships.

A broad definition of separation/divorce guides this study. For example, a woman does not need to be legally tied to a man to experience sexual assault during or after exiting a relationship. Further, many women cannot leave a relationship for a host of reasons but emotionally separate from their partners. Thus, here, I use the term *separation/divorce* to mean physically, legally, or emotionally exiting a marital/cohabiting relationship. Further, guided by empirical work done by Dr. Mary Koss and her colleagues in the late 1980s, the types of sexual assault described by 43 rural Ohio women was classified as follows:

- ***Sexual contact*** includes sex play (fondling, kissing, or petting) arising from menacing verbal pressure, misuse of authority, threats of harm, or actual physical force.
- ***Sexual coercion*** includes unwanted sexual intercourse arising from the use of menacing verbal pressure or the misuse of authority.
- ***Attempted rape*** includes attempted unwanted sexual intercourse arising from the use of or threats of force, or the use of drugs or alcohol.
- ***Rape*** includes unwanted sexual intercourse arising from the use of or threats of force and other unwanted sex acts (anal or oral intercourse or penetration by objects other than the penis) arising from the use of or threat of force, or the use of drugs or alcohol.

THEORETICAL FRAMEWORK

Developed by Walter DeKeseredy, McKenzie Rogness, and Martin Schwartz, the integrated theoretical model that informs this study includes the following variables: societal patriarchy; male proprietariness; exiting; threats to masculinity and patriarchal control; patriarchal male peer support; and separation/divorce sexual assault. Referred to by these sociologists as a feminist/male peer support model, some empirical support for it is presented in Chapter 4. Still, after carefully analyzing the results and reading more rural sociological and criminological literature, it is evident that further theoretical work needs to take in account factors such as rural social and economic transformations that have occurred since the end of the last century. Thus, in Chapter 5, a new theoretical model is offered, one that addresses this variable, as well as male peer support and rural challenges to masculine identity.

METHODS

As described in this report, researchers encounter many obstacles while conducting rural studies of woman abuse. However, some of these problems were overcome or minimized using a variety of methods. The first step was preparatory research. This involved several meetings, electronic mail exchanges, and in-depth telephone conversations with leading researchers in the field, local shelter staff, sexual assault advocates, police officers, mental health workers, and others with a vested interest in curbing separation/divorce sexual assault and other types of woman abuse. Then, techniques like those used by Dr. Lee Bowker approximately 24 years ago in Milwaukee were used to generate a sample. For example, an advertisement was placed twice in a free newspaper available throughout Athens County, Ohio. Also, posters about the study were pinned up in public places, such as courthouses, and were given to social service providers who came into contact with abused women.

In addition:

- Two local newspapers gave considerable coverage to the project.
- Ohio University sent out a press release to newspapers and other Ohio-based media.
- Three local radio stations and Ohio University's television station carried public service announcements about the study.
- The director of the local shelter and I appeared on a local television news show to discuss this project and broader issues related to it.
- The Ohio Domestic Violence Network and other agencies told interested parties (e.g., rural shelter workers) about the study and helped to recruit participants.
- Local shelter staff, a police department social worker, employees of the county sheriff's department, Planned Parenthood, Women's Center staff at a local two-year college, and employees of the local Sexual Assault Survivor Advocate Program informed possible respondents about the study.
- Ohio University sociologist Judith Grant told women who participated in her addiction study about this research.
- Index-like cards with the information provided in the recruiting poster were routinely placed on top of newspaper boxes inside stores and on sidewalks in Athens, Ohio.

From early March 2003 until early April 2004, two female research assistants carried cellular phones 24 hours a day to receive calls from women interested in participating in the study. Callers were told the purpose of the project and were then asked a series of screening questions to determine their eligibility to be interviewed. The main criteria were being 18 years of age or older and having ever had any type of unwanted sexual experience when they wanted to end, were trying to end, or after they had ended a relationship with a husband or live-in male partner. If they met the selection criteria, the women were invited to a semi-structured face-to-face interview at a time and place of their choosing, and they were paid $25.00 for their time. They were also given $7.75 for travel expenses and an index card listing the locations and phone numbers of local support services for survivors.

Female research assistants tape-recorded and transcribed all of the interviews. Most of them took about 90 minutes and a total of 43 women participated in this study. Posters placed in public places attracted most of our respondents ($n = 27$). Eight women called after exposure to ads or media stories about the study, and the same number were referred to us by individuals or organizations. Most respondents ($n = 30$) lived in Athens County, Ohio, three lived in Hocking County, Ohio, one lived in Vinton County, Ohio, and nine lived in other rural parts of the state. The mean age of the sample was 35 and the mean income for 2002 was $13,588. Sixty-five percent ($n = 28$) had some type of post-secondary education and close to half of the participants were unemployed. Of the 25 who had been married, all got divorced or legally separated, but only five remarried. Most of the respondents also had children.

FINDINGS

The key findings are categorized under these headings: types and timing of abuse; characteristics of men who sexually assaulted their ex-partners; consequences of separation/divorce sexual assault; and social support.

Types and Timing of Abuse

- Only a few respondents experienced just one of the above forms of separation/divorce sexual assault, and virtually all experienced rape or attempted rape.
- Most (80%) of the women were victimized by two or more variants of other types of abuse, such as physical violence and the destruction of prized possessions.
- Nineteen percent of the respondents stated that their partners abused their children and one woman believes that her ex-partner raped her as a means of killing her unborn child.
- Seventy-four percent (n = 32) of the respondents said that they were sexually assaulted when they expressed a desire to leave their relationships. Forty-nine percent (n = 21) were sexually abused while they were trying to leave or while they were leaving and 33% (n = 14) were victimized after they left.
- Compared to cohabiting women (33%, n = 6), married women (47%, n = 12) were more likely to report being abused while still in the relationship, before expressing a desire to exit, trying to exit, or exiting their relationships. At the next stage, when the women reported that they wanted to leave their abusive relationship, 20 of the 25 married women (80%) stated that they were sexually assaulted, while 12 of the 18 cohabiting women (67%) stated that their assaults occurred at this point in time.

Characteristics of Men Who Sexually Assaulted Their Ex-Partners

- Sixty-seven percent (n = 29) of the interviewees reported on a variety of ways in which their partners' male peers perpetuated and legitimated separation/divorce sexual assault. Three methods in particular stand out: frequently drinking with male friends, informational support, and attachment to abusive peers.
- Seventy-nine percent of the sample said that their partners strongly believed that men should be in charge and control of domestic household settings.
- Regardless of whether they consumed it in groups, 65% of the sample's estranged partners viewed pornography, and it was reported to be involved in sexually abusive events experienced by 30% of the interviewees.
- More than half (58.14%) of the women said that male offenders had guns and some perpetrators even threatened to use them.
- Over 65% (n = 28) of the women interviewed said that their partners used illegal drugs and that their consumption of these substances contributed to abusive behaviors.

Consequences of Separation/Divorce Sexual Assault

- Women experienced a wide range of negative outcomes, including low self-esteem, fear, nightmares, and a myriad of physical health problems.
- All of the survivors interviewed developed a host of adverse post-assault psychological outcomes, such as depression, sexual aversion, and fear.
- Many respondents mentioned physical scars.
- For many interviewees, exiting a relationship was financially devastating.

Social Support

- Data uncovered by this study strongly suggest that if there are high levels of collective efficacy in the respondents' communities, they do not function to prevent and deter separation/divorce sexual assault. For example, most of the interviewees (84%) stated that women experiencing unwanted sex in their community is a major problem and 81% reported that rape or sexual assault is also a serious problem.
- That 81% of the respondents stated that they personally know other women who were sexually assaulted provides further evidence that such victimization is a major problem in some rural Ohio communities and that little is being done to prevent it.
- Over half (58%) of the interviewees do not feel safe when they are at home.
- Eighty-four percent of the respondents stated that they could not count on their neighbors to help solve their personal problems.
- Sixty-seven percent of the sample did not get together with their neighbors in a typical week.
- Fifty-eight percent of the women turned to at least one friend for help, but most of their friends did not live near them. Further, 44% sought assistance from the police, and 40% received help from a local shelter.
- The interviewees' voices reveal that formal and better intervention by state authorities is more important for them than focusing on collective efficacy at this point in time.
- Only one of the respondents who turned to at least one element of the criminal justice system for help stated that it was the best assistance she received.
- Most interviewees turned to several different sources of social support.
- Most interview[ee]s found their friends to be the best source of social support.

SUGGESTIONS FOR FURTHER EMPIRICAL, THEORETICAL, AND POLICY WORK

This study shows that exiting or trying to exit a marital/cohabiting relationship increases women's chances of being sexually assaulted, especially if they are connected to patriarchal or abusive men. However, there is still much that we do not know about separation/divorce sexual assault in rural and urban communities. Certainly, much more empirical and theoretical work is needed. Of course, it is also necessary to develop policies and practices that meet the unique needs of women who are terrorized by men who will not let them leave and men who they have left.

New Directions in Empirical Work

Regardless of whether separation/divorce sexual assault studies are conducted in rural or urban settings, data gathered from men are needed to more precisely determine the factors that motivate them to be abusive. Moreover, representative sample surveys of rural and urban populations would help determine the incidence and prevalence of separation/divorce sexual assault. Such rural research is undoubtedly difficult to do, given the methodological obstacles discussed in Chapter 3. Further, there are many other groups of men and women who need to be included in future research, such as those who are immigrants, living in public housing, have physical disabilities, and so on.

This is one of the first studies to apply collective efficacy theory to woman abuse in intimate, heterosexual relationships. Obviously, more research is needed, including studying the perceptions and experiences of rural women who are not abused. Another point to consider is that almost all studies of collective efficacy/social disorganization and crime use quantitative techniques, such [as] analyses of census data. Nevertheless, many rural social problems are not easy to study using such methods, which is perhaps one of the key reasons why so few researchers focus on woman abuse in rural areas. Further, quantitative methods alone cannot adequately describe the complexities of rural woman abuse and community responses to it. Thus, it is essential to continue using other methods to examine community characteristics that affect separation/divorce sexual assault and other forms of woman abuse. One suggestion is to specifically design a qualitative project that focuses exclusively on the topics of central concern to this report and that uses in-depth interviews and participant observations of community relations.

POLICY RECOMMENDATIONS

The most common policy recommendations made by the 43 respondents are education, creating awareness, listening to the voices of survivors, criminal justice reforms, and subsidized housing. Based on data derived from these women, my previous empirical work, and a review of the extant literature on woman abuse in rural communities, I suggest that these and the following other policies be implemented as soon as possible and throughout all rural U.S. communities:

- Travel subsidies.
- Job training and education.
- Increased funding for rural service providers.
- The development of and support for small, community-based businesses and small industrial districts.
- Community capacity building.

The policies proposed by 43 rural Ohio women and me are not the only effective solutions to problems experienced by survivors of separation/divorce sexual assault. Rather, they are key elements of much need[ed] community-based, collaborative efforts. Policy development must also be highly sensitive to the ways in which broader social forces contribute to the harms identified in this report.

Application Exercise 4.2

Name of Student:________________
Student ID No.:________________
Course/Section No.:________________
Date:________________

1. Name three primary findings in "Sexual Assault During and After Separation/Divorce: An Exploratory Study."

2. What makes this an exploratory study, rather than a descriptive study?

3. The report gives several policy recommendations. Do you think these are appropriate given the methods described? Why or why not?

4. What future research directions are warranted given the results of these data?

5. If you were to design a follow-up study based on the research presented here, what kind of methods would you use? Be specific.
   a. How would you recruit your sample?
   b. How would you ensure confidentiality?

c. What specific risks are present with this kind of population?

d. What research design would you employ?

CHAPTER 5

Sampling and Design

One of the goals of any social science study is to describe or identify certain characteristics (variables) of some group or population in relation to those of another. When the population being studied is small, such as a group of 12 or 15 juveniles in a diversion program, the research could easily be accomplished by interviewing or observing all the patients. However, if the group to be studied is large, such as all U.S. adolescents using marijuana, it would be both impossible and highly inefficient to attempt interviewing, surveying, or observing all the individuals.

Fortunately, it is not necessary to systematically observe every member of a population (the full group with the characteristics of interest to the researcher). Rather, researchers need only to select a sample of this full population. If this sample is to represent the larger population accurately, it must be drawn carefully and according to certain rules of probability.

Typically, representative sampling strategies are used in survey research. However, the same basic strategies can be applied when identifying subjects for experimental studies, documents used in a textual content analysis, or people or places for observation (Berg, 2007).

The main objective of drawing a sample is to make inferences about the larger population from the smaller sample. Regardless of how carefully the sample is drawn, it is unlikely that it will be identical to the larger population from which it came. We can, however, reasonably expect that the sample will closely resemble the larger group. Since use of the smaller group allows the research to proceed, we must accept the possibility of slight discrepancies.

PROBABILITY SAMPLING

In a probability sampling strategy, the researcher specifies each segment of the population that will be represented in the sample. Basically, the sample is created by selecting units from the larger population. In a probability sample, the manner in which the sample units are selected is very important. The process usually entails drawing subjects from an identified population such that every unit in the larger population has precisely the same chance or probability of being selected as every other unit in that population. This process is known as *randomization*. In this process, the researcher assumes that, since every unit in the large population has precisely the same chance of being selected for the sample, characteristics possessed by the sample members resemble characteristics possessed by members of the larger population.

In order to accomplish this randomization and thereby achieve a *random sample* of participants for study, the researcher can use several different strategies. Among the most commonly used procedures is the random numbers table. Usually, the researcher arbitrarily selects a number with which to begin and then moves up, down, forward, backward, or across the table to continue selecting numbers. By identifying two points—a number for the vertical column and another for the horizontal row—we can locate a starting point for selecting a sample from a population listing.

Ten blocks of random numbers are arranged horizontally, and 10 are arranged vertically. Random numbers tables are usually found as appendixes of most statistics textbooks (see, for example, Appendix A, Chapter 8 of this book).

To illustrate use of a random numbers table, take a dollar bill from your pocket. Look at the first and last numbers of the serial number on the bill. These can be used as the vertical and horizontal guide numbers to enter a random numbers table. Let's say your numbers were 3 and 6. Go to the table and move to the third column of blocked numbers and the sixth row of blocked numbers. Now select any number between 1 and 5. Assume that you select 3. Now move across the row-3 numerals. This identifies your random number; let's say number 4.

At this point, some researchers would go through their list of people in the full population and identify every third name as part of the sample until the sample was filled. Other researchers would repeat this random-number selection and go through the list selecting the individual who corresponds to the randomly identified number from the table. This might mean selecting for a sample the 3rd, 8th, 12th, 15th, and so on. In the first case, the researcher would be conducting a systematic sampling strategy. You should be aware that systematic samples may be classified as probability or nonprobability samples, depending on how the starting point is selected and whether every possible element has an equal chance for inclusion. In the second case, the researcher would be using a simple random sampling protocol.

Other strategies for identifying a random sample may include placing all names of potential subjects in a hat, shaking them up, and simply drawing out names for the sample. Some researchers prefer to computerize their population list and have the computer randomly select some proportion of the full population. In general, there is no absolutely right or wrong way to identify a sample. The single principle that must be maintained is that every unit of the full population must have an equal chance of being drawn into the sample.

Stratified Cluster Sampling (Multistage Sampling)

In random or systematical probability sampling, we sample the actual individuals or elements intended for inclusion in the study. In stratified cluster sampling, we begin by grouping elements that share certain characteristics. These groupings or strata are then used as categories to divide the working population. Our sample involves elements from every stratum. Cluster sampling, then, involves dividing the population into several large groups or clusters. The sampling actually occurs as we draw elements from each of these larger clusters.

In other words, stratified cluster sampling involves several stages. The first stage is to divide the working population into various strata, and the second stage is to draw the sample from these strata. This process can be repeated as many times as necessary to cluster the elements of the population into appropriate categories.

For example, we might use inmates housed in U.S. jails as the working population to study jail rehabilitation efforts. One method of sample selection could be to use stratified cluster sampling. The first step would be to create a list containing the names of all jails in the United States. The second step would be to categorize these agencies according to some criteria; for instance, four regional categories could be used: North, South, East, and West. Now we could sample equally from each category using a simple random selection process.

Alternatively, we could determine the proportion of jails in each category and randomly draw a sample on the basis of those proportions. For instance, suppose that the North category contained 138 jails, the East 77, the South 175, and the West 160. Calculating the proportion for each category and rounding appropriately, the four categories would represent the following proportions, respectively:

Category	Number	Proportion (%)
North	138	25.1
East	77	14.0
South	175	31.8
West	160	29.1

Now assume that the time and budget allow us to have a sample of only 100 prisons and jails. Using appropriate rounding techniques, we would produce a sample of 100 jails as follows:

Category	Number of jails
North	25
East	14
South	32
West	29
Total	100 jails in sample

Sampling Error

Whenever we use probability samples, it is possible that the elements we include in a particular sample may produce findings identical to those of another sample drawn from the same population. This phenomenon, referred to as sampling error, arises because samples often vary slightly, even when two samples from the same population are drawn at the same time and under the same conditions.

For example, suppose we have a population of district attorneys from which to select a random sample for a questionnaire about the number of hours spent preparing for trial per case. It is possible that the mean hours spent in trial preparation are 3.5 hours. Yet even with repeated selection of different random samples, the mean of the sample may never equal exactly 3.5. The sample mean may be higher or lower than the population mean. However, if we select a number of different samples from the population and average the means of the samples, then the average mean should begin to approximate more closely the population's mean hours of trial preparation: 3.5.

It is also important to note that larger samples are more likely to offer mean scores that closely approximate the population means, since larger samples more closely represent the population.

Sample Size

Some researchers go by the general rule "More is better." Thus, the larger the sample, the better the results. However, in deciding how large a sample is sufficient, we cannot just say, "The larger, the better." To do so would be similar to answering the question "what time is it?" by saying "late."

Determining sample size depends on a number of different factors. First, size can be determined on the basis of how closely the sample approximates the population from which it is drawn. If the population is fairly homogeneous (e.g., all drug offenders in a given region), the sample can be smaller if the population is heterogeneous (e.g., all adults under correctional supervision in a given region). Considering this factor will ensure that the various characteristics in the heterogeneous population are represented in the sample.

A second useful guideline suggests that when statistics will be used, the sample should contain a minimum of 150 subjects. For greater statistical reliability, 250, 500, 1,000, or even 1,500 subjects should be used. As we increase the number of subjects, we also increase the degree to which the sample approximates the population and the accuracy of statistical procedures used in the analysis. Beyond 1,500 subjects, the amount of improved statistical accuracy is rather small.

The number of subjects actually included in a sample is often determined by factors of cost and time. The more subjects included, the greater the cost and time required both to collect and analyze data. When time and money are not an issue, most researchers seek as large a sample as possible, frequently exceeding 1,500 subjects.

NONPROBABILITY SAMPLING

Nonprobability samples usually find their way into studies where probability samples would be extremely expensive or when precise representativeness of the sample is not crucial. There are also many occasions when a full population cannot be completely defined. For example, Glassner and Berg (1980) sought to examine drinking patterns among American Jews. Since no complete list of Jews existed from which to draw a random sample, Glassner and Berg created a "master list" of Jews residing in one northeastern community. This list was quite comprehensive and was composed of a number of smaller lists obtained from various Jewish organizations and synagogues in the area. When complete, this list contained the names of over 3,500 Jewish families. Although Glassner and Berg used rigorous systematic sampling strategies, including use of a random numbers table to locate the *n*th name for each selection on the list, their overall sampling strategy was nonetheless a nonprobability strategy.

Nonprobability sampling strategies include a number of different protocols, including convenience, or accidental samples, purpose samples, snowballing techniques, and quota sampling.

Convenience Samples

Convenience, or accidental, samples are typically composed of subjects who are close at hand or easily accessible. For instance, it is fairly common for college and university professors to use students in their classes as subjects in survey research. This type of sample is attractive to some researchers because it tends to be inexpensive and easy to obtain. Hence, the researcher trades some degree of accuracy for increased efficiency.

Under certain circumstances, this strategy is an excellent means of obtaining preliminary information about some research question quickly and inexpensively. For example, if a researcher wanted to know about college drinking patterns, he or she could justify using a convenience sample or college students. If, however, the researcher was interested in knowing about drinking patterns among parolees, he or she could not use the college student sample and ask them to pretend that they are parolees when answering the questions. In other words, convenience samples must still be evaluated for appropriateness of fit for a study.

Another variation of the convenience sample is the *haphazard* sample, in which inhabitants of an area of investigation are surveyed or interviewed by virtue of their presence. This type of sample is common in some field research studies.

Purposive Samples

Sometimes when a researcher identifies a sample, his or her intention is to ensure that certain characteristics are represented. This is usually accomplished on the basis of a judgment or certain available information that the researcher possesses about some population or group. In some instances, *purpose samples* are selected after field investigation has ensured the location of people displaying attributes desirable for the study.

For example, if we were interested in studying car theft by adolescents involved in drug and alcohol use, it would be nearly impossible to select a random sample. After conducting a field study, however, we might be able to identify a cluster of youths who are involved in drugs and alcohol and who also steal or have stolen cars. Again, what the researcher may lose in generalizability, he or she will gain in accuracy of information by ensuring that the appropriate subjects have been obtained for the study.

Snowballing Techniques

In some situations, the use of *snowballing techniques* may be the best way to locate subjects with certain attributes or characteristics necessary in a study. The basic strategy involves first identifying several persons with relevant characteristics and interviewing or administering the survey to them; these subjects are then asked for the names of other persons who possess the same attributes they do.

For example, suppose we are interested in examining drug use or theft by nurses. By using a probability sampling strategy, we might identify few or no subjects (i.e., nurses who use or steal drugs). But through the use of informants, field investigations, or other strategies, we might identify a small number of nurses with these characteristics. By asking these subjects for referrals of additional nurses, the sample eventually "snowballs" from few subjects to many subjects.

Quota Samples

A *quota sampling* strategy is similar, in some ways, to a *stratified random sample.* Stratified random samples rely on various strategies of chance to fill variable cells, or stratum. The quota sample uses a nonprobability method or filling stratum in a sample in approximately the same proportions as in the full population.

For instance, we might be interested in studying fear of crime among people in the United States, with a special interest in fear among people who are aged. Since census data would give us reasonable estimates of the aged, young adult, and child populations in the United States, we could determine the proportions of people in these age groups. Next, we could select a region of the country and sample people in these three categories, or age cohorts, in the same proportions as represented in the census data. Quota samples work best with highly objective variables, such as age or socioeconomic status, rather than subjective variables, such as viewpoints or perceptions.

CAUSALITY

In quantitative research, one of the ultimate goals is the identification of a *cause*. In the so-called hard sciences, it is possible to control all the variables of an experiment and thus to prove causality with reasonable certainty. But in the social sciences, in the strictest sense, it is not possible to prove causality with certainty, given the complexities of social life and social reality. The social sciences typically use humans as subjects of study. Because human behavior is not absolutely predictable, it becomes impossible to predict accurately how, why, or when humans may act in certain ways. Also, because of ethical considerations, it is not appropriate to control or deceive subjects, endanger or harm them, or expose them to risk.

From a less strict perspective, causality cannot be established with certainty mathematically. For example, even though we may have thrown an apple into the air and watched it fall to the ground 99 times, we cannot be certain that the next time we toss the apple, it will fall to the ground. Perhaps a large bird might be lurking in the tree, watching hungrily as the apple goes up and down. The bird might swoop down and intercept the apple on the 100th toss. Or maybe the apple will be caught by an updraft, blown into the tree, and caught among the limbs, such that it will be unable to fall to the ground. Regardless of why the apple might not return to the ground, we cannot say for certain that it will.

Consider several more examples. If we flip a coin 99 times and get heads each time, there is no guarantee that the next time we flip the coin, it will come up heads. In fact, the laws of probability would suggest that it is more likely that the next toss will come up tails. Probability provides a predetermined degree of likelihood that something will happen; it does not provide certainty. At the racetrack, even if a horse has come in first during its last 15 races, we cannot be sure that, in race number 16, the horse will win. On the other hand, if we know that a horse has won its last 15 races, we will be more likely to bet on that horse than on a horse that has lost its last 15 races.

So it is with causality and probability. If we observe that the occurrence of a particular variable, *X*, is regularly followed by the occurrence of another variable, *Y*, it may be reasonable to assume that *X* causes *Y*. However, three conditions must be met in order to accept a causal statement:

1. ***Temporal requirement***—Variable *X* must precede variable *Y* in time.
2. ***Covariance requirement***—For every change that occurs in variable *X*, a subsequent change must occur in variable *Y*. In other words, if variable *X* increases, then variable *Y* must either increase or decrease. Thus, *Y* is dependent on *X*.
3. ***Elimination of alternative explanation requirement (spuriousness)***—The possibility must be eliminated that other factors actually cause variable *Y*. (In the social sciences, this is probably the most difficult requirement to meet.)

When these three conditions have been met, we generally accept that a cause-and-effect relationship exists between the two variables. In such a relationship, the *X* variable is identified as the *independent* variable and the *Y* variable as the *dependent* variable.

In the social sciences, not all relationships can be positively identified as causal. Certain variables that seem to occur at approximately the same time are said to be *concomitant*. Concomitance provides for plural explanations because it suggests that variables occur at approximately the same time as opposed to one variable causing the other. For example, many people eat lunch at approximately noon. We can ask, however, whether hunger occurs at noon or whether lunchtime has become ritualized at that hour. If lunchtime has become ritualized, then does the upcoming noon hour possibly trigger pans of hunger?

Therefore, in the social sciences, we traditionally talk about relationships and their strengths. In a causal relationship, we can statistically measure the strength of the relationship and the probability that it is significant.

VALIDITY AND RELIABILITY

Validity and *reliability* are two important considerations in research. Generally, it is believed that considerations of validity should precede considerations of reliability because validity examines the instrument of measurement while reliability addresses the consistency of response. Validity asks the question: Does the measurement instrument accurately measure the concept it is intended to measure? Reliability, on the other hand, considers the regularity of particular responses given by subjects. Consequently, if an instrument is reliable, it will provide fairly uniform and stable measures of responses, even when the same questions are asked in repeated studies. (This assumes that the questions have already been assessed as being valid.)

Types of Validity

Researchers can assess a wide variety of types of validity. In this section, we will highlight a few of the most common types, including *face, content, construct, predictive,* and *practical* validity.

FACE Face validity addresses whether a specific question appears, on the surface (i.e., "on the face of it"), to measure what the researchers intended. For example, suppose an exam is given to students in an introductory anthropology class. For previous exams in this class, the result has been a normal distribution of grades of a standard scale. In other words, the majority of the students passed the exam with various levels of success. This time, however, a majority of the students fail the exam. As students discuss the exam with the instructor in class, they discover a heading on the test that indicated it was really intended for an upper-level anthropology class. Somehow, the exams were switched. Therefore, this exam lacked face validity for the introductory class because it was not designed for them.

CONTENT Content validity assesses whether each item of the measurement instrument accurately measures the concept it was intended to measure. On a history test, for instance, suppose that a student answered questions 9 and 12 incorrectly and questions 14 and 17 correctly. When the exam is reviewed in class, he discovers that everyone else in the class got the same two questions wrong and the same two questions right. He also notices that all four questions relate to a topic that the instructor did not discuss in class and that was not covered in the assigned reading material. Naturally, none of the students has any concern about questions 14 and 17, since everyone got them right. But the students are concerned about the two questions they got wrong, numbers 9 and 12. The class points out to the instructor that these questions are not appropriate since they measure content not covered by lecture or reading material. In fact, the two questions that everyone answered *correctly* also lack content validity because they relate to the same subject material.

CONSTRUCT Construct validity is one of the most difficult types of validity to assess because it is basically theoretical in nature. Construct validity is concerned with whether individual questions actually measure the specific concept under study. It is also concerned with whether a set of questions that is used to create a scale assesses the full range of behaviors or responses that are intended to be assessed.

For example, suppose we are interested in assessing degree of liberalism. In compiling a set of questions designed for this purpose, we would need to include questions pertaining to all degrees or level of the characteristics. For instance, if we wanted to assess how the subject feels about minority groups, we could design a set of questions about how geographically close he or she would want minorities to reside. The first questions could ask, "Would it be acceptable to have minorities live in the same country with you?" The second question could ask about having minorities live in the same state, the same city, and so on, until the final question would ask about having minorities live next door. To be sure of the construct validity of this set of questions, we could submit the set to a panel of experts to review inclusiveness and determine whether geographic proximity of minorities is a reasonable measure of liberalism.

PREDICTIVE AND PRACTICAL Predictive validity addresses the accuracy of an instrument of measurement using checks outside the instrument itself. For example, most graduate schools rely on Graduate Record Examination (GRE) scores for admission and financial aid distributions decisions, expecting that candidates with high GRE scores will be successful, as measured by completing the graduate program. Thus, someone with a score of 1,400 out of 1,600 on the GRE is presumed to have a greater likelihood of completion than someone with a 1,000 score. Yet GRE scores lack predictive validity to the extent that many students with scores in the 1,000 range complete their graduate studies while not all those in the 1,400 range do. Therefore, records of successful completion rates constitute the test of predictive ability of the GRE.

Practical validity similarly checks validity outside the instrument. In this case, the researcher examines real-world situations being measured by the instrument and considers how well the results fit reality. For example, a research instrument may suggest that murderers tend to have red hair and wear size-14 shoes. If we were to examine the hair color and shoe size of a population of murderers, perhaps located in several different prisons, we could determine how much practical validity this suggestion has. If the population of murderers indeed has red hair and wears size-14 shoes, then the instrument has a high degree of practical validity. Conversely, if the population of murderers is generally blond and wears size-8 shoes, then the instrument has very low practical validity.

References

Berg, B. (2007). *Qualitative research methods for the social sciences.* Boston: Allyn & Bacon.

Glassner, B., & Berg, B. (1980). How Jews avoid alcohol problems. *The AmericanSociological Review, 45*(1), 647–664.

Exercise 5.1 Monitoring the Future:

NATIONAL RESULTS ON ADOLESCENT DRUG USE

Overview of Key Findings, 2007

Lloyd D. Johnston, Ph.D.

Patrick M. O'Malley, Ph.D.

Jerald G. Bachman, Ph.D.

John E. Schulenberg, Ph.D.

THE UNIVERSITY OF MICHIGAN
INSTITUTE FOR SOCIAL RESEARCH

NATIONAL INSTITUTE ON DRUG ABUSE
6001 EXECUTIVE BOULEVARD

BETHESDA, MARYLAND 20892
U.S. DEPARTMENT OF HEALTH AND HUMAN SERVICES
NATIONAL INSTITUTES OF HEALTH

INTRODUCTION

Monitoring the Future (MTF) is a long-term study of American adolescents, college students, and adults through age 45. The study, ongoing on an annual basis since its inception in 1975, is conducted by the University of Michigan's Institute for Social Research and is supported under a series of investigator initiated, competing research grants from the National Institute on Drug Abuse.

The need for a study such as MTF is evident. Substance use by American young people has proven to be a rapidly changing phenomenon, requiring frequent assessments and reassessments. Since the mid-1960s, when illicit drug use burgeoned in the normal youth population, it has remained a major concern for the nation. Smoking, drinking, and illicit drug use are leading causes of morbidity and mortality, both during adolescence as well as later in life. How vigorously the nation responds to teenage substance use, how accurately it identifies the substance abuse problems that are emerging, and how well it comes to understand the effectiveness of the many policy and intervention efforts largely depend on the ongoing collection of valid and reliable data. Monitoring the Future is designed to generate such data in order to provide an accurate picture of what is happening in this domain and why. It has served that function well for the past 32 years.

The 2007 MTF survey encompassed nearly 50,000 eighth-, 10th-, and 12th-grade students in over 400 secondary schools nationwide. The first published results are presented in this report. Recent trends in the use of licit and illicit drugs are emphasized, as well as trends in the levels of perceived risk and personal disapproval associated with each drug. This study has shown these beliefs and attitudes to be particularly important in explaining trends in use. In addition, trends in the perceived availability of each drug are presented.

A synopsis of the design and methods used in the study and an overview of the key results from the 2007 survey follow this introductory section. Next is a section for each individual drug class, providing figures that show trends in the overall proportions of students at each grade level (a) using the drug, (b) seeing a "great risk" associated with its use, (c) disapproving of its use, and (d) saying that they think they could get it "fairly easily" or "very easily" if they wanted to. The years for which data on each grade are available are 1975–2007 for 12th graders and 1991–2007 for 8th and 10th graders, who were first included in the study in 1991.

STUDY DESIGN AND METHODS

At the core of Monitoring the Future is a series of large, annual surveys of nationally representative samples of public and private secondary school students throughout the coterminous United States. Every year since 1975, a national sample of 12th graders has been surveyed. Beginning in 1991, the study was expanded to include comparable, independent national samples of 8th graders and 10th graders each year. The year 2007 marked the 33rd survey of 12th graders and the 17th survey of 8th and 10th graders.

Sample Sizes

The 2007 sample sizes were about 16,500, 16,400, and 15,100 in 8th, 10th, and 12th grades, respectively. In all, about 48,000 students in 403 secondary schools participated. Because multiple questionnaire forms are administered at each grade level, and because not all questions are contained in all forms, the number of cases upon which a particular statistic is based may be less than the total sample size. The tables here contain notes on the number of forms used for each statistic if less than the total sample is used.

Field Procedures

University of Michigan staff members administer the questionnaires to students, usually in their classrooms during a regular class period. Participation is voluntary. Parents are notified well in advance of the survey administration and are provided the opportunity to decline their son's or daughter's participation. Questionnaires are self-completed and formatted for optical scanning.

In 8th and 10th grades, the questionnaires are completely anonymous, and in 12th grade, they are confidential (to permit the longitudinal follow-up surveys of random subsamples of participants for some years after high school). Extensive, carefully designed procedures are followed to protect the confidentiality of subjects and their data. All procedures are reviewed and approved on an annual basis by the University of Michigan's Institutional Review Board (IRB) for compliance with federal guidelines for the treatment of human subjects.

Measures

A standard set of three questions is used to determine *usage* levels for the various drugs (except for cigarettes and smokeless tobacco). For example, we ask, "On how many occasions (if any) have you used marijuana...(a) in your lifetime? (b) during the past 12 months? (c) during the last 30 days?" Each of the three questions is answered on the same answer scale: 0, 1–2, 3–5, 6–9, 10–19, 20–39, and 40 or more occasions.

For the psychotherapeutic drugs (amphetamines, sedatives [barbiturates], tranquilizers, and narcotics other than heroin), respondents are instructed to include only use ". . . on your own—that is, without a doctor telling you to take them." A similar qualification is used in the question on use of anabolic steroids.

For cigarettes, respondents are asked two questions about use. First they are asked, "Have you ever smoked cigarettes?" (the answer categories are "never," "once or twice," and so on). The second question asks, "How frequently have you smoked cigarettes during the past 30 days?" (the answer categories are "not at all," "less than one cigarette per day," "one to five cigarettes per day," "about one-half pack per day," etc.). Smokeless tobacco questions parallel those for cigarettes.

Alcohol use is measured using the three questions illustrated above for marijuana. A parallel set of three questions asks about the frequency of being drunk. A different question asks, for the prior two-week period, "How many times have you had five or more drinks in a row?"

Perceived risk is measured by a question asking, "How much do you think people risk harming themselves (physically or in other ways), if they . . ." "try marijuana once or twice," for example. The answer categories are "no risk," "slight risk," "moderate risk," "great risk," and "can't say, drug unfamiliar."

Disapproval is measured by the question "Do YOU disapprove of people doing each of the following?" followed by "trying marijuana once or twice," for example. Answer categories are "don't disapprove," "disapprove," and "strongly disapprove." In the 8th- and 10th-grade questionnaires only, a fourth category, "can't say, drug unfamiliar," is provided and is included in the calculations.

Perceived availability is measured by the question "How difficult do you think it would be for you to get each of the following types of drugs, if you wanted some?" Answer categories are "probably impossible," "very difficult," "fairly difficult," "fairly easy," and "very easy." For 8th and 10th graders only, the additional answer category, "can't say, drug unfamiliar," is offered and included in the calculations.

OVERVIEW OF KEY FINDINGS

In recent years, the trends in drug use have become more complex and thus more difficult to describe. A major reason for this increased complexity is that cohort effects have emerged, beginning with the increases in drug use that occurred during the early 1990s. "Cohort effects" refer to lasting differences between class cohorts that stay with them as they advance through school and beyond. These effects result in the various grades reaching peaks or valleys in different years, and thus the various age groups are sometimes moving in different directions at a given point in history. We have seen such cohort effects for cigarette smoking throughout most of the life of the study, but such effects were much less apparent for the illicit drugs until the past decade and a half. The 8th graders have been the first to show turnarounds in illicit drug use: They were the first to show the upturn in use in the early 1990s and the first to show the decline in use after 1996. They have generally shown the greatest proportional declines from recent peak levels of use, attained for the most part during the 1990s, while the proportional declines have generally been the least at 12th grade.

A number of drugs showed modest continuing declines in use in 2007, although few of the one-year changes reached statistical significance. These included marijuana and all of the stimulant drugs other than cocaine. Most of the other drugs held steady in their use in 2007, generally following decreases in their use in prior years. Only one of the many classes of drugs under study showed any sign of increase in use this year—ecstasy (MDMA).

Drugs Decreasing in Use

The use of ***any illicit drug*** in the 12 months preceding the survey (annual prevalence) is down by more than four tenths among 8th graders since the recent peak for that grade in 1996. Tenth and 12th graders reached their recent peaks a year later than the 8th graders; from their 1997 peaks, use is down by about a quarter among 10th graders, but by only about 15% so far among 12th graders. In the one-year interval from 2006 to 2007, only the 8th-grade level had a statistically significant decline in any prevalence period in this index (specifically, in lifetime and annual prevalence); nevertheless, gradual declines did continue in all grades, with 8th-grade lifetime use showing the largest decline of 1.9 percentage points to 19%. In 2007, the lifetime prevalence rates for this index were 19%, 36%, and 47% in grades 8, 10, and 12, respectively. In other words, just under half of American secondary school students today have tried an illicit drug by the time they near high school graduation.

A number of specific drug classes showed continuing declines this year in at least one grade. These include ***marijuana***, ***amphetamines***, ***Ritalin*** specifically, ***methamphetamine***, and ***crystal methamphetamine***. (Alcohol and cigarettes, discussed in a separate section below, also showed some significant declines.)

Marijuana use tends to drive the overall illicit drug index because it is by far the most prevalent of the illicit drugs. Therefore, marijuana shows a very similar pattern of change to that for any illicit drug. In 2007, the annual prevalence of marijuana use fell by a significant 1.4 percentage points among 8th graders to 10.3%, and by a nonsignificant 0.6 percentage points among 10th graders to 24.6%. Annual marijuana use among 12th graders leveled at 31.7%.

Amphetamine use is well below recent peak levels in all three grades under study. Eighth and 10th graders reached their peak levels in annual prevalence in 1996 and since then have shown declines of more than one half and one third, respectively. Twelfth graders, on the other hand, did not reach their recent peak level until 2002, and have declined by one third since then. The decline in use has decelerated at 8th grade since 2004, though there was a nonsignificant 0.5-percentage-point drop this year; at 10th grade, use stabilized after 2005. Twelfth graders have continued to show a gradual decline in recent years (down 0.6 percentage points in 2007, nonsignificant), once again suggesting that a cohort effect is at work.

Ritalin is a specific prescription amphetamine. Its use outside of medical supervision was first measured in the study in 2001; use has been falling since then, with total declines of between one quarter and one half at each grade level. In 2007, 2.1% (8th grade), 2.8% (10th grade), and 3.8% (12th grade) report having used Ritalin without medical instruction at least once in the prior 12 months.

Methamphetamine use was not included in the study until 1999. Since then it has shown a rather steady decline in all three grades—a decline that has now reached about two-thirds in all three grades. That decline continued in 2007, significantly so in both 8th and 12th grades.

Crystal methamphetamine (***ice***) reached its lowest point this year since 1992. Its use is measured only among 12th graders; their annual prevalence this year is 1.6%, down by about half from the peak year of 2002.

Drugs Holding Steady

Among the many drugs showing very little change in 2007 at any grade level were ***LSD***, ***hallucinogens other than LSD***, ***cocaine***, ***crack cocaine***, ***heroin***, ***narcotics other than heroin***, ***OxyContin*** and ***Vicodin*** specifically, ***sedatives***, ***tranquilizers***, three so-called "club drugs" (***Ketamine***, ***Rohypnol***, and ***GHB***), and ***steroids***. In each case, annual prevalence rates are below where they were at their recent peaks, but no appreciable further decline occurred at any grade level for these drugs in 2007. ***LSD*** use—which had shown very sharp declines in annual prevalence between 1999 and 2004, accompanied by a sharp decline in the perceived availability of the drug—has shown little further decline at any grade level. Annual prevalence rates are now very low—at 1.1% in grade 8, 1.9% in grade 10, and 2.1% in grade 12. During the period of decline, perceived risk and disapproval of LSD use did not change in ways that would have been expected if they were driving the change in use (that is, they did not increase); on the other hand, perceived availability did change in the expected direction, showing a sharp decline.

Hallucinogens other than LSD, taken as a class, show much less decline in recent years than LSD; but they are still somewhat below their recent peak levels. (Psilocybin, also known as "shrooms" or "magic mushrooms," is the most widely used of these drugs today.) Annual use changed very little in 2007. Annual prevalence ranges from 1.6% in 8th grade to 4.8% in 12th grade.

The one stimulant drug that did not show a decline this year was ***cocaine***. Cocaine use reached a recent peak among teens in the late 1990s, declined for a year or two, and has held relatively level in recent years. Today, annual prevalence ranges between 2% and 5% in grades 8, 10, and 12.

Crack cocaine use previously declined some in all three grades but showed no further decline this year. Annual prevalence now ranges between 1.3% and 1.9% across the three grades; these rates are down by between a quarter and one half from what they were at their recent peaks.

Heroin use finally fell below its recent peak levels in all three grades by 2001. Since then use has held quite steady. Annual prevalence of heroin use is now slightly below 1.0% in all three grades.

Narcotics other than heroin, taken as a class, are reported only for 12th graders. After increasing substantially since the early 1990s, use of this class of drugs has appeared to level over the past few years. Still, the annual prevalence rate stands at 9.2%. Vicodin and OxyContin, two important analgesics in the narcotic drugs class, are discussed below.

OxyContin use was first measured in 2002. The 2007 figures for all three grades are slightly higher than they were in 2002, but the trend lines have been somewhat erratic. For the three grades combined, there was no change in annual prevalence in the past year. Annual prevalence rates in 2007 for OxyContin use are 1.8%, 3.9%, and 5.3%. In other words, 1 in every 20 high school seniors has at least tried this powerful narcotic drug in the past year.

Similarly, ***Vicodin*** use shows no systematic change in use this year, and the observed rates remain close to recent peak levels. Annual prevalence rates in 2007 are higher than they are for OxyContin: 2.7%, 7.2%, and 9.6% in 8th, 10th, and 12th grades, respectively.

Sedative (barbiturate) use, which is reported only for 12th grade, did not reach its recent peak until 2005, when annual prevalence reached 7.2%. It is down slightly to 6.2% in 2007.

Tranquilizer use increased steadily for nearly a decade, from 1992 to about 2000 among 10th and 12th graders (and from 1991 through 1996 among 8th graders). Thereafter it declined, but this year there was no further decline. Thus, the decade-long upward march in tranquilizer use in the upper grades ended, some modest downward trending occurred, and now that decline seems to be over. Use among 8th graders, which has been much lower, started declining after 1996 and has changed very little since 1998. Annual prevalence rates now lie between 2.4% in grade 8 and 6.2% in grade 12—only modestly below their recent peak levels.

Three "club drugs"—***Ketamine***, ***Rohypnol***, and ***GHB***—have all had quite low prevalence rates in recent years and showed some declines. In 2007, however, there was little systematic change in annual prevalence for any of these three drugs.

Anabolic steroid use reached peak levels by 2000 in 8th and 10th grades, and by 2002 in 12th grade. Since those peak levels, annual prevalence has declined by one half in the lower grades and over four tenths in 12th grade; those declines began in 2001 among 8th graders, in 2003 among 10th graders, and not until 2005 among 12th graders. In 2006 and 2007, steroid use remained relatively unchanged. The annual prevalence figures in 2007 were 0.8%, 1.1%, and 1.4% in grades 8, 10, and 12, respectively.

Drugs Showing Signs of Increased Use

Only one drug showed signs of increased use this year—***ecstasy (MDMA)***—and the increase was modest and not significant. Another drug, ***inhalants***, provided mixed signals, so we discuss it in this section.

Ecstasy (MDMA) use declined substantially at all three grade levels after 2001, apparently as a result of a considerable rise in perceived risk of using this drug. However, while some further decrease occurred in 2006 in 8th grade, there was a nearly significant increase of 1.1 percentage points at 12th grade (to 4.1%), and annual prevalence at 10th grade had been increasing a bit over the prior two years. In 2007 there was some further increase in use at 10th and 12th grades, and the prior gradual decline at 8th grade ended. Of perhaps more concern, perceived risk and disapproval of ecstasy use have been declining in the two lower grades over the past three years, and perceived risk at 12th grade leveled in 2006 and declined in 2007. In 2007 all three grades showed some decline in perceived risk and disapproval. Given that changes in these important attitudes and beliefs are often leading indicators of changes to come in actual use, there is the concern that newer arrivals to adolescence do not have an appreciation of the dangers of using this drug and will be more likely to initiate use as a result.

Inhalants constitute another class of drug, which has shown a worrisome decline in perceived risk, and it exhibited a mixed pattern of change this year. After 1995, inhalant use had been declining at all three grades. Then in 2003 we reported a significant increase in inhalant use among the 8th graders, and in 2004 all grades showed some increase in annual prevalence, though none was statistically significant. In 2005, there occurred some further increase in grade 12. This pattern of increase may have reflected a cohort effect working its way up the age spectrum, as we have seen for several other drugs. In 2006 and 2007 the pattern of changes has been mixed, with the increase in use continuing at 10th grade, but with some decline occurring at 8th and 12th grades. Of particular concern for the future, however, is the fact that among the 8th and 10th graders, perceived risk had been falling steadily for five years, after peaking in 2001. In 2007, that decline halted in 8th grade but continued at 10th. (Twelfth graders are not asked about the risks of inhalant use.) We believe that this recent trend may reflect generational forgetting (discussed below) of the dangers of this drug, as newer cohorts replace the older ones who had been exposed to the anti-inhalant ads in the middle 1990s, leaving the newer cohorts vulnerable to a resurgence of use.

Over-the-Counter Cough and Cold Medicines

In response to a possible emergent trend, a new question was included in the study for the first time in 2006 about the use of over-the-counter cough and cold medicines for the purpose of "getting high." The drugs in these classes that are abused usually contain dextromethorphan, a cough suppressant that can cause alterations of consciousness and mood when taken in high doses. Street names for these drugs include "DXM," "Dex," and "skittles." The proportions of students reporting having used these drugs during the prior year for the purpose of getting high were 4%, 5%, and 7% in grades 8, 10, and 12, respectively, in 2006. These rates remained the same in 2007, with the exception that use at 12th grade declined by one percentage point; so at this point this problem behavior does not seem to be increasing further. Because these drugs are available over the counter, students may not fully recognize the dangers of using them, even in high doses. Perceived risk is not assessed, but we believe it is possible that the increasing attention to these drugs and their dangers, particularly by the media over the past few years, may have succeeded in stemming the growth in their use.

Implications for Prevention

The wide divergence in historical trajectories of the various drugs over time helps to illustrate the point that, to a considerable degree, the determinants of use are often specific to the drugs. These determinants include both the perceived benefits and the perceived risks that young people come to associate with each drug. Unfortunately, word of the supposed benefits of using a drug usually spreads much faster than information about the adverse consequences. The former—supposed benefits—takes only rumor and a few testimonials, the spread of which has been hastened greatly by the media and the Internet. It usually takes much longer for the evidence of adverse consequences (e.g., death, disease, overdose reactions, addictive potential) to cumulate and then be disseminated. Thus, when a new drug comes onto the scene, it has a considerable "grace period" during which its benefits are alleged and its consequences are not yet known. We believe that ecstasy was the most recent beneficiary of such a grace period, which lasted until 2001, when perceived risk for this drug finally began to rise sharply. To a considerable degree, prevention must occur drug by drug, because people will not necessarily generalize the adverse consequences of one drug to the use of other drugs. Many beliefs and attitudes held by young people are specific to the drug. The figures in this *Overview* on perceived risk and disapproval for the various drugs—attitudes and beliefs that we have shown to be important in explaining many drug trends over the years—amply illustrate this assertion. These attitudes and beliefs are at quite different levels for the various drugs and, more importantly, often trend differently over time.

"Generational Forgetting" Helps Keep the Epidemic Going

Another point worth keeping in mind is that there tends to be a continuous flow of new drugs onto the scene and of older ones being "rediscovered" by young people. Many drugs have made a comeback years after they first fell from popularity, often because young people's knowledge of their adverse consequences faded as generational replacement took place. We call this process "generational forgetting." Examples include LSD and methamphetamine, two drugs used widely in the beginning of the broad epidemic of illicit drug use, which originated in the 1960s. Heroin, cocaine, PCP, and crack are some others that made a comeback in the 1990s after their initial popularity faded. At present we see a danger that LSD and ecstasy may be about to exhibit the effects of generational forgetting of their potential for adverse consequences.

As for newer drugs emerging, examples include the nitrite inhalants and PCP in the 1970s; crack and crystal methamphetamine in the 1980s; and Rohypnol, GHB, and ecstasy in the 1990s. The perpetual introduction of new drugs (or of new forms or new modes of administration of older ones, as illustrated by crack, crystal methamphetamine, and noninjected heroin) helps to keep the country's "drug problem" alive. Because of the lag times described previously, during which evidence of adverse consequences must cumulate and be disseminated before they begin to deter use, the forces of containment are always playing "catch up" with the forces of encouragement and exploitation. Organized efforts to reduce the "grace period" experienced by new drugs would seem among the most promising responses for minimizing the damage they will cause. Such efforts regarding ecstasy by the National Institute on Drug Abuse and others appeared to pay off.

The psychotherapeutic drugs now make up a larger part of the overall drug picture than was true 10 years ago, in part because use has increased for many of them over that period, and in part because use of a number of street drugs has declined substantially since the mid-1990s. It seems likely that young people are less concerned about the dangers of using these drugs outside of medical regimen than they are about the dangers of using the illegal drugs, quite likely because the former are widely used for legitimate medical purposes. Increasingly, prescription psychotherapeutic drugs are being advertised directly to the consumer, which also may imply that they can be used with low risk.

Cigarettes and Alcohol

The statistics for use of the licit drugs—cigarettes and alcohol—are also a basis for considerable concern. Nearly half (46%) of American young people have tried cigarettes by 12th grade, and nearly a quarter (22%) of 12th graders are current smokers. Even as early as 8th grade, nearly a quarter (22%) have tried cigarettes, and 1 in 14 (7.1%) has already become a current smoker. Fortunately, there has been some real improvement in these smoking statistics over the last 10 or 11 years, following a dramatic increase earlier in the 1990s. Much of the recent improvement was simply regaining the ground lost in the early 1990s, but by 2007 that has been more than accomplished.

Thirty-day prevalence of ***cigarette*** use reached its recent peak in 1996 at grades 8 and 10, capping a rapid climb from the 1991 levels (when data were first gathered on these grades). In the decade between 1996 and 2007, current smoking has fallen considerably in these grades (by 66% and 54%, respectively). For 12th graders, peak use occurred a year later, in 1997, and has had a more modest decline so far of 41% by 2007. However, because of the strong cohort effect that we have consistently observed for cigarette smoking, we expect the 12th graders to continue to show declines, as the lighter-using cohorts of 8th and 10th graders become 12th graders. Overall increases in perceived risk and disapproval of smoking appear to have contributed to this downturn. Perceived risk increased substantially and fairly steadily in all grades from 1995 through 2004, after which it leveled in 8th and 10th grades, but continued rising in 12th until 2006, after which it leveled. Disapproval of smoking had been rising steadily in all grades since 1996. After 2004, the rise decelerated in the lower grades through 2006—again, reflecting a cohort effect in this attitude.

It seems likely that some of the attitudinal change that has occurred for cigarettes is attributable to the adverse publicity suffered by the tobacco industry in the 1990s, as well as a reduction in cigarette advertising and an increase in antismoking advertising reaching children. But price is also likely to have been an important factor; cigarette prices rose appreciably in the late 1990s and early 2000s as cigarette companies tried to cover the costs of the tobacco settlement, and as states increased excise taxes on cigarettes.

Unfortunately, the declines in smoking in all grades have decelerated considerably, and current daily use showed no further decline in 2007 in the two upper grades. Very likely a slowdown in price increases, as well as declines in the funding of antismoking campaigns at both the national and state levels, have contributed to these developments. In 2007 use among 8th graders decreased significantly, use among 10th graders dropped very slightly, and use by 12th graders leveled. We believe it likely that the larger proportional declines in the lower grades will make their way into the upper grades as the cohort effect makes its way up the age spectrum.

Smokeless tobacco use had also been in decline in recent years, continuing into the early 2000s, but the decline appears to have ended for the upper grades. The 30-day prevalence rates for smokeless tobacco are now down by about half from their peak levels.

Alcohol use remains extremely widespread among today's teenagers. Nearly three quarters of students (72%) have consumed alcohol (more than just a few sips) by the end of high school; and about two fifths (39%) have done so by 8th grade. In fact, more than half (55%) of the 12th graders and nearly a fifth (18%) of the 8th graders in 2007 report having been drunk at least once in their life.

To a considerable degree, alcohol trends have tended to parallel the trends in illicit drug use. These include a modest increase in binge drinking (defined as having five or more drinks in a row at least once in the past two weeks) in the early and mid-1990s, though it was a proportionally smaller increase than was seen for most of the illicit drugs. Fortunately, binge drinking rates for the nation's teenagers leveled off seven to ten years ago, just about when the illicit drug rates began to turn around, and in 2002 a drop in drinking and drunkenness began to appear in all grades. The decline continued into 2005 for drinking at all grades (as well as for prior month drunkenness among 10th and 12th graders). In 2007, current use of alcohol continued to decline for 12th grade, declined some in 8th grade, and leveled among 10th graders.

The longer-term trend data available for 12th graders show that alcohol usage rates, and binge drinking in particular, are substantially below where they were at the beginning of the 1980s. Most of the improvement occurred during the 1980s, before being partly offset by increases in the first half of the 1990s; fortunately, the recurrence of a downturn in recent years pretty much offset the ground lost in the 1990s.

Where Are We Now?

Clearly, the problem of substance abuse among American young people continues to remain sufficiently widespread to merit concern. Today, nearly half of them (47%) have tried an illicit drug by the time they finish high school. Indeed, if inhalant use is included in the definition of illicit drug use, nearly a third (28%) have done so as early as 8th grade—when most students are only 13 or 14 years old. More than 1 in 4 (26%) have used some illicit drug other than marijuana by the end of 12th grade, and nearly 1 in 5 (19%) of all 12th graders reported doing so during the 12 months prior to the survey.

Of course, if we look at the situation from the perspective of helping to deter future use, we may want to emphasize the considerable proportions of youth who do not use each of these drugs and who disapprove of their use. For example, 74% of seniors today made it through the end of high school without ever using an illicit drug other than marijuana, and more than half (58%) did so without ever trying marijuana. Further, the great majority personally disapprove of using most of the illicit drugs, as has been true for many years.

ANY ILLICIT DRUG

Monitoring the Future routinely reports three different indexes of illicit drug use—an index of "any illicit drug" use, an index of the use of "any illicit drug other than marijuana," and an index of the use of "any illicit drug including inhalants." In this section we discuss only the first two; the statistics for all three may be found in the tables.

In order to make comparisons over time, we have kept the definitions of these indexes constant, even though some new substances appear as time passes. The index levels are little affected by the inclusion of these newer substances, however, primarily because most individuals who use these newer substances are also using the more prevalent drugs included in the indexes. The major exception has been inhalants, the use of which is quite prevalent in the lower grades. Thus, after the lower grades were added to the study in 1991, a special index was added that includes inhalants.

Trends in Use

In the late 20th century, young Americans reached extraordinarily high levels of illicit drug use by U.S. as well as international standards. The trends in lifetime use of any illicit drug are given in the first panel on the facing page. By 1975, when the study began, the majority of young people (55%) had used an illicit drug by the time they left high school. This figure rose to two thirds (66%) by 1981 before a long and gradual decline to 41% by 1992—the low point. After 1992 the proportion rose considerably, reaching a recent high point of 55% in 1999; it stands at 47% in 2007.

Trends for annual, as opposed to lifetime, prevalence appear in the second (upper right) panel. Among 8th graders, a gradual and continuing falloff occurred after 1996. Peak rates since 1991 were reached in 1997 in the two upper grades and declined little for several years. However, since 2001 both upper grades have shown declines, which continued in 2007.

Because marijuana is much more prevalent than any other illicit drug, trends in its use tend to drive the index of any illicit drug use. Thus we have an index that excludes marijuana, and shows the proportions of high school students who use the other, so-called "harder" illicit drugs. The proportions who have used any illicit drug other than marijuana in their lifetime are shown in the third panel (lower left). In 1975, over one third (36%) of 12th graders had tried some illicit drug other than marijuana. This figure rose to 43% by 1981, then declined for a long period to a low of 25% in 1992. Some increase followed in the 1990s as the use of a number of drugs rose steadily, and it reached 30% by 1997. In 2001 it was 31%, but this reflected a slight artifactual upward shift in the estimate due to a change in the question wording for "other hallucinogens" and tranquilizers. Since 1997, the rate has fallen some to 26% in 2007. The fourth panel presents the annual prevalence data for the same index, which shows a pattern of change over the past few years similar to the index of any illicit drug use, but with much less pronounced change since 1991.

Overall, these data reveal that, while use of individual drugs (other than marijuana) may fluctuate widely, the proportion using any of them is much less labile. In other words, the proportion of students prone to using such drugs and willing to cross the normative barriers to such use changes more gradually. The usage rate for each individual drug, on the other hand, reflects many more rapidly changing determinants specific to that drug: how widely its psychoactive potential is recognized, how favorable the reports of its supposed benefits are, how risky the use of it is seen to be, how acceptable it is in the peer group, how accessible it is, and so on.

SUBGROUP DIFFERENCES

Understanding the important subgroup variations in substance use among the nation's youth allows for more informed considerations of substance use etiology and prevention. In this section, we present a brief overview of some of the major demographic subgroup differences.

Space does not permit a full discussion or documentation of the many subgroup differences on the host of drugs covered in this report. However, the much longer Volume I in this series—including the one published in 2007 and the one forthcoming in 2008—contains an extensive appendix with tables giving the subgroup prevalence levels and trends for all of the classes of drugs discussed here. Chapters 4 and 5 in Volume I also present a more in-depth discussion and interpretation of those subgroup differences. Comparisons are made by gender, college plans, region of the country, community size, socioeconomic level (as measured by the educational level of the parents), and race/ethnicity. Monitoring the Future Occasional Paper 67—to be succeeded by Occasional Paper 69 (forthcoming)—is available on the study's Web site (www.monitoringthefuture.org), and provides in graphic form the many subgroup trends for all drugs. The reader may wish to access the graphic version of this material available in this online occasional paper, because it is so much easier to comprehend the findings with a pictorial display of the subgroup trend data over time than with the tabular material provided in Volume I.

Gender

Generally, we have found males to have somewhat higher rates of illicit drug use than females (particularly, higher rates of frequent use), and much higher rates of smokeless tobacco and steroid use. Males generally have had higher rates of heavy drinking; however, in their 30-day prevalence of alcohol use at 8th grade, the girls overtook the boys in 2002 and have had higher rates since. At 10th grade, girls overtook boys in 2005 and have remained equivalent since. The genders have had roughly equivalent rates of cigarette smoking (although among 12th graders the two genders have reversed order twice during the life of the study). In 2007, 30-day smoking fell among 8th- and 10th-grade females, resulting in lower rates than among males. The gender differences, in which males end up with higher rates of use, appear to emerge as students grow older. In 8th grade, females actually have higher rates of use for some drugs. Usage rates for the various substances generally tend to move much in parallel across time for both genders, although the absolute differences tend to be largest in the historical periods in which overall prevalence rates are highest.

College Plans

While in high school, those students who are *not* college-bound (a decreasing proportion of the total youth population) are considerably more likely to be at risk for using illicit drugs, drinking heavily, and particularly smoking cigarettes. Again, these differences are largest in periods of highest prevalence. In the lower grades, the college-bound showed a greater increase in cigarette smoking in the early to mid-1990s than did their non-college-bound peers.

Region of the Country

The differences associated with region of the country are sufficiently varied and complex that we cannot do justice to them here. In the past, though, the Northeast and the West tended to have the highest proportions of students using any illicit drug, and the South the lowest (although these rankings do not apply to many of the specific drugs and do not apply to all grades today). In particular, the cocaine epidemic of the early 1980s was much more pronounced in the West and Northeast than in the other two regions, although the differences decreased as the overall epidemic subsided. While the South and West have generally had lower rates of drinking among students than the Northeast and the North Central (Midwest), those differences have narrowed somewhat in recent years. Cigarette smoking rates have consistently been lowest in the West (except in 2004 among 8th graders, when the Northeast was just as low, and in 2007, when the Northeast was the lowest). The upsurge of ecstasy use in 1999 occurred primarily in the Northeast, but that drug's newfound popularity then spread to the three other regions of the country in 2000.

Population Density

There have not been very large or consistent differences in overall illicit drug use associated with population density over the life of the study, helping to demonstrate just how ubiquitous the illicit drug phenomenon has been in this country. Crack and heroin use generally have not been concentrated in urban areas, as is commonly believed, meaning that no parents should assume that their children are immune to these threats simply because they do not live in a city.

Socioeconomic Level

The average level of education of the student's parents, as reported by the student, is used as a proxy for socioeconomic status of the family. For many drugs the differences in use by socioeconomic class are very small, and the trends have been highly parallel. One very interesting difference occurred for cocaine, the use of which was *positively* associated with socioeconomic level in the early 1980s. That association had nearly disappeared by 1986, however, with the advent of crack, which offered cocaine at a lower price. Cigarette smoking showed a similar narrowing of class differences, but this time it was a large *negative* association with socioeconomic level that diminished considerably between roughly 1985 and 1993. In more recent years, that negative association has reemerged in the lower grades as use declined faster among students from more educated families. Rates of binge drinking are roughly equivalent across the classes in the upper grades (but not in 8th grade), and this rough equivalence has existed for some time among 12th graders.

Race/Ethnicity

Among the most dramatic and interesting subgroup differences are those found among the three largest racial/ethnic groups—Whites, African Americans, and Hispanics. Contrary to popular assumption, at all three grade levels African-American students have substantially lower rates of use of most licit and illicit drugs than do Whites. These include any illicit drug use, most of the specific illicit drugs, alcohol, and cigarettes. In fact, African Americans' use of cigarettes is dramatically lower than Whites' use; and this is a difference that emerged largely during the life of the study (i.e., since 1975). Hispanic students have rates of use that tend to fall between the other two groups in 12th grade—usually closer to the rates for Whites than for African Americans. Hispanics do have the highest reported rates of use for some drugs in 12th grade—crack, heroin with and without a needle, methamphetamine, and crystal methamphetamine. In 8th grade, they tend to come out highest of the three racial/ethnic groups on nearly all classes of drugs (amphetamines being the major exception). One possible explanation for this change in ranking between 8th and 12th grade may lie in the considerably higher school dropout rates of Hispanic youth. Thus, more of the "drugprone" segment of that ethnic group may leave school before 12th grade compared to the other two racial/ethnic groups. Another explanation could be that Hispanics are more precocious in their initiation of these types of behaviors. Again, we refer the reader to Occasional Paper 69 (forthcoming) at www.monitoringthefuture.org for a much more complete picture of these complex subgroup differences and how they have changed over the years.

Application Exercise 5.1

Name of Student:______________

Student ID No.:________________

Course/Section No.:____________

Date:______________________

1. "Monitoring the Future" discussed the design, methods, and field procedures for assessing adolescent substance abuse in the United States. Given the information on sampling that was provided, is an appropriate sample size used? Why or why not?

2. Why is a random sample used in this research?

3. What alternate methods could be used to recruit subjects?

4. Is this the most appropriate way to assess adolescent substance use? Justify your answer.

5. How might you be able to *triangulate* the results from the "Monitoring the Future" study?

Exercise 5.2 Women in Parole:

Respect and Rapport (Convenience Sampling)

Connie Ireland, Ph.D., & Bruce Berg, Ph.D.

ABSTRACT

While the number of females in law enforcement has increased in recent years, research suggests that the uniquely gendered contributions of females are minimized in favor of traditional modes of law enforcement, emphasizing physical presence, authoritative commands, and demonstrative control. This research examines women in parole, using in-depth interviews with a small convenience sample of female parole agents in California. Subjects discuss their experiences as parole agents from the perspective of women in a predominantly male occupation. Overwhelmingly, subjects emphasize traditionally associated female traits of intuition, verbal communication, and relationships, over physical tactics. Subjects emphasize the importance of building respect and rapport with parolees in multiple contexts, including in the parolees' homes, with the families of parolees, and at parolees' places of employment. Subjects suggest that this approach ensures their personal safety and enhances parolee compliance, especially when compared to their subjective account of experiences by male parole agents.

INTRODUCTION

With few exceptions, scholarship on females in law enforcement has singularly focused on women in policing. This literature richly details the entrance of women into law enforcement fields and documents the gender myths, legal battles, and prevalent harassment experienced by female police officers (Berg & Budnick, 1986; Martin, 1979). While little research has directly examined these experiences for women in other law enforcement careers, recent research suggests female parole agents report similar harassment, marginalization and gendered adaptations as their policing counterparts (Ireland & Berg, 2006; Palacios & Ireland, 2005).

During the 1980s, research suggested women's performance of their law enforcement duties emphasized stereotypic feminine traits such as verbal communication and problem solving skills in lieu of more stereotypic masculine traits of strength and physical presence. For example, Homant and Kennedy (1985) found that female police officers were frequently more *sympathetic* to victims of spousal abuse than male officers. Van Wormer (1981) found that female police officers frequently used *communication skills* rather than force and accomplished their duties in ways superior to their male counterparts (see also Berg, 1992; Christie, 1999). The current research examines the extent to which this performance orientation is shared by women working as parole agents.

Data for this article are derived from analysis of twelve semi-structured interviews collected for a larger study examining various broad domains of female parole agents in California (see Ireland & Berg, 2006). The current article focuses on gendered performance of duties as perceived by female parole agents, including their perceptions of guns, fear/safety, and modes for ensuring parolee compliance. These gendered experiences are embodied in the grounded themes of, "respect and rapport."

LITERATURE REVIEW

A thorough search of the literature on parole reveals a void in scholarship on female parole agents. The scant literature on parole in general focuses primarily on changes in prison release mechanisms or supervision of parolees in the field. One journal printed a special edition dedicated to women in corrections, encompassing anecdotal stories and memoirs of early female correctional pioneers but failed to include any mention of female parole agents (Women Working in Corrections, 2005). With rare exception (Ireland & Berg, 2006; Palacios & Ireland, 2005), literature focuses solely on females in policing or corrections/custody positions (see Feinman, 1994; Martin, 1996; Van Wormer & Bartollas, 2000), virtually ignoring females in probation and parole. Many of the issues relevant to females in policing and custody positions—such as hiring/training issues, sexual harassment issues, pay disparity, and socialization challenges—are also relevant to female parole agents. For example, law enforcement research suggests that female police officers perform their duties in a gendered way, yet only one study to date has examined the extent to which this phenomenon is true among female parole agents (Ireland & Berg, 2006). This article seeks to examine the extent to which female parole agents report using traditionally female traits, namely respect and rapport building, in discharging their duties.

As discussed, existing literature does not adequately examine females in parole. As such, the literature available for comparison comes predominantly from the law enforcement literature. The use of this auxiliary literature base provides some context and substance to areas in parole where no literature yet exists. Furthermore, it seems an appropriate staring point for comparison, since parole agents carry peace officer status and, as such, are similar in nature to police officers whose primary function similarly is public safety. However, parole agents are not line staff, in the same manner that patrol officers are. Given the experience required to become a parole agent, and given their degree of authority and autonomy in the field, they are closer in rank to field lieutenants than to street patrol (Breedlove, 2005). Further, parole agents manage specialized caseloads comprised entirely of convicted felons. Put simply, parole agents, technically, are sworn peace officers; as such, it seems reasonable to examine the large literary area of women in law enforcement, in order to assess and compare female parole agents; this is especially true in the general absence of empirical research specifically focusing on parole agents.

Nearly thirty years of research on females in law enforcement documents the well-established belief that policing is man's work. Lonsway (2003) describes this as the "myth of physical prowess," wherein police work regularly requires heated pursuits, wrestling dangerous suspects into submission, physically intervening in private disputes which become public ones, rescuing victims from flaming vehicles, and other such formidable activities. According to this paradigm, policing is best left to males, who are more physically capable of strenuous activity and better able to assert themselves in order to take control over difficult and stressful crime scene situations. In practice, most police policies equate brute strength and physical endurance with competence (Benton, 2005). This deeply ingrained construct fuels hostility toward sworn females in law enforcement, which is consistently reported in the literature (Fletcher, 1995; Pagon & Lobnikar, 1996; Warner, 1989). On the other hand, those in traditionally female positions in law enforcement, such as clerical and dispatch staff, are generally accepted by male officers (Pagon & Lobnikar, 1996; Warner, 1989). So long as females fill traditionally female roles that require "caregiving, emotionality, clerical skills and subservience," they too are accepted by their male colleagues (Berg & Budnick, 1986, p. 315; Sims, Scarborough, & Ahman, 2003).

Despite the enduring belief that policing requires substantial physical prowess, a considerable body of research documents the fact that police work is largely sedentary, with regular demands for keen perception and communication skills, and only rare requirements of physical exertion, let alone brute force or strength. In fact, no research has yet documented physical strength as the primary requirement for effective and safe police work (Bell, 1982; Garcia, 2003). Despite this disjuncture between the myth and reality of physical strength in policing, 88.7% of police agencies require physical agility testing as a primary tool to ensure hiring of capable officers. Lonsway (2003, p. 241) calls this the "most fundamental mistake that police agencies make," primarily because physical agility requirements favor physical strength over other essential assets such as thinking capacity, communication skills, problem solving ability, and observation skills. As Belknap (1996) aptly states, "as a result of policing being viewed as 'men's work,' the positive contributions that policewomen may offer (such as using less force) have often been ignored, while physical strength is emphasized" (p. 215). Ironically, while police academies began shifting emphasis towards decision making and communications and away from physical strength in the 1970s, the reality that women do well in these areas continues to escape police departments, parole agencies, and researchers.

By the 1970s, the need for traditionally female traits such as communication and sensitivity in law enforcement became apparent to some discerning scholars (Darien, 2002). Simultaneously, widespread concerns about racial and gender discrimination in the workplace emerged. Women and people of color earned significant gains with the passage of federal employment legislation in the United States (Greene, 2000) and Canada (Tougas, Rinfret, Beaton, & de la Sablonniere, 2005); these laws provided for protection against racial and gender discrimination in the workplace. In policing, these laws became policy through requirements for hiring females and minorities to fill formal and informal quotas (Fletcher, 1995). Police departments reluctantly hired women, not because they embraced gender integration in policing, but as a result of the combined pressure from women's rights groups and federal courts (Pagon & Lobnikar, 1996). This trend of females entering law enforcement by way of legal mandate was also seen in Canada (Tougas et al., 2005), Europe (Price, 1996), and India (Natarajan, 2001), leading to small but steadily rising rates of women in policing.

Throughout the 1980s and 1990s, the number of women in law enforcement grew, including women serving as parole agents; many of these women also held higher ranking positions in policing than ever before, as a consequence of court mandates requiring agencies to hire women as fully operational, sworn officers in the field (Zhao, Herbest & Lovrich, 2001; National Center for Women in Policing, 1999). The rate of females in sworn positions grew by nearly one half a percent each year between 1973 and 1999 (Lonsway, Carrington, Aguirre, Wood, Moore, Harrington, Smeal & Spillar, 2002).

Compared with policing agencies, little has been written about women in corrections; yet, the proportion of women in corrections is about twice that of women in law enforcement. In full, women represent between 26.3% and 33% of all correctional staff nationwide (Pastore & Maguire, 2003). While women are more prevalent in corrections, in general, these numbers largely represent women in custodial positions that are typically lower paid, and considered of lower status, than most sworn law enforcement positions (Lonsway et al., 2002).

The literature demonstrates that a consistent concern remains among male officers and administrators, namely, can women adequately perform the job? Voluminous research documents that female police officers' competence is commensurate with or exceeds that of their male counterparts in both physical and emotional fitness (Sims et al., 2003; Price, 1996). Perlin, Mather, and Turner (2005, p. 861) bio-medically examine physical competence of women in the military, concluding that "women are equal to men in the physical and cognitive aspects of military readiness, including . . . tolerance of gravity forces, the ability to respond to stress, and the ability to survive in extremes of heat and cold." Friedl (2005, p. 764) examined multiple tests of female readiness for military combat, which demands much greater physical performance than law enforcement duties, and states, "several important assumptions about female physiology and occupational risks were found to be astoundingly wrong." Specifically, in the areas of acute health risks, G-force/flight safety, and personal readiness, the assumed female biomedical inferiority to males in combat was unsupported by extensive laboratory research examining this issue. In other words, women were as physically capable of military combat as were males.

Despite the myth that physical strength, lacking in some women, is required in the profession of law enforcement, a number of studies document that women are as capable of performing the routine duties of police officers as men (Balkin, 1988; Garcia, 2003). As Van Wormer (1981) pointed out over 25 years ago, women are arguably more capable than their male counterparts in areas that require greater concern, patience, understanding, and communication skills; they are also less likely to use excessive force, misconduct, and cynicism than males. Policing styles practiced by females are arguably the "most desirable qualification for a police officer working under a community-policing program" (Garcia, 2003, p. 339). Similarly, female officers can provide insight, perception, and understanding to agencies employing a problem oriented philosophical orientation (problem oriented policing or POP).

Several studies document specific performance differences between genders. The literature suggests that females often employ a style of policing that is generally more effective than that of males—albeit less argumentative and dependent upon physical prowess. Specifically, females rely less upon physical force, are more effective at diffusing volatile situations, are more efficient at de-escalating violent citizens, and are less frequently involved in excessive force incidents than male officers (Bureau of Justice Assistance [BJA], 2001). Furthermore, females possess better communication skills and foster community cooperation and trust more readily than male officers (BJA, 2001). Female officers are less likely to be named in a citizen complaint, allegation, or civil lawsuit than male officers, and they respond more effectively to domestic violence incidents than their male counterparts (Lonsway et al., 2002). Female police officers tend to be less aggressive than male officers, manage violent confrontations better, are more pleasant and respectful to community members, and have better communication skills overall than men (Brown, 1996).

Females are also less likely to be involved in *any* force during the course of their sworn duties. Garner, Buchanan, Schade, and Hepburn (1996) found arrests involving male officers and male suspects had the highest rate of force used, while arrests involving female police officers and female suspects had the lowest. Hoffman and Hickey (2005) found that female officers had a lower rate of weapon use and a lower rate of suspect injury than male officers.

In sum, previous research suggests females perform law enforcement duties in a gendered way, but that this gendered way benefits the occupation of policing. Female officers employ greater communication skills and less force than male officers, creating what seems to be a more successful approach, than traditionally male, aggressive, physically dominated policing styles. Female police officers gain greater suspect compliance, with fewer injuries, and fewer community complaints than male police officers.

In a manner similar to that used to examine gendered performance among female police officers, the current research is an initial examination of gendered styles of performance from the perspective of female parole agents. Toward this end, the current research examines the extent to which female parole agents employ similar strategies in the performance of their field duties as described in the law enforcement literature. The current research explores what female parole agents say about their reliance upon communication skills, problem solving, empathy, and respect, in terms of the performance of their daily activities and duties.

This research addresses the following research questions. First, what performance style(s) do female parole agents subjectively perceive as beneficial in carrying out their duties with parolees in the field? Second, do female parole agents see their occupational approach as gendered, and if so, in what way(s)? Third, to what extent do female parole agents describe their reliance upon various gendered or stereotypically associated tools (such as weapons) and interpersonal skills (such as communication) to ensure personal safety, community safety, and parolee compliance? Fourth, what are the subjective experiences of female parole agents regarding the importance of weapons, communication skills, and relationships with parolees?

METHODOLOGY

The current study is based on data from a convenience sample of twelve female parole agents in California. The United States Correctional Museum (a pseudonym) provided an initial list of seventeen potential subjects to the principal investigator for an upcoming museum exhibit honoring noteworthy female contributions in law enforcement. A parole agent working for the correctional museum generated a list of women in parole known to that agent and whom he thought might be willing to participate. The list initially included women he believed to be correctional pioneers in California, including the first four women hired in corrections occupations within the state. Researchers contacted all seventeen women by telephone. Of these, thirteen women consented to participate in the study; two women were unavailable, and two women declined to participate. Of these thirteen initial subjects, three women were excluded from analysis because two were former parolees and one was the wife of a deceased parole agent. Two replacement subjects were contacted by the principal investigator of this study; both consented to participate. The replacement subjects were known to the principal investigator through unrelated parole research and also had longstanding careers in corrections.

Data Collection

Each subject was interviewed by a team of two research assistants who used a semi-structured questionnaire to explore specific aspects of the subject's life and career. During each interview, one research assistant conducted the interview and the other operated audio/visual recording equipment. Each research assistant prepared detailed written notes immediately upon conclusion of each interview.

The length of interviews ranged from 30 minutes to 4 hours. A portion of each interview was both audio and video recorded. The video tapes averaged 30 minutes in length; the audio tapes averaged two hours in length. The recordings were transcribed verbatim prior to analysis.

Analysis Plan

Both audio and video tapes were transcribed subsequent to the interviews. These were combined with the detailed notes prepared by each research assistant. Upon review of all notes and transcriptions, a biography for each subject was prepared, which included personal background information, employment history, and particularly poignant comments/quotations. Thematic content analysis was used to analyze the comments made by subjects during their interviews (Berg, 2007). This involved creating a coding frame of potential themes about gender issues in the performance of parole duties, and then slotting subject comments into their appropriate thematic categories. Examples of the various themes discussed in this research were lifted at random from the thematic categories in which they were placed in to avoid *case making* in our analysis (Berg, 2007). Among other findings discussed below, the data described female parole agents' overwhelming practice of gendered supervision styles characterized by intuition, verbal skills, and relationship building as a basis of supervising parolees.

FINDINGS AND ANALYSIS

As is common in qualitative research, discussion of specific research findings are [is] interwoven with the analysis of those findings. Thus, this section includes both discussion of identified themes and the meaning of those trends in a broader context. Overall, the findings are similar to those suggested by law enforcement literature, namely that females bring arguably unique (and at minimum stereotypically associated), gendered skills to their parole positions. Subjects in this study describe intentional efforts to ensure their personal safety and to successfully manage difficult parolees in the community by relying upon traditionally female associated traits including intuition, verbal communication, and the ability to both develop and effectively use respect and rapport with their parolees.

Respect and Rapport

Subjects' management of parolees in the community was shaped by gendered supervision styles. The theme that emerged throughout the data is a predominant reliance on cultivating respect and rapport to ensure long term safety and elicit parolee compliance. Subjects explained that they believed that this pattern of respect and rapport built a broad safety net around them during their parole agent activities. Further, the use of respect and rapport fostered an astonishing degree of parolee compliance.

Although most subjects specifically referred to the importance of respect and rapport in terms of the benefits of these attributes for creating safe and effective work environments, the true significance of this approach in dealing with parolees is apparent when considering the descriptive accounts shared by the subjects, with regard to how they defined these terms.

RESPECT. Subjects overwhelmingly described the belief that respecting a parolee (through words and actions) resulted in more cooperative parolees. Conversely, disrespecting parolees (e.g., using degrading terms, embarrassing them in front of their families, etc.) resulted in uncooperative and even combative parolees. Subjects emphasized that they intentionally used fairness, dignity, consistency, and professionalism in all of their dealings with their parolees. Subjects articulated the importance of respecting parolees in the parolee's home, their places of employment, and when with their families.

Interestingly, the female agents in this study reported cooperative arrests throughout the course of their careers. Although there were rare exceptions, subjects reported that nearly all of the arrests they personally made involved a minimum of conflict. Subjects also reported that only under rare circumstances did they require the assistance of other (male) parole agents or police officers when effecting a field arrest. Eight of the twelve subjects reported their belief that male parole agents used force in arrests to a far greater extent than they and their female associates did when undertaking field activities—including arrests.

In practice, respect was often displayed with a kind of pseudo-social worker attitude. Donita, for example, a Parole Agent I with 2 years' experience, reported: "I believe parolees are human beings that took a wrong road and need assistance."

Charity's ten year correctional career included time supervising juveniles and parolees. She echos Donita's social-rehabilitative view of parole: "I never really had what I considered an evil person on parole. Never. Well, I finally figured out if I could enhance their lives somewhat, they no longer got in trouble."

Jane has a 42 year correctional history including supervising youths in juvenile hall, serving as a parole agent, and as a parole unit supervisor. She was recently appointed to a state level parole board position. She states the following of her approach with parolees:

> *If you treat them with dignity and respect, then you'll get that in return for the most part. You really need to treat people with respect, give them some dignity. Parolees, if you treat them well and you do your job, even when you have to lock them up, they will respect you and understand that you are just doing your job. If you treat them like a piece of crap, that's what you're going to get back.*

Rita, a 25 year parole veteran with the sex offender caseload, states it this way: "I respect their homes; it was rare that I would take police officers to the home to arrest a parolee. I only did that when a parolee was a real danger and other options [pause] were not successful. I did everything I could to avoid a situation becoming dangerous."

RAPPORT. Subjects also described a process by which repeated interactions characterized by respect in the field leads to rapport with parolees. In other words, rapport is the fruit of longstanding respect. The harmonious working relationship that characterizes rapport yields parolee compliance, agent safety, and trust/information from parolees' family and the community.

RAPPORT AND PAROLEE COMPLIANCE. Lourdes, a parole supervisor and firearms instructor supervising sex offenders in Los Angeles, recounts the following story. She attempts to illustrate the benefits of establishing respect and maintaining rapport in achieving parole agent safety and parolee compliance. She states,

> *I remember they [the police] were trying to arrest one of my guys. The guy was a dangerous little character. Some guy didn't want to drink with him so he got a little upset and shot him between the eyes and killed him, and he had [the police] just running all over the place trying to figure out where he was. The police department called me and said my guy was a suspect, I said 'he's at work.' So I drove to his work with them, told them to wait outside. They said, 'wait outside? You're going in there by yourself?' I went inside and told him, 'you need to come outside.' He said, 'you found out, huh?' I said, 'uh-huh.' I said, 'I'm not going to embarrass you in here so you walk out and it will be okay.' So, I get him to the car and brought him to the homicide detectives and said, 'here's your guy.' But that's because you need to establish rapport with them.*

Donita employs the same respect and rapport to achieve parole agent safety and parolee compliance. Knowing that technical violations generally result in temporary removal and prompt return to the community, Donita has a long range view of parole supervision. She relates an incident in which she planned to arrest a parolee on an alcohol violation: "He wanted to stay out for Halloween weekend [with his kids]. Instead of taking him in, I told him to report back on Monday at a specific time. He showed up."

RAPPORT AND PAROLE AGENT SAFETY. In addition to fostering compliance, eight subjects emphasized respect and rapport in ensuring long term personal safety. Claudia, the gubernatorial appointee, states, "I have encountered situations where a parolee has actually been protective of me, either against people in the neighborhood or other individuals in the home. I think it all boils down to the respect you have garnered as a result of the relationship you develop with this individual."

Lourdes is one of three agents who describes specific incidents in which her parolees "watch her back" in the community. She states:

> *when there is a [good] relationship there, a lot of times when the agent is not paying attention, the parolee is paying attention, and the parolee will have the agent's back. If you treat your parolees firm, fair and consistent, your parolee will watch out for you. A lot of times my parolees would tell me when I go to the projects to see them,"you're not supposed to come at this time; 7 o'clock at night is too late for you to be in the projects."*

The safety gained through good rapport also extended to the parole agents' property. Lourdes relates:

> *I had a car that broke down in the projects, and I told one of my high control parolees, "watch that car—don't let them jack the car." A week later I saw the state car still there. The tow truck driver was too scared to go into the projects and pull the car out. The only thing I lost was the hubcaps. I asked my parolee, "you didn't watch my hubcaps?" He said, "you don't know how*

> *hard it was to make sure they didn't take that car." We've had other incidents when agents lost backpacks out of their car, had slashed tires, because they [the community] don't want law enforcement there. But if you treat your parolees right, they know you're not playing games with them; they'll do what they need to do.*

RAPPORT, FAMILIES, AND COMMUNITIES. Seven subjects emphasized the importance of knowing the parolees' families in order to obtain useful information and also to secure protection while out in the community.

Rita, who has served as a police reservist, a parole agent, and supervisor, supervised a high risk sex offender caseload. She states it is "important to really know the parolees; knowing their families is critical. When you are doing home visits, the first person opening the door was usually the parolee's mother, father, or grandmother. [I] depend on family for safety."

Letty has a 30 year correctional career as a prison guard, a parole agent, supervisor, administrator, and warden. She states:

> *One of the things I found when in the field, was that the families always protected me. If I went into an area, they'd make sure I went away from their house all in one piece. It was very protective, there was a [pause] respect or a feeling that they had about the parole agent, but I never felt intimidated by the community.*

Jane, who is completing her 42 year parole history with a term on a state parole board, reiterates this point. She states, "if you get a real good rapport with a family, they become your eyes and ears. So when you're not there, they'll call you, 'Oh, Ms. Garcia [pseudonym]! It's time for you to take him to jail! He's doing this, this, this and that!'"

CONCLUSIONS AND IMPLICATIONS

This research lends support to the notion of a gendered performance of duties by female parole agents, quite similar to that described in the literature regarding female police officers. Female parole agents in this study described a variety of ways in which they used stereotypically associated female attributes such as intuition, communication skills, respect, and rapport to effect parole compliance, arrest dangerous felons, garner community support, and ensure their personal safety in the field. Subjects emphasized using their communication skills over their weapons and described believing that they achieved greater compliance than their male counterparts. Subjects in this study underscored the essential importance of relationship building, established by practicing techniques intentionally intended to foster respect and gain rapport. Jane, who has served 42 years in correctional employment, best crystallizes the theme:

> *Our whole thing was rapport. Rapport with the parolee, rapport with his or her family and good working relationship with the police so if we have a really nasty arrest, the guy was a potentially violent person, you have the backup to deal with it. You know the parolee, you know the family, know all the community resources.*

The style of gendered parole supervision demonstrated in accounts offered by the subjects in this study emphasized relationships building, over a more demanding, authoritarian style, in order to achieve personal safety in the field and parolee compliance to laws and parole conditions. The subjects practiced respect, characterized by courtesy and empathy, in their interactions with parolees and parolees' families, homes, and places of employment. In turn, subjects describe their perception of this respect evolving into rapport, whereby parole agent, parolee, and the community were engaged in a dynamic mutual relationship which respondents describe as beneficial to all concerned. Parole agents describe having gained increased compliance and personal safety through rapport; while parolees are described as having gained respect, dignity, understanding, and consideration for reasonable exceptions. The community, according to the subjects, achieved enhanced safety derived from these non-violent parolee-community interactions.

Despite obvious cautions, findings in the current research suggest several important policy implications. First, these findings should encourage policies that support enhanced relational approaches for those under community correctional supervision. Practices such as motivational interviewing, which trains supervision staff in positive behavioral reinforcement of those supervised, may well be a viable solution to the revolving door of criminal justice. Second, these findings suggest that such changes as reducing caseload size, thereby allowing parole agents more time and more frequent opportunities for positive interaction with their charges, may actually increase officer safety, improve parolee compliance, and foster successful reintegration of offenders back into the community. Third, other innovative approaches that emphasize respect and rapport building should also be explored. While some critics may view these recommendations as unreasonably "soft" goals when dealing with serious and violent felons in the community, it must be emphasized that these findings suggest an attitude of respect and rapport—not a position of weakness, laissez-faire supervision or an unwillingness to introduce physical strength—promotes the positive outcomes described herein. While legislating attitude may be difficult, it may be an essential element to bring effective community corrections to the 21st century.

References

Balkin, J. (1988). Why policemen don't like policewomen. *Journal of Police Science & Administration, 16*, 29–38.

Belknap, J. (1996). Policewomen, policemen, or both? Recruitment & training implications for responses to woman battering. *Journal of Contemporary Criminal Justice, 12*(3), 215–234.

Bell., D. J. (1982) Policewomen: Myths & realities. *Journal of Police Science & Administration, 10*, 112–120.

Benton, S. (2005). New female sheriff laying down the law. *American City & County, 120*(1), 24–24.

Berg, B. L. (1992). *Law enforcement: An introduction to police in society.* Boston: Allyn & Bacon.

Berg, B. L. (2007). *Qualitative research methods for the social science.* Boston: Allyn & Bacon.

Berg, B. L., & Budnick, K. J. (1986). Defeminization of women in law enforcement: A new twist in the traditional police personality. *Journal of Police Science & Administration, 14*, 314–319.

Breedlove, J. (2005). Personal interview.

Brown, J. (1996). Integrating women into policing: A comparative European perspective. *Policing in Central & Eastern Europe: Comparing Firsthand Knowledge with Experience from the West.* College of Police & Security Studies: Slovenia.

Bureau of Justice Assistance. (2001). *Recruiting & retaining women.* Washington, D.C.: Author.

Bureau of Justice Statistics. (2006). *Sourcebook of Criminal Justice Statistics.* Retrieved May 15, 2008, from http://www.albany.edu/sourcebook/

California Department of Corrections and Rehabilitation. (2007). *Division of adult parole operations.* Department of Human Resources.

Christie, G. (1999). Gender issues in police communications: Emotional decoding & job factors—police and nurses compared. Paper presented at the 2nd Australasian Women & Policing Conference, University of Queensland (July).

Crank, J. P. (2003). *Understanding police culture* (2nd ed.). Cincinnati, OH: Anderson Publishing Company.

Darien, A. (2002). The alter ego of the patrolman? Policewomen & the discourse of difference in the NYPD. *Women's Studies, 31*(5), 561–609.

Feinman, C. (1994). *Women in the criminal justice system* (3rd ed.). Westport, CT: Praeger Publishing Division.

Fletcher, C. (1995). *Breaking & entering.* New York: Simon & Schuster, Inc.

Friedl, K. E. (2005). Biomedical research on health & performance of military women: Accomplishments of the defense women's health research program (DWHRP). *Journal of Women's Health, 14*(9).

Garcia, V. (2003). Difference in the police department. *Journal of Contemporary Criminal Justice, 19*(3), 330–344.

Garner, J. H., Buchanan, J., Schade, J., & Hepburn, J. (2006). *Understanding use of force by & against the police: Research in brief.* National Institute of Justice, Washington D.C.

Greene, H. T. (2000). Black females in law enforcement. *Journal of Contemporary Criminal Justice, 16*(2), 230–239.

Hoffman, P., & Hickey, E. (2005). Use of force by female police officers. *Journal of Criminal Justice, 33*(2), 145–151.

Homant, R. J., & Kennedy, D. B. (1985). Police perceptions of spouse abuse: A comparison of male & female officers. *Journal of Criminal Justice, 13*, 29–47.

Ireland, C., & Berg, B. (2006). Women in parole: Gendered adaptations of female parole agents in California. Unpublished manuscript.

Lonsway, K. (2003). Tearing down the wall: Problems with consistency, validity, & adverse impact of physical agility testing in police selection. *Police Quarterly, 6*(3), 237–277.

Lonsway, K., Carrington, S., Aguirre, P., Wood, M., Moore, M., Harrington, P., et al. (2002). *Equality denied: The status of women in policing: 2001.* Beverly Hills, CA: National Center for Women & Policing.

Lyman, M. D. (2004). *The police: An introduction* (3rd ed.). Upper Saddle River, NJ: Prentice Hall.

Martin, S. E. (1979). Policewomen & policewomen: Occupational role, dilemmas & choices of female officers. *Journal of Police Science & Administration, 7*, 314–323.

Martin, S. E. (1996). *Doing justice, doing gender: Women in law enforcement and criminal justice occupations.* Thousand Oaks, CA: Sage Publishing.

Natarajan, M. (2001). Women police in a traditional society: Test of a western model of integration. *International Journal of Comparative Sociology, 42*(1), 211–233.

National Center for Women & Policing (1999). *Equality denied: The status of women in policing: 1998.* Los Angeles: National Center for Women & Policing, Feminist Majority Foundation.

Pagon, M., & Lobnikar, B. (1996). Reasons for joining & beliefs about policing among Slovenian female police rookies. *Policing in Central & Eastern Europe: comparing firsthand knowledge with experience from the West.* College of Police & Security Studies: Slovenia.

Palacios, N., & Ireland, C. (2005). Women in parole: Respect & rapport. Presented at the annual conference of the Academy of Criminal Justice Research in Long Beach, California.

Pastore, A. L., & MaGuire, K. (2003). *Sourcebook of criminal justice statistics.* Washington, D.C.: U.S. Department of Justice, Bureau of Justice Statistics

Perlin, J., Mather, S., & Turner, C. (2005). Women in the military: New perspectives, new science. *Journal of Women's Health, 14*(9), 861–862.

Price, B. (1996). Female police officers in the United States. *Policing in Central & Eastern Europe: Comparing firsthand knowledge with experience from the West.* College of Police & Security Studies: Slovenia.

Sims, B., Scarborough, K., & Ahman, J. (2003). The relationships between police officers' attitudes toward women & perceptions of police models. *Police Quarterly, 6*(3), 278–297.

Tougas, F., Rinfret, N., Beaton, A., & de la Sablonniere, R. (2005). Policewomen acting in self-defense: Can psychological disengagement protect self-esteem from the negative outcomes of relative deprivation? *Journal of Personality & Social Psychology, 88*(5), 790–800.

Van Wormer, K. (1981). Are males suited to police patrol work? *Police Studies, 31*, 41–44.

Van Wormer, K., & Bartollas, C. (2000). *Women & the criminal justice system.* Boston: Allyn and Bacon, Inc.

Warner, R. (1989). Affirmative action in times of fiscal stress & changing value priorities: The case of women in policing. *International Personnel Management Association, 18*(3), 291–310.

Morton, J. B. (2005). ACA and women working in corrections. *Corrections Today, 67*(6), 86–111.

Zhao, J., Herbest, L., & Lovrich, N. (2001). Race, ethnicity & the female cop: Differential patterns of representation. *Journal of Urban Affairs, 23*(3), 243–257.

Application Exercise 5.2

Name of Student:______________

Student ID No.:________________

Course/Section No.:_____________

Date:____________________

1. "Women and Parole" details the design, methods, procedures, and results of a study of female parole agents in California. Given the information on sampling provided, is an appropriate sample size used? Why or why not?

2. Why is a convenience sample used in this research?

3. What alternate methods could be used to recruit subjects?

4. Is this the most appropriate way to access female parole agents? Justify your answer.

5. How might you be able to *triangulate* the results from the "Women in Parole" study?

CHAPTER 6

Technologies of Observation

Have you ever been stopped while walking through a mall and asked a series of questions about some deodorant, breakfast food, or product packaging? Or have you ever been asked at the conclusion of a semester to evaluate the performance of one of your teachers? If you have, then you have participated in a *survey.*

Simply put, a survey is a means of collecting a great deal of aggregate data in a very brief period of time. The term *survey* also may be used to refer to information obtained in more qualitative interview strategies. To differentiate between formal, structured, questionnaire-type surveys and more nominal-level interviews, we will refer to the former as *questionnaire-based surveys* and the latter as *interviews.*

QUESTIONNAIRE-BASED SURVEYS

Questionnaire-based surveys are especially useful when working with representative samples (see Chapter 5). One of the major strengths in this type of survey is that it allows the researcher to examine a large sample of subjects, and when the sample is representative of some group, the research findings can be generalized to large populations.

A questionnaire should be developed to fulfill a specific research need or to address a particular research question. Many naive researchers construct questionnaires that have not been adequately conceptualized and operationalized. Such haphazard attempts—no matter how well intentioned—are seldom very useful in terms of generating meaningful findings and conclusions. The most common error inexperienced researchers make is not asking the right questions or asking the right questions so imprecisely that they become fatuous. These sorts of flaws in research can be avoided during the design stage if the investigator is thoughtful and careful. We will discuss this in greater detail later in this chapter when talking about survey construction.

In some questionnaire-based surveys, respondents may answer written questions that they *self-administer* after reading all included instructions. In other questionnaire-based surveys, respondents answer questions asked by a researcher who administers the survey, explains the instructions, and is present in the event that the subject has questions of his or her own. Surveys can also be administered by telephone, with researchers either calling subjects or staffing phone lines to which subjects can call. Questionnaires may be distributed in a variety of ways: hand delivered, mailed, picked up at some organizational meeting, and so on. A *cover letter*, describing the research and inviting the subject to participate, typically accompanies a questionnaire.

Cover Letters

Cover letters usually are written on official university or organization letterhead to ensure the potential subject of true institutional affiliation. The purpose of the cover letter is to introduce the subject to the researcher and the research project and to legitimate both. The letter should be sufficiently enticing to persuade the respondent to complete the survey. Cover letters typically strive to explain the importance of each subject's opinion and the research value of having his or her completed survey. Cover letters also usually state that there are no right or wrong answers to any questions and that all answers will remain anonymous and confidential. Cover letters also provide information about possible risks and benefits (such as incentives) to the subject, which often forms the basis of *informed consent* documents.

Self-Administered Questionnaires

Self-administered questionnaires are given to respondents with the expectation that each person will be able to read and understand the questions, possesses the knowledge and willingness to answer them, and will take the time to do so. Self-administered questionnaires may be completed by individuals who are alone or in groups.

Mailed Questionnaires

A mailed questionnaire provides the researcher with a means of contacting a large number of respondents over an extensive geographic area in a fairly expedient and inexpensive manner. With this type of questionnaire, each respondent answers the questions and returns the survey only if he or she has been convinced of its importance and is sufficiently motivated to do so. In order to motivate respondents in mailed surveys, researchers must write interesting and convincing cover letters.

One of the most difficult aspects of a mailed questionnaire is obtaining a large enough return rate to make the study meaningful. Response rates from an initial mailing may be well below 50%. However, this rate can and must be improved with follow-up mailings; some researchers use as many as three follow-up mailings (Cook, Heath, & Thompson, 2000).

In order to avoid unnecessary mailing costs and duplication of completed surveys, the researcher must develop some means of checking who has and has not returned a survey. Some researchers place an inconspicuous code number on the return envelope near the zip code. By checking envelopes containing returned surveys against a master mailing list, the researcher can avoid sending follow-up surveys to these people. Since the code number is on the outside of the envelope, the survey itself can be removed before the envelope is checked against the list, thus maintaining subject anonymity.

Advantages to Questionnaires

Collecting data through a questionnaire strategy has a number of significant advantages. First, the questionnaire-based survey is economical. It yields a great deal of information, or bits of data, in a short period of time, and because it is mailed to subjects, it can cover a broad geographic area. Second, given the anonymity it provides, some people are likely to be more truthful answering a self-administered questionnaire than they would be while responding to other types of surveys (Carini, Hayek, Kuh, Kennedy, & Ouimet, 2003; Harrison, Haaga, & Richards, 1993; Sudman & Bradburn, 1981). A third advantage to the questionnaire is that it can be completed at whatever pace the subject chooses. In other words, if the phone rings or any other distraction or interruption occurs, the questionnaire may be put aside until time allows for its completion. This is not possible with some other data-gathering strategies, such as a researcher-administered questionnaire or an interview in which the investigator remains until the questionnaire or interview has been completed.

Disadvantages to Questionnaires

Of course, questionnaire-based surveys have several disadvantages as well. Among the most serious is the potential limitation on data because of the restrictions such surveys place on the depth of questioning. Because the questions are formally structured and written on the page, no deviation or follow-up questioning is possible (besides the questions that were considered at the time the questionnaire was originally developed). Another disadvantage to the questionnaire is that it must be relatively short in order to ensure that most subjects will complete the entire survey. As a result, questionnaires lack the depth of coverage possible with other means of data gathering, such as face-to-face interviews, which often exceed an hour to complete and may last up to 6–8 hours. Although some questionnaires are quite lengthy, usually they are kept relatively brief.

INTERVIEWS

Interviews frequently are conceived as *conversations with a purpose* (Berg, 2007): to gather information, or, as with questionnaires, bits of data. The research interview is a much underestimated device for gathering data. Most students inaccurately believe that because they have been asking and answering questions all their lives, conducting an interview should be a simple task. In truth, the interviewer cannot simply ask questions in the same manner one would in a normal conversation.

One important reason for this distinction is founded on Erving Goffman's (1967) terms *evasion tactics* and *deference ceremonies*, or avoidance rituals. In normal conversation, you might utter some word, phrase, or statement that invokes the other party's need to avoid this area. Usually, the other party will offer some audible or visual cue that he or she does not want to discuss this area. In exchange, you will *defer* and demonstrate an intrinsic respect for the other party by moving the conversation away from the sensitive area. Berg (2007) argues that in these deference ceremonies, there is an unspoken understanding that this deference will be reciprocated in future communication.

Such a deference exchange in a research interview is untenable. Frequently, the very information that the respondent is attempting to avoid is the information sought in the research. The key factoring an interview is *control.* The conversation must at all times be under the control of the interviewer. This is not to suggest that the interviewer should be callous and unfeeling. Rather, the interviewer must develop strategies to maintain control and facilitate the smooth transition from one question to the next. To do so involves learning ways of temporarily deferring but later returning to sensitive areas (see Berg, 2007).

Types of Interviews

The inexperienced researcher may assume that every interview is the same, which is quite inaccurate. Some sources classify interviews as those that are *directive* and those that are *nondirective* (Abrahamson, 1983). Other sources use terms such as *formal* and *informal* (Fitzgerald & Cox, 1987). Babbie (2007) and Berg (2007) provide three major categories of interviews: *standardized* (formal or directed), *unstandardized* (informal or nondirective), and *semistandardized* (guided semistructured).

STANDARDIZED INTERVIEWS A standardized interview uses a formal, structured interview schedule in which questions are asked the same way with each subject: precisely as worded in the schedule, in exactly the order in which the questions appear. The objective is to standardize the stimulus so that responses will be comparable (Babbie, 2007; Berg, 2007). In addition to a standardized schedule of interview questions, a formal interview is usually prearranged so that both the interviewer and subject are aware that an interview is to occur.

While standardized interviews offer the advantage of asking questions that are readily comparable among subjects during analysis, interviews have several disadvantages. First, the requirement to adhere rigidly to the order and phrasing of questions in the interview schedule can potentially damage the interviewer's rapport with the subject. For example, neither the interviewer nor the subject can digress from the question series as ordered in the interview schedule. This restriction will inhibit the subject from freely discussing information (albeit relevant to the study question) that does not immediately relate to the question being asked. Further, the subject will be prevented from digressing to topics he or she might find personally gratifying to discuss but that are not relevant to the study.

Second, because the questions are developed entirely outside the interview process, they can seem artificial. If the subject senses this, it may affect how he or she sees the interviewer and the articulated purpose for the interview. If the situation becomes too artificial, the subject may be inclined to avoid speaking truthfully or completely about important areas for the research.

In brief, the potential disadvantage of the structured interview is the potential loss of information. Nuances of conversation that might have proven important, that have yielded otherwise unanticipated areas of investigation, or that might have been simply serendipitous discoveries, will have been lost. The principal advantage of the structured interview, like the questionnaire-based survey, is standardization of stimuli and, consequently, responses.

UNSTANDARDIZED INTERVIEWS In contrast to the strict rigidity of the standardized interview, the unstandardized interview does not use a formal schedule of questions. The unstandardized interview usually begins with a question that is intended to orient the respondent to the general area of research interest. Beyond that orienting question, which is usually conceived of in advance, the interviewer must adapt, develop, and generate questions and probes appropriate to the given interview situation.

Unstandardized interviews are extremely useful during the course of *field research* and are frequently used to augment researchers' observational notes. The use of unstandardized interviews in fieldwork allows researchers to better understand the situations, people, and events that they observe and to access valuable information that might otherwise be missed.

The principal disadvantage of unstandardized interviews is their inability to offer comparability between subjects. In other words, because the same set of stimuli has not systematically been provided to every subject, their responses are not necessarily analytically comparable.

SEMISTANDARDIZED INTERVIEWS Midway between the extremes of the standardized and the unstandardized interview is the semistandardized interview. This style of interviewing uses a series of predetermined questions that are systematically asked of each respondent exactly as written on an interview schedule. However, in a semistandardized interview, the researcher may periodically deviate from the order of questioning and may even digress from the scheduled questions entirely. This digression allows the interviewer to pursue information far beyond what is provided by the answers to prepared standardized questions. Digression also allows the interviewer to create a more fluid informational exchange during the interview, thereby increasing rapport and the quality of responses.

The chief advantage of the semistandardized interview is its flexibility. The interviewer has more freedom to elicit greater knowledge and information from the respondent than is provided by the rigid, standardized interview structure. Nonetheless, the researcher is still able to analyze the responses to the scheduled questions, which are systematically comparable.

CONSTRUCTING QUESTIONNAIRES AND INTERVIEW SCHEDULES

The development of questionnaires and interviews begins in a similar manner. First, the researcher must decide on the nature of his or her research and whether it will be better served by a questionnaire or an interview. Second, the researcher must create a list of all the broad categories of interest to the study. For example, assume that the researcher is interested in studying spouse abuse and, in particular, abused women. The broad research categories for such a survey might include the following:

1. Demographics
2. Basic family background information
3. History of victimization (outside the family)
4. History of victimization (inside the family)
5. Friendship and social patterns
6. Knowledge about spouse abuse
7. Perceptions of self-esteem and efficacy
8. Resources

Next, the researcher must develop questions that are relevant to each category and that have been operationalized to represent and measure concepts appropriate for the research. The purpose of these questions will be to elicit information corresponding to the subjects' views and attitudes.

In effect, as the researcher creates questions to measure concepts related to each broad category, he or she is developing a draft of the instrument. The basic structure of each question will be determined on the basis of decisions made by the researcher. Clearly, the decision to develop a questionnaire, rather than an interview schedule (or vice versa), makes an initial determination about the structure of the questions. Surveys are usually characterized by the use of *closed-ended* or *forced-response* questions, whereas interviews typically use *open-ended* questions.

Closed-Ended or Forced-Response Questions

A closed-ended question offers several choices of answers to the respondent. These answers are those that the researcher believes are the likely choices, but the option "other" is often included to provide for alternatives. The question and corresponding answers must all be carefully and clearly worded to assume that the subject understands them and can identify a response from those provided. Closed-ended questions are used regularly in questionnaire-based surveys and sometimes in interviews as well.

The obvious advantage to closed-ended questions is the ease with which they can be coded. They can be computerized effortlessly, without the time-consuming creation of logs of corresponding numbers and categories. The corresponding disadvantage, however, is that the subject must fit his or her response into one of the options provided. Thus, the researcher forces the subject (sometimes imprecisely) to identify an answer from among the alternatives predetermined by the researcher, not the subject. Hence, the label *forced response* is sometimes applied to closed-ended questions.

Open-Ended Questions

Open-ended questions are designed to provide subjects with the latitude of responding with the greatest amount of fluidity and personal discretion. For example, if a researcher were to ask a sample of college students what constitutes "date rape," they might respond with a variety of characteristics, such as forced sexual contact, forced vaginal penetration, unwanted genital touching, taking sexual advantage of an intoxicated partner, sexual contact preceded by violence, and so on. In other words, the researcher can expect a lexicon of responses, reflecting various nuances of how college students see and understand date rape. Later, after receiving the subjects' answers, the researcher can categorize and subsequently analyze these various responses.

Open-ended questions are most useful when investigators are interested in learning how certain groups of people think about given issues. Interviews are largely composed of open-ended questions, although several closed-ended questions may also be included. When open-ended questions are used in questionnaires, the usual intent is to elicit brief statements and not lengthy, complete explanations about certain events. Conversely, in interview schedules, open-ended questions are the norm and may be followed by a number of probes that will draw out full descriptions of certain events or issues.

Coding open-ended questions used in questionnaires is somewhat more difficult than coding closed-ended responses. Since questionnaire responses are usually brief, they are likely to be categorized and the categories numerically coded in a process sometimes referred to as *data reduction*. In this process, nominal data are transformed into numerical codes, making them more comparable with the data obtained from closed-ended responses.

When used in interviews, open-ended questions are coded using some variation on thematic content analysis (Berg, 2007). When using content-analytic strategies, the nominal and textual character of the data may be preserved and displayed.

ETHNOGRAPHY

So far, this chapter has described several similarities between two major techniques of data collection: questionnaire-based surveys and interviews. As we move on to discuss *ethnography*, we will see a number of vivid contrasts. Surveys and interviews can be conducted virtually anywhere, administered by the respondent or the researcher, and completed at virtually any hour of the day. But ethnographic research, by definition, can only be conducted when and where the phenomenon under consideration naturally occurs.

Ethnographic research is sometimes referred to as *natural scientific research* (Denzin & Lincoln, 2008) or simply *field research* (Berg, 2007; Guy, Edgley, Arafat, & Allen, 1987). Even though definitions of ethnographic research vary somewhat, one element common to all is that ethnography "places the researchers in the midst of whatever it is they study" (Berg, 2007, p. 172). Some textbooks label as "ethnographic" any research that takes the investigator into the field or natural setting. This type of research can be contrasted with that in which an investigator identifies a sample of subjects and artificially brings them into his or her study through the use of questionnaires or interviews. Ethnographic research moves the investigator into the natural setting that his or her potential subjects inhabit. The subjects then come to the researcher, who works in their setting in a fluid and reflexive manner.

The Ethnographic Record

Spradley (1979) suggests that a wide variety of items can be used effectively when conducting ethnographic research: photographs, recordings (audio and video), relevant newspaper and magazine articles, interviews, surveys, and, of course, direct observations. In effect, any documentation of the phenomenon under investigation should go into the ethnographic record.

Note that many textbooks limit their discussions to *field research* and *observations in field research.* There is nothing intrinsically wrong with this; surely, many of the data collected in field studies or ethnographies are observational. Yet the types of data included in field studies should not be restricted. A wide variety of material may be useful and relevant to the study of certain phenomena. Nonetheless, one major means of gathering data in the field is observation.

Observations in Field Settings

Observation is usually a central means of collecting data in ethnographic studies. Observations may vary in their degree of structure and reflect the kinds of settings or types of events, people, and behaviors under investigation. One researcher may enter the field with a very clear focus and goals for his or her research, whereas another may enter the field with virtually no aim other than to discover how inhabitants of the setting live, work, and play together. Researchers may also immerse themselves by participating in the ongoing situations they are investigating; or they can *dance* with data in an effort to experience it (Janesick, 2003).

A classic example of an ethnographic study that uses observation as a major data-gathering technique is Laud Humphreys's (1970, 1975) analysis of homosexual encounters in a public bathroom. Humphreys used a bathroom in a California public park as his research setting. Serving as a lookout and voyeur, or "watch queen," Humphreys observed various sexual interactions between men in the bathroom. Humphreys's research led to the social scientific acceptance of homosexual activities as a lifestyle and behavioral choice, rather than as a biological dysfunction.

Many textbooks credit the *Chicago School* (the sociology department at the University of Chicago during the 1920s through early 1940s) with spawning observational research strategies. The nature of observational research is to place oneself in a setting in a manner that will (1) allow the researcher to visually observe as much interaction between parties as possible or (2) provide the researcher access to participate in interactions among parties without seriously disrupting the process.

In the first case, the researcher's role is called the *nonparticipant observer*, and in the second case, the *participant observer.* Each of these perspectives or researcher roles offers a slightly different view of the setting. The nonparticipant observer is free to devote all his or her attention to observing the interactions, events, and processes under investigation. The participant observer must split his or her time between strictly observing and actually participating. The advantage of being a nonparticipant observer is obtaining a potentially more comprehensive description of observable details. The advantage in being a participant observer is that not only does the researcher observe and record the event, but he or she also experiences the emotions and interests of the people under study.

UNOBTRUSIVE RESEARCH

Much of the research conducted by social scientists relies on direct contact with subjects, whether observing them in their natural setting, interviewing them in a convenient location, or having them complete some sort of questionnaire. This type of contact with subjects is described by many research textbooks as being intrusive in subjects' lives. Given the questioning that usually occurs in research about the validity of results and reliability of data, we might ask whether intrusion in some manner taints or biases the eventual analytic results.

An alternative to this intrusive approach to collecting data is *unobtrusive*, or *nonreactive*, data collection. To a large extent, all unobtrusive strategies use a variation of observation. In this case, however, the researcher observes various traces of human activity and behavior (Berg, 2007; Shaughnessy & Zechmeister, 1990). *Traces* refer both to the accumulation of various byproducts left by people, whether intentionally or inadvertently, and to the erosion caused by people or natural phenomena (i.e., weathering). For instance, graffiti left on urban city walls may represent simple names or *tags* or it may represent symbolic communications including threats of death to specific people (Kephart & Berg, 2002). Through traces, researchers can observe what factors motivate people to behave in certain ways, how people structure their daily lives, how different cultural or political ideologies affect people's behavior, and so forth.

Textbook descriptions of unobtrusive measures sometimes conjure in the minds of readers the images of detectives using clues and bits of physical evidence to solve complicated crimes.

In fact, this is not unlike the use of unobtrusive measures in research. However, you don't need to be Sherlock Holmes to conduct unobtrusive social scientific research. A number of strategies can be used to conduct unobtrusive research. Webb et al. (1966, 1981), Berg (2007), and to a large measure, Shaughnessy and Zechmeister (1990) establish three major categories: archival strategies, accretion measures, and erosion measures.

Archival Strategies

Archives can be defined as any "running record" (Webb, Campbell, Schwarz, & Sechrest, 2000), regardless of the location or means of housing the record. Archives include birth and death certificates kept in a local courthouse; books and documents shelved in a library; videotapes displayed in a video-rental store; admission, disposition, and discharge records stored in a hospital computer; and even rows of tombstones in a graveyard. Records may be maintained by individuals, public institutions, private corporations, governments, and even social organizations. Hence, archives may be public or private, easy or difficult to access.

For example, incident reports and initial complaint reports are usually held in municipal police departments and can be accessed easily. Reports of sexual assaults and crimes involving juveniles are usually held in these same police departments, but access may be restricted or denied to researchers. Nonetheless, all these files represent a kind of public archive.

Private archives may be represented by personal libraries or private collections of documents held by various institutions, including libraries. Private archives may also include diaries and autobiographies, letters, home movies/videos, and various artistic endeavors (e.g., drawings, sketches, doodles). When these various documents occur naturally, without being prompted by an investigator, they are called *unsolicited documents*. In other situations, documents may be the products of requests or solicitations by investigators, in which case they are called *solicited documents.*

An example of an unsolicited private document might be the daily journal or diary of a serial killer on death row. Information such as this might be very useful to an investigator interested in understanding what serial killers think about or perhaps what motivates them. An example of a solicited document might also be a diary written by a serial killer but one that an investigator requested the inmate to create. The specific difference between an unsolicited and solicited document, therefore, is whether it was self-initiated or created at the behest of a researcher.

Using archival records has a number of advantages. First, archival records can usually be accessed with relatively little expense and difficulty. They are a source of data that is immediately available to the investigator, one that doesn't require survey construction, pilot tests, or similar concerns. Second, archival documents are nonintrusive, which means that there is no chance of research reactivity or potential biasing effects when conducting archival research. Third, the use of archival data along with data collected by other techniques (e.g., surveys, observations, interviews) can augment and validate analyses and findings.

Researchers must, of course, be mindful of several disadvantages when working with archival data, the most serious of which is the possibility of omissions or misleading inclusions. Webb et al. (2000) refer to problems regarding selective deposits and selective survival. *Selective deposits* refer to documents that have possibly been edited or altered in some manner. *Selective survival* describes documents in which portions are missing, rendering the documents incomplete. Regardless of whether these alterations to archival documents have occurred intentionally or inadvertently, researchers must carefully consider the biases and potential informational gaps that might result.

Accretion and Erosion Strategies

When researchers examine the physical artifacts and traces of human activity in a field setting, these items provide measures of accretion or erosion. *Accretion* is the building up or accumulation of materials and products, and *erosion* is the wearing away or deterioration of materials.

ACCRETION MEASURES Ecological concerns have increased rapidly in recent years. Because of these concerns, the examination of certain types of human traces may be advantageous and also provide clues to contemporary social culture. In this case, *traces* refer to items that people have disposed of—garbage. There is, in fact, a national movement in the United States to recycle various items such as glass, paper, cardboard, plastic, and metals, which requires separating them into designated containers. The materials collected through recycling provide a wealth of potential unobtrusive data.

Nearly 40 years ago, Sawyer (1961) employed a similar version of "garbageology" to examine rates of liquor sales in Wellesley, Massachusetts, a so-called dry town (i.e., no liquor stores were permitted). Sawyer obtained estimates of liquor sales by sifting through the garbage at the town dump and counting the number of discarded liquor bottles.

It would be interesting (and somewhat cleaner) to replicate such a study today by examining the contents of recycling containers. We could investigate which neighborhoods or communities consume what proportion of beer, wine, and hard liquor. We might even be able to identify certain ethnic or religious clusters of people through their alcohol consumption. For example, in communities in which disproportionate amounts of kosher wines have been identified, we might have uncovered a cluster of Jewish families. In short, the examination of alcohol bottles disposed of in recycling containers could yield a number of interesting findings.

EROSION MEASURES Erosion measures include evidence that indicates selective wear or use on some object or material. In most research, erosion measures, like accretion measures, are used along with other techniques for corroboration.

Erosion measures provide interesting documentation occurrences in natural settings. In one well-quoted study, Edward Shils examined erosion at the Chicago Museum of Science and Industry (Berg, 2007; Webb et al., 1981). In his study, Shils learned that the vinyl tiles around an exhibit of live, hatching chicks had to be replaced approximately every six weeks, whereas the tiles around other exhibits went unchanged for years. A comparative examination of the rates of tile replacement throughout the museum produced rough estimates of how attractive the visiting public found certain exhibits.

The actual difference between accretion and erosion measures is not always clear-cut. In some cases, what one researcher might identify as an *accretion* measure might be called an *erosion* measure by another researcher. For example, in the previous discussion of the naturally occurring accretion of disposed alcohol containers, we could argue that since the containers were originally filled with alcoholic beverages and are now empty, they are an erosion measure. To some extent, then, this designation is a matter of perspective, and whether the measure is called an accretion or erosion measure amounts to unnecessary terminological hairsplitting.

Another interesting perspective involves use of both naturally occurring and more controlled measures of accretion or erosion by some researchers. In this type of case, the investigator arranges a situation in which some accretion or erosion measure that he or she has created can be measured along with any naturally occurring measures. For example, Friedman and Wilson (1975) placed dots of glue between adjacent pages at different intervals throughout textbooks before students purchased them for a given course. At the conclusion of the semester, the researchers collected the books and examined them.

First, they examined each glued pair of pages in each textbook and recorded how many there were and which had been separated. Next, the researchers noted the frequencies and locations of passages that students had underlined. These underlined segments provided the researchers with a natural accretion measure, which could be compared along with the controlled erosion measure; the glued pages. What the researchers found was quite surprising: Analysis of both the naturally occurring and controlled measures suggested that students more often read the first several chapters than the remaining chapters of their textbooks.

The use of various unobtrusive measures provides a rich and interesting source of data. The kinds of unobtrusive measures available to researchers are limited only by their imagination. As a stand-alone data set, a single unobtrusive measure may be questionable in some cases, but when used with other data-collection strategies, each technique tends to strengthen the other. This procedure is referred to as data *triangulation.*

TRIANGULATION

The term *triangulation* was originally used in geographic-surveying activities, map making, navigation, and military applications. In these fields, triangulation involves using three known points or objects to draw sighting lines toward an unknown point or object. Usually, the three sighting lines intersect, forming a small triangle called the *triangle of error*. The best estimate of the true location of the new point or object is the center of the triangle, assuming that the three lines are about equal in error. Although sightings can be done with two lines intersecting at one point, a third line permits a more accurate estimate of the location of the unknown point or object.

Triangulation was first used in the social sciences as a metaphor describing a form of *multiple operationalism* or *convergent validation* (Berg, 2007; Campbell, 1956; Campbell & Fisk, 1959). In this context, triangulation largely was used to describe multiple data-collection technologies designed to measure single concepts or constructs (data triangulation).

If your instructor asked all the students in your class to look out of the window and describe what they saw, the results might be quite diverse. For instance, one person might see a "large" tree; another, a "tall, oaklike" tree; a third, a "spreading, green, shady" tree; and a fourth, a "pin-oak" tree. In short, each person might see a slightly different facet of the same tree, yet their descriptions would all share some basic essence: a tree. If we took these observations together, we would be better able to visualize what the students saw: in this case, a tall, green, spreading, pin-oak tree.

So it is with triangulation. When researchers use multiple lines of action, they are able to improve the final results. Doing so increases the validity of a research project by demonstrating that similar conclusions have been obtained when using diverse lines of action. Findings that are largely bound to a single method may be difficult to accept and not taken very seriously. Method-bound results may be artifacts of a given technique and not true findings. While it is unlikely that multiple lines of action will result in identical findings, multiple lines of action should offer sufficient overlap and similarity to make the findings quite convincing, as demonstrated by the example of the pin-oak tree.

References

Abrahamson, M. (1983). *Social research methods.* Englewood Cliffs, NJ: Prentice Hall.

Babbie, E. (2007). *The practice of social research.* (11th ed.). Belmont, CA: Wadsworth.

Berg, B. L. (1995). *Qualitative research methods for the social sciences* (2nd ed.). Boston: Allyn & Bacon.

Berg, B. L. (2007). *Qualitative research methods for the social sciences* (6th ed.). Boston: Allyn & Bacon.

Campbell, D. T. (1956). *Leadership and its effects upon the group.* Columbus, OH: Ohio State University Press.

Campbell, D. T., & Fisk, D. W. (1959, March). Convergent and discriminant validation by the multivariate-multi-method matrix. *Psychological Bulletin, 56,* 81–105.

Carini, R. M., Hayek, J. C., Kuh, G. D., Kennedy, J. M., & Judith, A. O. (2003). College student response to Web and paper survey: Does mode matter? *Research in Higher Education, 44*(1), 1–19.

Cook, C., Heath, F., & Thompson, R. L. (2000). A meta-analysis of response rates in Web or Internet-based surveys. *Educational and Psychological Measurement, 60,* 821–826.

Denzin, N., & Lincoln, Y. S. (2008). *The landscape of qualitative research* (3rd ed.). Thousand Oaks, CA: Sage.

Fitzgerald, J. D., & Cox, S. M. (1987). *Research methods in criminal justice.* Chicago: Nelson-Hall.

Friedman, M. P., & Wilson, R. W., (1975). Application of unobtrusive measures in a study of textbook usage by college students. *Journal of Applied Psychology, 60,* 659–662.

Goffman, E. (1967). *Interaction rituals.* New York: Anchor Books.

Guy, R. F., Edgley, C. E., Arafat, I., & Allen, D. E. (1987). *Social research methods.* Boston: Allyn & Bacon.

Harrison, E. R., Haaga, J., & Richards, T. (1993). Self-reported drug use data: What do they reveal? *The American Journal of Drug and Alcohol Abuse, 19*(4), 423–441. Retrieved October 20, 2008, from http://www.informaworld.com/10.3109/00952999309001632

Humphreys, L. (1970). *Tearoom trade.* Chicago: Aldine.

Humphreys, L. (1975). *Tearoom trade: Impersonal sex in places* (enlarged ed.). Chicago: Aldine.

Janesick, V. J. (2003). The choreography of qualitative research design. In N. K. Denzin & Y. S. Lincoln (Eds.), *Strategies of Qualitative Inquiry* (2nd ed., pp. 46–79). Thousand Oaks, CA: Sage.

Kephart, T., & Berg, B. L. (2002, February). Gang graffiti analysis: A methodological model for data collection. Presented at the Annual Meeting of the Western Criminal Justice Society, San Diego, CA.

Sawyer, H. G. (1961). *The meaning of numbers.* Paper presented at the Association of Advertising Agencies.

Shaughnessy, J. J., & Zechmeister, E. B. (1990). *Research methods in psychology.* New York: McGraw-Hill.

Spradley, J. P. (1979). *The ethnographic interview.* New York: Holt, Rinehart & Winston.

Sudman, S., & Bradburn, N. M. (1981). *Asking questions: A practical guide to questionnaire design.* San Francisco: Jossey-Bass.

Webb, E. J., Campbell, D. T., Schwartz, R. D., & Sechrest, L. (1966). *Unobtrusive measures: Nonreactive research in the social sciences.* Chicago: Rand McNally.

Webb, E. J., Campbell, D. T., Schwartz, R. D., Sechrest, L., & Grove, J. B. (1981). *Nonreactive measures in the social sciences.* Boston: Houghton Mifflin.

Webb, E. J., Campbell, D. T., Schwarz, R. D., & Sechrest, L. (2000). *Unobtrusive Measures* (Revised Edition). Thousand Oaks, CA: Sage.

Exercise 6.1 Cybercrime in the United States

67 Percent of Responding Businesses Detected Cybercrime in 2005

Department of Justice
Office of Justice Programs
Bureau of Justice Statistics
September 17, 2008
www.ojp.usdoj.gov/bjs

WASHINGTON—Among 7,818 businesses responding to the National Computer Security Survey (NCSS), 67 percent detected at least one cybercrime in 2005, the Justice Department's Bureau of Justice Statistics (BJS) announced today. Nearly 60 percent of businesses detected one or more cyber attacks, 11 percent detected cyber thefts and 24 percent detected other computer security incidents. Computer viruses were the most common type of cyber attack, detected by 52 percent of reporting businesses.

The NCSS documents the nature, prevalence and impact of cybercrimes against businesses in the United States. Survey respondents represented 7,818 businesses out of the 7.3 million businesses identified nationwide in 2005. Of businesses reporting the number of incidents, 43 percent detected 10 or more cyber attacks, theft or other security incidents during the year. Computer viruses were about 7 percent of the incidents and cyber thefts were less than 1 percent. Other computer security incidents (92 percent)—primarily spyware, adware, phishing, and spoofing—were the most common.

The effects of these crimes were measured in terms of monetary loss and system downtime. Ninety percent of the businesses providing information sustained monetary loss. Cyber thefts accounted for more than half of the loss and cyber attacks for about a third. Approximately 68 percent of victims of cyber theft sustained monetary loss of $10,000 or more. By comparison, 34 percent of victims of cyber attacks lost $10,000 or more.

System downtime affected 89 percent of businesses that provided downtime information. Sixty percent of system downtime was caused by computer viruses, 8 percent by denial of service, vandalism or sabotage, and 32 percent by other computer security incidents. System downtime lasted longer than 24 hours for about a third of victimized businesses.

Among survey respondents, businesses with the highest prevalence of cybercrime in 2005 included telecommunication businesses (82 percent of such businesses), computer system design businesses (79 percent) and manufacturers of durable goods (75 percent).

Nearly 75 percent of businesses victimized by cyber theft said that insiders—such as employees, contractors or vendors working for the business—were responsible for the crime. More than 70 percent of businesses victimized by cyber attacks or other computer security incidents said the suspected offenders were outsiders (hackers, competitors and other non-employees).

Overall, 15 percent of victimized businesses said they reported cybercrimes to law enforcement authorities. Six percent of businesses detecting cyber attacks reported the incidents to authorities, compared to more than 50 percent of businesses detecting cyber thefts.

The President's National Strategy to Secure Cyberspace directs the Department of Justice to develop better data on the nature and prevalence of cybercrime and electronic intrusions. The NCSS was developed by the Bureau of Justice Statistics in partnership with the Department of Homeland Security. The Justice Department's Computer Crime and Intellectual Property Section and the Computer Intrusion Section of the Federal Bureau of Investigation Cyber Division also collaborated on the project.

The NCSS data collection was conducted over a seven-month period in 2006. A nationally representative sample of 35,600 businesses representing 36 economic sectors received the survey. Twenty-three percent of the selected businesses responded. Though the responses are not nationally representative, the NCSS is the largest survey conducted to date. Detailed findings for each of the 36 sectors are provided in this report.

The report, *Cybercrime against Businesses, 2005* (NCJ 221943), was written by BJS statistician Ramona R. Rantala. Following publication, the report can be found at http://www.ojp.usdoj.gov/bjs/abstract/cb05.htm.

For additional information about the Bureau of Justice Statistics' statistical reports and programs, please visit the BJS Web site at http://www.ojp.usdoj.gov/bjs.

The Office of Justice Programs, headed by Acting Assistant Attorney General Jeffrey L. Sedgwick, provides federal leadership in developing the nation's capacity to prevent and control crime, administer justice, and assist victims. OJP has five component bureaus: the Bureau of Justice Assistance; the Bureau of Justice Statistics; the National Institute of Justice; the Office of Juvenile Justice and Delinquency Prevention; and the Office for Victims of Crime. In addition, OJP has two program offices: the Community Capacity Development Office, which incorporates the Weed and Seed strategy, and the Office of Sex Offender Sentencing, Monitoring, Apprehending, Registering, and Tracking (SMART). More information can be found at http://www.ojp.gov.

[This document can be accessed at http://www.ojp.usdoj.gov/bjs/pub/press/cb05pr.pdf]

Application Exercise 6.1

Name of Student:________________

Student ID No.:________________

Course/Section No.:________________

Date:________________

1. The "Cybercrime" press release distributed by the Bureau of Justice Statistics (Exercise 6.1) discusses the prevalence and impact of cybercrime in the United States. According to the article, two-thirds (67%) of all businesses detected at least one cybercrime in 2005, most notably *cyber theft, computer viruses, spyware, adware, phishing,* and *spoofing*. How would **you** define the following terms?
   cyber theft: ________________
   computer virus: ________________
   spyware: ________________
   adware: ________________
   phishing: ________________
   spoofing: ________________
2. Now, ask another person (a classmate, colleague, friend, or family member) how they would define the following terms:
   cyber theft: ________________
   computer virus: ________________
   spyware: ________________
   adware: ________________
   phishing: ________________
   spoofing: ________________
3. Suppose you were a researcher and wanted to study cybercrime in the United States. What process would you use to operationalize these terms? Discuss what resources you would use in doing this.
   ____
4. Next, please carry out the process you have identified in question 3 to operationalize the cybercrime terms. When you have completed this process, write the operational definitions of terms below.
   cyber theft: ________________
   computer virus: ________________
   spyware: ________________
   adware: ________________
   phishing: ________________
   spoofing: ________________
5. Compare the terms as you've operationalized them with those of a classmate. What differences do you see between the two lists? Are there any instances in which something would be considered a cybercrime under one set of definitions, but not under another? Please explain.
   ____

Exercise 6.2 Correctional Populations in the United States, 1997

U.S. Department of Justice
Office of Justice Programs

Janet Reno, ATTORNEY GENERAL

Daniel Marcus, ACTING ASSOCIATE ATTORNEY GENERAL

Mary Lou Leary, ACTING ASSISTANT ATTORNEY GENERAL

Jan M. Chaiken, Ph.D., DIRECTOR, BUREAU OF JUSTICE STATISTICS

NOVEMBER 2000, NCJ 177613

METHODOLOGY

The U.S. Census Bureau conducted the 1997 Survey of Inmates in State Correctional Facilities (SISCF) for the Bureau of Justice Statistics (BJS) and the 1997 Survey of Inmates in Federal Correctional Facilities (SIFCF) for BJS and the Bureau of Prisons. From June through October, 1997, inmates were interviewed about their current offense and sentences, criminal histories, family and personal backgrounds, gun possession and use, prior drug and alcohol use and treatment, educational programs, and other services provided while in prison. Similar surveys of State prison inmates were conducted in 1974, 1979, 1986, and 1991. Federal inmates were surveyed for the first time in 1991.

Sample Design

The samples for the SISCF and SIFCF were taken from a universe of 1,409 State prisons and 127 Federal prisons enumerated in the 1995 Census of State and Federal Adult Correctional Facilities or opened between completion of the census and June 30, 1996. The sample design for both surveys was a stratified two-stage selection; first, selecting prisons, and second, selecting inmates in those prisons.

In the first stage, correctional facilities were separated into two sampling frames: one for prisons with male inmates and one for prisons with female inmates. Prisons holding both genders were included on both lists.

In the sampling of State facilities, the 13 largest male prisons and 17 largest female prisons were selected with certainty. The remaining 1,265 male facilities and 261 female facilities were stratified into 14 strata defined by census region (Northeast except New York, New York, Midwest, South except Texas, Texas, West except California, and California). Within each stratum facilities were ordered by facility type (confinement and community-based), security level (maximum, medium, minimum, and none), and size of population. A systematic sample of prisons was then selected within strata with probabilities proportionate to the size of each prison.

For the sample of Federal prisons, one male prison and two female prisons were selected with certainty. The remaining 112 male facilities were classified into 5 strata defined by security level (high, medium, low, minimum, and administrative). The 20 remaining female facilities were stratified into 2 strata by security level (minimum and not minimum). Within security level, facilities were ordered by size of population and then selected with probability proportionate to size.

For the State survey 280 prisons were selected, 220 male facilities and 60 female facilities. Of the 280 facilities 3 refused to allow interviewing and 2 closed before the survey could be conducted. Overall, 32 male facilities and 8 female facilities were selected for the Federal survey, and all participated.

In the second stage, inmates were selected for interviewing. For State facilities interviewers selected the sample systematically using a random start and a total number of interviews based on the gender of the inmates and the size of the facility. For Federal facilities, a sample of inmates was selected for each facility from the Bureau of Prisons central list, using a random start and predetermined sampling interval. All selected drug offenders were then subsampled so that only a third were eligible for interview. As a result, approximately 1 in every 75 men and 1 in 17 women were selected for the State survey, and 1 in every 13 men and 1 in every 3 women were selected for the Federal survey. A total of 14,285 interviews were completed for the State survey and 4,041 for the Federal survey, for overall response rates of 92.5% in the State survey and 90.2% in the Federal survey.

The interviews, about an hour in length, used computer-assisted personal interviewing (CAPI). With CAPI, computers provide questions for the interviewer, including follow-up questions tailored to preceding answers. Before the interview, inmates were told verbally and in writing that participation was voluntary and that all information provided would be held in confidence. Participants were assured that the survey was solely for statistical purposes and that no individual who participated could be identified through use of survey results.

Estimates of Prisoner Counts

Based on the completed interviews, estimates for the entire population were developed using weighting factors derived from the original probability of selection in the sample. These factors were adjusted for variable rates of nonresponse across strata and inmates' characteristics and offenses. The sample for the State survey was adjusted to midyear custody counts for June 30, 1997, from data obtained in the National Prisoner Statistics series (NPS-1A). The sample from the Federal facilities was weighted to the total known sentenced custody population at midyear 1997.

Excluded from the estimate of Federal inmates were unsentenced inmates and those prisoners under Federal jurisdiction but housed in State and private contract facilities. Those prisoners who were under State jurisdiction, yet held in local jails or private facilities, were excluded from the estimated number of State prisoners. As a result, the estimated prisoner counts do not match those in other BJS data series.

The estimated prisoner counts vary according to the particular data items analyzed. Estimates are based on the number of prisoners who provided information on selected items.

Accuracy of the Estimates

The accuracy of the estimates presented in this report depends on two types of error: sampling and nonsampling. Sampling error is the variation that may occur by chance because a sample rather than a complete enumeration of the population was conducted. Nonsampling error can be attributed to many sources, such as nonresponses, differences in the interpretation of questions among inmates, recall difficulties, and processing errors. In any survey the full extent of the nonsampling error is never known. The sampling error, as measured by an estimated standard error, varies by the size of the estimate and the size of the base population.

Estimates of the standard errors have been calculated for the 1997 surveys. (See appendix Tables 2 and 3 [see original report for tables].) For example, the 95-percent confidence interval around the percentage of State inmates who ever used drugs is approximately 83.0% plus or minus 1.96 times 0.4% (or 82.2% to 83.8%).

These standard errors may also be used to test the significance of the difference between two sample statistics by pooling the standard errors of the two sample estimates. For example, the standard error of the difference between black and white State prison inmates for the percent reporting a binge drinking experience would be 1.2% (or the square root of the sum of the squared standard errors for each group). The 95-percent confidence interval around the difference would be 1.96 times 1.2% (or 2.4%). Since the difference of 21.6% (53.5% minus 31.9%) is greater than 2.4%, the difference would be considered statistically significant.

The same procedure can be used to test the significance of the difference between estimates from the two surveys. For example, the standard error of the difference between Federal and State prison inmates for the percent reporting prior drug use would be 1.1%. The 95-percent confidence interval around the difference would be 1.96 times 1.1% (or 2.1%). Since the difference of 10.1% (83.0% minus 72.9%) is greater than 2.1%, the difference would be considered statistically significant.

All comparisons discussed in this report were statistically significant at the 95-percent confidence level. To test the significance of comparisons not mentioned in this report, use percentages in text or tables and numbers of inmates. These standard errors should be used only for tests on all inmates. Comparisons of male and female inmates require different standard errors.

[This document can be accessed at http://www.ojp.usdoj.gov/bjs/pub/pdf/cpus9704.pdf]

Application Exercise 6.2

Name of Student:_______________

Student ID No.:_______________

Course/Section No.:_______________

Date:_______________

1. The BJS report presented in Exercise 6.2 is based on the 1997 *Survey of State Inmates in State Correctional Facilities (SISCF)*. This report details the sampling procedure used to interview inmates for the survey. Based on the survey methods discussed, do you believe that the results are generalizable to the inmate population nationwide? Why or why not?

2. The inmate survey is based on face-to-face interviews. How might face-to-face interviews impact the inmate responses?

3. Suppose you were a researcher and wanted to follow up on this study. In addition to the face-to-face interviews conducted in the SISCF, what other methods would you employ to find out about inmate histories, families, substance use, firearms, educational programs, and services received while in custody?

4. Why might the use of an alternate method, called *triangulation*, be useful in examining issues for prison inmates?

CHAPTER 7

Data Organization and Analysis

The subject of data organization and analysis can be examined from two broad perspectives: quantitative and qualitative. In order to answer a research question, the researcher should consider which methodological technique of data collection, organization, and analysis—quantitative or qualitative—would best serve this purpose? The nature of the research question itself should suggest which strategy is most suitable.

By design, *quantitative* strategies employ an analysis that is numerical in nature. Typically, when quantitative data-analysis strategies are used, the data are ordinal-, interval-, and possibly ratio-level variables. Statistical tests are used to measure relationships and determine their significance. When using quantitative strategies, researchers often collect data from large numbers of individuals. In quantitative strategies, surveys with closed-ended questions are typically given to a large number of individuals.

In addition to the standard data-collection techniques of surveys and interviews, numerous creative techniques have been employed in doing qualitative research. In the classic work *Unobtrusive Measures: Nonreactive Research in the Social Sciences*, Webb and colleagues (1966, 2000) describe a number of innovative techniques that can be used to collect data, including examples of studies that use assessments of erosion and accretion measures. The use of erosion measures is illustrated by a study comparing the rates of wear of floor tiles in front of different exhibits at the Chicago Museum of Science and Industry; the purpose of the study was to determine the popularity of various exhibits (Webb et al., 1966, pp. 36–37). The use of accretion measures in quantitative analysis is illustrated by a study of the settings of radio dials in cars; the settings of cars brought into repair shops were recorded to determine the popularity of individual radio stations (p. 39). These are just two examples of the innovative data-collection techniques that can be employed in quantitative data collection.

Qualitative data-collection, organization, and analysis strategies are typically nonnumeric in nature. Data that are analyzed using qualitative strategies are typically nominal-level variables (the lowest level of variables; Bailey, 1982). Qualitative strategies often produce data that are of considerable depth but (because of the depth) include far fewer individuals than are typically included in quantitative strategies. In qualitative studies, structured interviews are used as well as techniques that incorporate nonobtrusive means of observation and data collection, such as field notes, artifacts, newspaper articles, and participant observation.

While there are a number of similarities between quantitative and qualitative strategies, there are also enough significant differences to warrant separate discussions of the two.

QUANTITATIVE DATA

Types/Sources

In quantitative research, there are two general types of data: primary data and secondary data. Each type can be described according to its source.

Primary data are original data, collected specifically to answer a research question or questions. They are often referred to as "raw data," because they have not previously been collected, analyzed, or interpreted.

In some instances, depending on the type of research question being asked, collecting primary data may be the only way to answer the question. For instance, *biometric security measures* are a relatively new correctional component. Examples of biometric security measures include retina and fingerprint scans used to identify inmates and staff in correctional institutions (Jain, Hong, & Pankanti, 2000) and the use of Body Orifice Security Scanners (BOSS) to detect contraband hidden in oral, vaginal, or anal cavities (TheSourceNY, 2008). If a researcher was interested in examining the impact of biometrics on institutional security, the researcher would have to collect primary data, since it is unlikely that any existing database would provide the needed information. Likewise, a researcher attempting to replicate a certain study would need to collect primary data and compare them to those in the original study.

Secondary data were originally collected for another purpose but are also suitable for answering a current research question or questions. The researcher must determine whether existing data contain the information necessary to answer his or her new question. Because these data have already been collected, organized, analyzed, and interpreted, the use of secondary data can save a research staff countless hours of work as well as precious dollars.

A number of state and federal agencies regularly collect the data they need to compile statistics and produce reports. In addition to being used in-house, these data sets are often made available to outside researchers who wish to analyze them for other purposes. For example, the U.S. Bureau of the Census collects a tremendous amount of information when it surveys the national population every 10 years. The data are made available to the public for use in a variety of research conducted outside the census bureau. The Bureau of Justice Statistics likewise makes available the data it collects on crime.

In some cases, a question can be answered using either primary or secondary sources. For example, *electronic monitoring* has been actively employed in various probation/parole jurisdictions for more than a decade. This technique uses an electronic bracelet on an offender's wrist or ankle to help monitor the whereabouts of an individual who is on probation or parole. If a researcher was interested in examining the impact of electronic monitoring on the life of the parolee or probationer, the researcher could collect primary data or perform secondary analysis of existing data.

Getting Started

Most scholars agree that data analysis should be planned at the beginning of a project rather than at the end (Berg, 2006; Hagan, 2006; Maxfield & Babbie, 2005). This is a sound advice for all researchers, regardless of how much experience they may have. Knowing the type of data analysis that will be undertaken once the data have been collected will help direct the researcher in selecting what type of data are needed and in what form they should be collected.

When possible, an early step in data collection should be the precoding of responses to facilitate data entry and verification later. Precoding takes place after the questions have been developed. The precoding of questionnaires is directly related to the types of questions the researcher plans to ask. Closed-ended questions lend themselves to precoding. In fact, the codes can be listed right on the questionnaire so that when the data are being entered into a file, the data-entry person needs only to follow the codes. When coding takes place after the questionnaire has been completed, a column on the right-hand side is left blank for this purpose.

Coding actually consists of assigning a numerical value to a particular answer to a question. For example, suppose that a question asked an individual's gender. If the individual responded "female," that answer could be coded "0," and if the individual responded "male," that answer could be coded "1." If the question asked the respondent's years in college, the coding could be as follows:

Freshman = 1

Sophomore = 2

Junior = 3

Senior = 4

Graduate student = 5

For most closed-ended questions, this type of coding scheme is relatively easy to initiate.

What about questions that respondents fail to answer? The standard approach to this problem is to assign either "9" or a "99" to each unanswered question to signify missing data. When the data are analyzed, the computer can be directed to ignore these entries and concentrate on the responses from individuals who did answer the questions. If a respondent failed to answer a majority of the questions, it would probably be advantageous for the researcher to eliminate that response set from the analysis.

To document these kinds of coding decisions, the researcher must prepare a *codebook*, which is a detailed account of the questions, the codes assigned to the answers, and the format in which the codes appear. (If the data are secondary, they should come with a prepared codebook.) The codebook generally describes the variables in a data set and the response options of those variables.

Once the data have been entered and verified, they are ready for analysis. Typically, the first run done is a *one-variable run*. This means that each question on the survey instrument is listed by the computer, and the number for each response is presented. For example, using the gender question from above, the printout would show (1) how many respondents indicated they were female or male, (2) what percentage of all respondents each figure represents, and (3) how many individuals responded to the question. Given this information for the entire survey, the researcher would have a general sense of the spread of responses on individual variables.

This printout also serves as another means of verifying the data. If the response for one of the questions seems out of character with the range of possible answers, the researcher will know to look for a coding or data-entry problem. Once he or she is satisfied with the correctness of the data, the researcher can run more sophisticated types of data analysis to address the research questions the study was undertaken to answer.

QUALITATIVE DATA

Qualitative research data come in a wide variety of types, including photographs, tape and video recordings, field notes, interviews, artifacts, drawings, books, and even newspaper and magazine articles. In this section, the discussion will be limited to the organization of *textual data*. A considerable amount of qualitative data either exists as text or can be transformed through description to some form of text.

Do not interpret the previous statement to suggest that photographic data, for example, must be reduced and limited to textual analysis. Certainly, examination of images, or visual ethnography, is an important and worthwhile type of data analysis (Berg, 2008; Wang, 2000). However, the authors believe that the largest amount of qualitative research currently being undertaken by social scientists in the United States involves textual data. Operating from this orientation, we will begin by considering how to organize textual data.

Organization

Organization of qualitative research characteristically means considering words, and a great many words, at that. The basic underlying organizational scheme in any qualitative analysis is to reduce the amount of raw data without simultaneously losing content meaning. As Miles and Huberman (1994) express, researchers need methods for data management and analysis that are systematic and explicit. In other words, researchers need to arrange data in systematic ways that allow for quick location and retrieval of specific elements.

During the past four decades or so, this desire for systematic arrangement and retrieval has evolved considerably. At one time, qualitative researchers created various "hard copy" *filing* or *indexing* systems to organize, store, and retrieve data. To do so involved making numerous copies of data records (e.g., interview transcriptions, letters, field notes) and organizing them in paper folders, piles, and even cardboard boxes. In turn, these folders, piles, and boxes were coded in some systematic manner to allow researchers to identify and index their contents. This identification procedure also allowed for various sorts of cross-referencing of topics.

Over the years, more and more qualitative researchers have moved away from paper-and-folder systems for coding and indexing and toward the use of computers. And as the technology has changed, so, too, has the vocabulary describing it. For example, the term *word crunching* (Dennis, 1984) has slowly crept into the vocabularies of many qualitative researchers to describe the reduction of data bulk and use of computerized methods for accessing and retrieving textual data. Computer programs have been developed that specifically address or are dedicated to the organization and analysis of textual data. Some programs have been designed to perform content analysis, for instance, while others have been created to help in the development of grounded theory (Maietta, 2006; Weitzman and Miles, 1995). Among the most popular types of dedicated qualitative programs are those designed to assist in the storing and analysis of ethnographic data (Dicks & Mason, 1998).

Many researchers, however, co-opt and adapt commercial data and word-processing programs to suit their various qualitative-analytic needs. Today, most social scientists are at least sufficiently computer literate to use word-processing systems, which provide several significant tools. Most word-processing systems have an indexing function and a means of searching for terms or specific characters (discussed later in this chapter). Word processors also facilitate text revision, such as quickly "cutting and pasting" (i.e., copying and moving) blocks of text; when desired, this text can be stored as a new electronic file or printed out as revised "hard copy." In short, word-processing systems offer innovative qualitative researchers a fairly versatile means of organizing and analyzing textual data.

Getting Started

The researcher begins the process of qualitative data analysis by preparing and organizing the data. If he or she has conducted interviews using a tape recorder, the first task will be to *transcribe* the interview tapes. Ideally, the researcher should transcribe the interview data directly into a computer, and the data should be transcribed verbatim. Quite literally, this means that if the subject makes a clicking sound with his or her mouth, the transcriber should indicate that such a sound was made. If a telephone rings in the background, the transcriber should indicate parenthetically that the phone rang. If a dog barks and can be heard on the tape, even this should be included in the transcription. The idea is to recreate the entire interview situation, not merely the verbal exchange between interviewer and subject.

Because transcription is a lengthy and sometimes tedious process (as well as expensive, if a transcriber is hired), extraneous sounds heard during an interview are ignored by some researchers. For expediency, the researcher may choose to eliminate anything that is not directly a question or an answer. In cases in which a consistent interview schedule has been used, the researcher may even transcribe shorthand versions of questions and write out full representations of the answers. The guiding principle behind any of these possible arrangements is to preserve the most detail in the briefest possible form.

The researcher working with field notes should convert the shorthand jottings he or she made in the field to full field notes. (See Berg, 2007, for a description of full field notes.) Such full notes will likely have been prepared during the course of the investigation, so by the analysis stage of research, the data will largely have been entered and will be ready for coding and indexing.

When working with artifacts, photographs, drawings, or other nontextual data, the researcher needs to prepare a written account that describes these items in detail. This account can then be used as a textual record of the objects and artifacts. Once material has been entered into a word processor, it can be indexed using the function provided by most systems. Indexed terms can be used to locate various classification categories, specific words, classes of key terms, and themes. Most indexing systems provide the dual capacity of identifying specific words where they appear in text or listing more general key terms or phrases on pages where material is present. For instance, in a page of text on drug use, marijuana and cocaine may be discussed in some detail. The researcher will likely identify the words *marijuana* and *cocaine* and might also key the page with the term *drugs*, even though this particular word is not literally shown on the page. This indexing process provides two benefits:

1. It allows the researcher to move to a slightly more abstract line of thinking during her or his analysis.
2. It provides a type of cross-referencing that will quickly allow the researcher to search for and retrieve discussions of related terms—for instance, in the example, any type of drug.

Using key words indexing also allows the researcher to work with various analytic themes or classes of words, which facilitates intentionally listing thematic categories that represent specific concepts examined by certain questions. Indexing data in this way also makes it possible to locate structured questions from the instrument, as well as their corresponding responses. Answers to questions can be compared across subjects or aggregated to calculate the magnitude of a particular pattern of response.

References

Bailey, K. D. (1982). *Methods of social research* (2nd ed.). New York: Free Press.

Berg, B. L. (2006). *Qualitative research methods for the social sciences* (5th ed.). Boston: Allyn & Bacon.

Berg, B. L. (2007). *Qualitative research methods for the social sciences* (6th ed.). Boston: Allyn & Bacon.

Berg, B. L. (2008). Visual ethnography. In L. M. Given (Ed.), *The Sage encyclopedia of qualitative research methods* (pp. 934–938). Thousand Oaks, CA: Sage.

Dennis, D. L. (1984). Word crunching: An annotated bibliography on computers and qualitative data analysis. *Qualitative Sociology, 7*(1/2), 148–156.

Dicks, B., & Mason, B. (1998). Hypermedia and ethnography: Reflections on the construction of a research approach. *Sociological Research Online* 3 (3). Retrieved October 10, 2008, from http://www.socresonline.org.uk/socresonline/3/3/3.html

Hagan, F. E. (2006). *Research methods in criminal justice and criminology* (7th ed.). Boston: Allyn & Bacon.

Jain, A., Hong, L., & Pankanti, S. (2000). Biometric identification. *Communications of the ACM, 43*(2), 90–98.

Maietta, R. (2006). State of the art: Integrating software with qualitative analysis. In L. Curry, R. Shield, & T. Wetle (Eds.), *Improving aging and public health research: Qualitative and mixed methods.* Washington, D.C.: American Public Health Association and the Gerontological Society of America.

Maxfield, M. G., and Babbie, E. (2005). *Research methods for criminal justice and criminology* (4th ed.). Belmont, CA: Thompson Higher Education.

Miles, M. B., & Huberman, A. M. (1994). *Qualitative data analysis: An expanded sourcebook* (2nd ed.). Beverly Hills, CA: Sage.

TheSourceNY. (2008). *Body orifice security scanner: A safe non-intrusive method of detecting objects concealed in body cavities.* Retrieved October 19, 2008, from http://www.bodyorificescanner.com/

Wang, C. (2000). *Strength to be: Community visions and voices.* Ann Arbor, MI: University of Michigan Press.

Webb, E. J., Campbell, D. T., Schwartz, R. D., & Sechrest, L. (1966). *Unobtrusive measures: Nonreactive research in the social sciences.* Chicago: Rand McNally.

Weitzman, E. A., & Miles, M. B. (1995). *Computer programs for qualitative analysis.* Thousand Oaks, CA: Sage.

Application Exercise 7.1

Name of Student:________________

Student ID No.:_________________

Course/Section No.:______________

Date:__________________________

Using the library in your college or university, locate the Sunday editions of *LA Times* or *NY Times* for the past two months. Next, find all of the articles that describe a crime or criminal event.

1. List all of the categories of crime indicated in a *headline* for each article.
2. Create a tally sheet (a sheet with each of these categories listed on it) and show how many times each category of crime appears in headlines.
3. Read through each article, and identify specific terms that describe the people involved in the criminal event (the suspects, the victims, the witnesses). Create a tally sheet for each of these terms.

Application Exercise 7.2

Name of Student:________________

Student ID No.:________________

Course/Section No.:________________

Date:________________

Visit a public location such as a beach, park, or library. Enter the field for three separate five-minute observation periods. Carefully write field notes for each one of these observations. *Warning:* PUBLIC BATHROOMS MAY NOT BE USED IN THIS EXERCISE. Remember to draft your full notes as quickly as possible after withdrawing from the field. Your notes should range in length from about two to three double-space-typed pages for each five-minute interval of observation.

CHAPTER 8

Policy Implications

ETHICS VERSUS POLITICS

Ethical and political issues are sometimes thought of as being closely related. However, they are not the same issue. One way to differentiate between the two is to link *ethical* concerns with methodological design and *political* concerns with the use of research findings. For example: Does the design include activities that in any way injure subjects or place them at serious risk of injury? Is participation voluntary or coercive? Are there undue invasions of privacy? Will the research further deteriorate conditions for subjects or the environment?

These questions about research design clearly fall in the purview of ethical issues. How findings are used, how they were intended to be used, and what impact they may have on people, such as those used as subjects (e.g., drug users who were not actual subjects in the study), are all political issues. For instance, suppose a researcher makes arrangements with police officers to take urine samples from suspected violent felons immediately after release. This activity would raise "red flags" for both ethical and political reasons. Depending on the purpose of the research, however, the issues would vary.

Assume that the researcher wants to find out whether these violent felons used drugs and/or alcohol when committing their crimes in order to better identify precursors of violent behavior. The researcher would naturally need to get informed consent from each suspected felon prior to obtaining the urine sample. The researcher would also need to offer the usual types of confidentiality assurances and provide security for all records and urine analysis data. These are all important ethical concerns.

What if, however, the researcher's purpose is to establish a data set in order to argue that some violent criminals are polydrug users and should be sentenced more severely than single-drug users who become violent? Now, the researcher enters the world of politics.

In the truest sense, ethical considerations are not entirely separate from political ones, but they are distinguishable. How researchers plan to use findings from their own research seems to be reasonably within their control. How others who pay for or read about research in scientific journals use those findings is not so easily controlled, however. These issues can be difficult for researchers, especially inexperienced ones, to reconcile. As Punch (1986, pp. 13–14) suggests, too often, academics, textbooks, and journal articles espouse an image of conducting social research for students that is "neat, tidy, and unproblematic." Yet experienced researchers immediately recognize that such an image is idealistic, not realistic.

The argument here is *not* that every researcher must search his or her soul constantly throughout the design and implementation of a project. Such silly and naive sentimentality is itself a false image of research. There are enormous differences between revealing the innermost thoughts and trepidations contained in one's research diary (a journal routinely kept by many social scientists during research) and addressing certain political and ethical concerns.

The following sections will review a number of the general and largely pragmatic issues involved in the politics of research. The soul searching will be left to each individual researcher's conscience.

GATEKEEPERS AND THE POWERFUL

Why a researcher chooses a particular topic and slant, how he or she gains access to subjects and settings, and even which data-gathering techniques he or she selects may all have political overtones. Many studies describe in detail the enormous significance of their findings and argue that the topic was chosen for some lofty humanitarian reasons. Students of research often develop images of people such as Margaret Mead, Franz Boas, and Bronislaw Malinowski, intrepidly going off into the wild to study primitives and literally getting dirty with data. The fact is, though, that much of today's research (when it is not the secondary analysis of nearly sterile data sets) is research by *convenience* and *accessibility.*

Convenience can be a legitimate reason to undertake research, particularly when linked to accessibility and a topic that is research worthy. Yet some researchers fear that their findings will not be taken seriously if it is discovered how conveniently the data were collected. In truth, on occasion, social scientists simply find themselves in the right place, at the right time.

Adler (1985) describes how she learned that her next-door neighbor was a drug smuggler and how through him, she gained access to the world of middle-level drug smugglers. Certainly, the study of drug smuggling is important and respectable research that needs to be undertaken. Because of the circumstances, Adler found herself in a convenient position to undertake that study. Had she intentionally sought to locate a drug smuggler to use as a guide to the world of drug smuggling, she may not have been successful.

Many researchers gain access to research settings because of personal relationships with *gatekeepers*, who are usually people with special information, connections, or control over some setting (Berg, 2007; Bogdan & Taylor, 1975). Given these assets, gatekeepers often have the ability to facilitate research or to disrupt, slow, or even prevent it from occurring. When Berg (1990a, 1990b) was interested in studying training in a police academy, he sought the advice of one of his students, who was a state police officer. While discussing the project with the student, Berg (1990a, 1990b) learned that not only was the student an officer but the president of the State Police Association. Because of the student's relationship with the police commissioner, Berg (1990a, 1990b) was given considerable access to seven police academy programs (including several that, coincidentally, were located five minutes from his home, further increasing the convenience quotient of the research; Berg, 1990a, 1990b).

Access can also be affected when researchers enter the realm of the *powerful* or *elite*. Researchers have, in fact, seldom penetrated these largely uncharted territories (Punch, 1986). Instead, most researchers have focused on what may be labeled *holding categories*, or low-level and marginal social groups. There are, for example, few empirical studies on powerful and elite individuals, such as corporate executives, crime bosses, drug kingpins, congress people, high-ranking police and military personnel, and so forth. On the other hand, there are countless studies on people from the lower social strata or who have marginal qualities or interests: drug addicts, the poor, the mentally impaired, patrons of topless bars and porno shops, and so on.

Some researchers believe that it is not adequate simply to conduct research on categories of people who are easy to access. But gaining access to study the powerful and elite poses many potential pitfalls. Persons of power would likely be able to control what areas of their lives a researcher could access.

These problems with accessing the elite are somewhat analogous to the problems a researcher faces when entering a correctional setting with the permission of the warden. Although the warden may give the appearance of cooperation, the researcher can never be certain that he or she will have *full access* to every location in the prison that he or she desires to explore. In the name of security, the warden may limit where the researcher can go, with or without a correctional officer escorting him or her. Even when given access, the researcher may find inmates and prison workers to be inhibited, resistant, or uncooperative, due to their knowledge of the warden's cooperation with the researcher.

INSTITUTIONAL REVIEW BOARDS

Another political factor in research is the institutional review board (IRB), an internal agency or institutional mechanism designed to assess research proposals and ensure protection of human subjects. Usually, members of the institution or agency are placed on a panel that reads research plans and considers whether they can be undertaken legally, safely, and ethically (see also Chapter 2).

Ideally, when an IRB determines that there may be problems with a research design, it notifies the researcher and discusses its concerns. If the researcher can assuage the board's concerns, perhaps by modifying the design, permission to undertake the study will probably be given. If, on the other hand, no agreement can be obtained between the researcher and the IRB, the institution or agency will not allow the researcher to carry out the study under its name or using its resources.

In a utopian sense, the IRB is there to protect those people (subjects) who might not otherwise be able to protect themselves. From this view, the IRB is a benevolent protector. Of course, this view suggests that the subjects of most research studies are unprotected or powerless.

One of the complaints many researchers utter when submitting proposals to IRBs is that the people sitting in judgment over their designs may never themselves have conducted research. Some IRB members may be clinicians whose methods are somewhat different from those of social scientists. Other members may, at one time, have eroded their ability to make legitimate assessments and offer quality advice. It is interesting to note that members of IRBs are often selected on the basis of convenience or because they volunteer, not because of their experience, skills, or knowledge.

Thus, the politics of IRBs sometimes take on a game-like appearance: The researcher tries to hammer out a proposal that will meet the demands of the IRB, even when the design may not make good methodological sense to him or her. In this situation, the researcher might tell the IRB whatever it takes to get the design approved but then do what he or she wants or believes is correct in carrying out the project.

Under such devious circumstances, we might be tempted to question the integrity of the researcher. We must be cautious, however, and consider the actions of the IRB that may have motivated the researcher to compromise his or her integrity. We might also question the appropriateness of some actions of IRBs when members clearly have little or no empirical experience or their skills have become dull from lack of use.

Regrettably, no uniform standards can be established that would ensure an appropriate and equitable review of all research proposals. Since every research project has different benefits and problems, no single criterion of ethical appropriateness or safety can be applied. What can be done, however, is to staff IRBs with members who have, at minimum, some recent experience in conducting empirical research and who have themselves operated ethically. Perhaps seats on IRBs should also be elected positions, rather than appointed ones. Then individuals who were qualified and maybe even dissatisfied with previous board actions could run for positions.

THE USE OF RESEARCH FINDINGS

When we read research studies, we assume that the information and findings they present are accurate. Researchers operate on the assumption that as long as they tell the truth, they will be believed. In fact, all researchers are charged with the responsibility of providing accurate information, all the time. To do otherwise would mean undermining the amount of confidence people place on study results. But just how applicable or generalizable those findings may be is a separate question.

Just because a given research finding is accurate and truthfully presented does mean that it is useful. The terms *accurate* and *truthfully presented* do mean that it is useful. The terms *accurate* and *useful* are not synonyms. Although used similarly in lay parlance, scientifically, we know that usefulness speaks to practical application, whereas *accuracy* suggests correctness.

We have all heard reports about caffeine, nicotine, saccharin, NutraSweet®, and cholesterol, specifically, that high concentrations of these products have caused blindness, cancer, and heart attacks in laboratory animals (chiefly rats). These studies were undertaken carefully and seem to yield highly accurate results—about rats. But do these results translate accurately for humans?

On the surface, examples such as these may seem somewhat extreme. Nonetheless, they do illustrate the validity of these questions: Do research findings apply in real-world settings? Is there genuine reason to believe that these studies have practical implications that can be generalized to humans?

For instance, when a study has been conducted on delinquent youths in Syracuse, what implications will the results have for youths in California? If fear of crime is studied among blind people living in Pennsylvania, will the findings be relevant to sighted persons living in the same state? What about blind people living in Michigan?

In effect, the issue becomes as follows: To what extent will results generalize to different locations and situations? How exact must situations be before findings from a study in one situation can be used to explain phenomena that occurred in another situation? Concerns such as these are often discussed in research books, as they regard dimensions of the sample and various demographics of people in the sample. But there are other "nonpeople" dimensions, or what Katzer, Cook, and Crouch (1991, p. 176) call *ecological representativeness*: elements of a study beyond the level of people.

Ecological representativeness includes, for example, instrumentation: Would the same results have been obtained if an in-depth interviewing strategy had been used instead of a questionnaire? What if a telephone interview had been used instead of a face-to-face one? Would the results have differed if the methodological design had been triangulated and included both multiple data-gathering strategies and multiple researchers? What would have happened if the wording or order of the questions in the interview schedule had been altered? Might different kinds of subjects have been obtained if the study had been conducted in the winter instead of the summer? Would a researcher of the opposite gender have come to the same conclusions?

These kinds of questions should be considered along with more traditional questions about the researcher's sampling strategy. In some studies, in which the researcher had meticulously identified a representative sample, generalizability at the people who use research findings and who consider their possible implications must also consider other dimensions: ecological representativeness.

Since it would be impossible outside the confines of theory to design a study that generalized across all dimensions, researchers usually work with what they view as the most important dimension: people. In fact, many times, the other "nonpeople" elements may not matter much. Environments may be essentially alike; other data-gathering strategies may offer more or less information but not necessarily different findings, and so forth. People, however, will assuredly have differences. When a researcher develops a careful sampling procedure, readers of the results can be relatively confident about generalizing those findings along the people dimension. Even when a study uses a sample other than a representative one (e.g., an accidental, purposive, or weighted sample), the people dimension is usually covered. In an effective report, the researcher will describe the extent of limitations on generalizing results at the people level.

At times, however, the other dimensions *do* matter. In these instances, using other elements would create differences in the results. Although the researcher may not adequately consider the differences that will prevent consumers of research from generalizing findings to their situations, consumers should do so. Thus, the next obvious question is as follows: What should we look for when determining the degree of generalizability of research findings?

The crux of generalizability is the removal or suppression of obvious differences between the phenomenon and situation described in the research and those in which the results are to be applied. If we can demonstrate that the differences between the study situation and the application situation are relatively minor, then the results can safely be applied.

Sometimes, it is easier to consider how situations are *similar* than it is to determine how they are *different*. For example, since researchers are usually concerned with the people dimension, they may report demographic comparisons between their sample and some larger populations. When comparisons show similarities among proportions of males to females, educational levels, age cohorts, economic levels, religious affiliations, and related characteristics, generalizability may be relatively easy to establish. In other cases, however, there may be differences that matter but that are not as obvious. In these situations, we must assess the adequacy of methods used by the investigator, the theoretical arguments offered, and the kinds of evidence presented.

In an absolute vacuum, any minor change in the research environment could alter the results of a study. In the real world of research, however, things are not quite that sensitive. The reader must consider the likelihood that the results would have differed had alternative theories been applied, different data-gathering strategies been employed, or various other measures of strength and association been used.

It is important for inexperienced researchers to keep in mind that there is no single best way to evaluate the usefulness of a study's findings. The evaluation process is based largely on the concerns of the research consumer. A study that is determined unsuitable for one consumer may be just right for another. In some cases, then, the differences between a study and a particular application situation do not invalidate the results overall. Of course, in other situations, identifying a faulty method or theory or an incorrect measure may indicate that a research report is unacceptable in any situation. There is, however, no foolproof way to undertake the enterprise of research, and readers should be cautious when evaluating application plausibility and generalizability.

GENDER AND RESEARCH POLITICS

In the past three decades, female scholars have entered the top ranks of the social and behavioral sciences. This relatively recent emergence of women in the sciences reflects that the predominant form of social structure in modern history has been patriarchal: male-dominated families, governments, and lineages. The major mechanism used to maintain this structure has historically been to keep women in positions subordinate to men, including subordinated intellectual roles.

The processes, theories, and products of the social sciences have been deeply influenced by this ideological mechanism. Early criminologists were almost entirely male. In fact, relatively few female social scientists were in the forefront of social science history. Agnew and Pyke (1987, p. 242) echo White's (1975) suggestion that "variables such as the decreased likelihood of sponsorship, lack of role models, atypical (interrupted) career paths, and exclusion from the 'old boys network' all operated to dissuade women from careers in science."

While social scientists are trained to consider certain relevant issues regarding gender, including researcher reactivity, gender performance, attitudes, educational levels, earning capacity, and other demographic characteristics, certain personal views held by the researcher may affect or even bias the study results, either intentionally or unconsciously. Historically, most criminological research and theory had been built upon a patriarchal (and chiefly white, western European) ideological foundation that suggested the following:

1. Females are different from males along most variable divisions.
2. These differences have a basic biological origin.
3. Men's position on variables is superior (Agnew & Pyke, 1987; Pyke, 1982).

Beginning in the 1970s, women criminologists emerged to change the path of criminological theory. Adler's (1975) early feminist criminological theory held that the feminist gains of the 1970s were matched with a rise in women's criminality. According to Adler, "women have demanded equal opportunity in the fields of legitimate endeavors, a similar number of determined women have forced their way into the world of major crime such as white collar crime, murder and robbery" (Adler, 1975, p. 3). This was, and remains, a controversial perspective; yet, it marks the entrance of women into the field of criminology. Chesney-Lind (2004) remains one of the most prolific women scholars focusing on female criminality, noted for her assessment of the "add girls and stir" approach historically seen in the study of females and crime. While not an exhaustive list, other notable female criminologists who have made substantial contributions to criminological theory and practice over the last three decades include drug court research by Turner, Susan, Greenwood, Fain, & Deschennes (1999), Wilson, Gottfredson, and Najaka's juvenile delinquency research (2001), Morash's work on gender and crime (2005), Petersilia's work in corrections (2003), Bloom, Owen, and Covington's work with female offenders (2003), and Taxman, Perdoni, and Harrison's research in the area of substance abuse (2007).

When we read a research report and assess its relative merits, gender bias is an important factor to consider. Bias may arise from the way in which the researcher's personal orientations affect the construction of a question or focus. For example, consider the following series of statements:

1. Girls are less aggressive than boys.
2. Girls are arrested for shoplifting less frequently than boys.
3. Girls are physically weaker than boys.

In addition to the Europatriarchal cultural bias obvious in all of these statements, there is an inherent inaccuracy: They suggest that *all* females are more whatever than *all* males.

Such forms of language bias may be culturally ingrained and operate unconsciously. Nonetheless, they create an inferential bias that should be considered when evaluating research findings.

In addition, bias may be reflected in the topic selected for investigation or the way in which results are presented. Until about the last 30 years, serious research on gender roles, women deviants, and even occupational motivations among women has been all but nonexistent. In the past, when studies examined these issues, they involved comparisons with men, often showing preferences for male subjects (Agnew & Pyke, 1987; Carlson, 1971; Pyke, Ricks, Stewart, & Neeley, 1975). These early studies predominantly used male samples and were more likely to be generalize to females than studies using only female subjects (Agnew & Pyke, 1987; Greenglass & Stewart, 1973). This early problem and the subsequent overgeneralizations from research involving exclusively male subjects led to Chesney-Lind's (2004) assertion that such research was approached from a "add girls and stir" perspective. Contemporary social science literature more adequately addresses gender in criminal justice and criminological research.

Ideally, we could study research in which phenomena had been studied from a variety of ideological orientations (e.g., Europatriarchal, feminist, egalitarian). If a finding was consistent from these different perspectives, readers' confidence in it could be much greater. At present, however, increasing the sensitivity of the social sciences to address gender bias should promote more objective research.

References

Adler, F. (1975) *Sisters in crime*, New York: McGraw-Hill.

Adler, P. (1985). *Wheeling and dealing*. New York: Columbia University Press.

Agnew, N. M., & Pyke, S. W. (1987). *The science game* (4th ed.). Englewood Cliffs, NJ: Prentice Hall.

Berg, B. L. (1990a). First day at the police academy: Stress reaction training as a screening-out technique. *Journal of Contemporary Criminal Justice, 6*(2), 89–105.

Berg, B. L. (1990b). Who should teach police? A typology and assessment of police academy instructors. *American Journal of Police, 9*(2), 79–100.

Berg, B. L. (2007). Qualitative research methods for the social sciences (6th ed.). Boston: Allyn & Bacon.

Bloom, B., Owen, B., & Covington, S. (2003). *Gender-responsive strategies: Research, practice, and guiding principles for women offenders.* (NCJ Publication No. 201301). Rockville, MD: National Criminal Justice Reference Service.

Bogdan, R., & Taylor, S. J. (1975). *Introduction to qualitative research methods.* New York: Wiley.

Carlson, R. (1971). Where is the person in personality research? *Psychological Bulletin, 75*, 203–219.

Chesney-Lind, M. (2004). *Girls, delinquency, and juvenile justice.* Belmont, CA: Wadsworth/Thompson Learning.

Greenglass, E., & Stewart, M. (1973). The underrepresentation of women in social psychological research. *Ontario Psychologist, 5*, 21–29.

Katzer, J., Cook, K. H., & Crouch, W. W. (1991). *Evaluating information.* New York: McGraw-Hill.

Morash, M. (2005). *Understanding gender, crime, and justice.* Thousand Oaks, CA: Sage.

Petersilia, J. (2003). *When prisoners come home: Parole and prisoner reentry.* New York: Oxford University Press.

Punch, M. (1986). *The politics and ethics of field work.* Beverly Hills, CA: Sage.

Pyke, S. W. (1982). Confessions of a reluctant ideologist. *Canadian Psychology, 23*, 125–134.

Pyke, S. W., Ricks, F. A., Stewart, J. C., & Neeley, C. A. (1975). The sex variable in Canadian psychological journals. In M. Wright (Chair), *The status of women psychologists.* Symposium presented at the meeting of the Ontario Psychological Association, Toronto, Canada.

Taxman, F. S., Perdoni, M., & Harrison, L. (2007). Treatment for adult offenders: A review of the state of the state. *Journal of Substance Abuse Treatment, 32*(3), 239–254.

Turner, S., Greenwood, P., Fain, T., & Deschennes, E. (1999). Perceptions of drug court: How offenders view ease of program completion, strengths and weaknesses, and the impact on their lives. *National Drug Court Institute Review, II*(1), 61–86.

White, M. S. (1975). Women in the professions: Psychological and social barriers to women in science. In J. Freeman (Ed.), *Women: A feminist perspective* (pp. 227–237). Palo Alto, CA: Mayfield.

Wilson, D. B., Gottfredson, D. C., & Najaka, S. S. (2001). School-based prevention of problem behaviors: A meta-analysis. *Journal of Quantitative Criminology, 17*(3), 247–272.

Exercise 8.1

Report: U.S. Executions, Death Sentences on Decline

Matthew Barakat

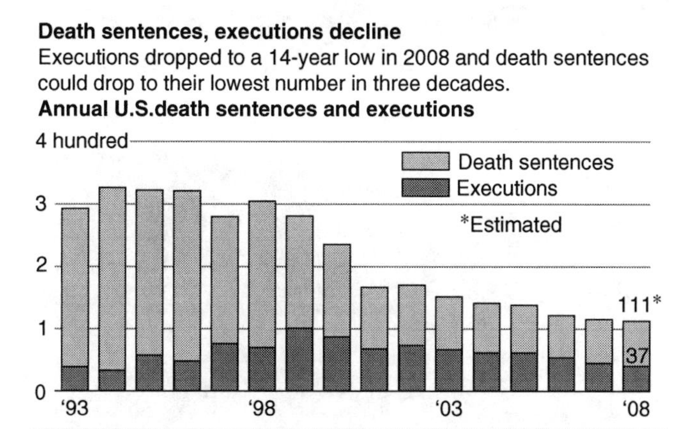

WASHINGTON (AP)—New death sentences in the United States were at or near a three-decade low this year and the number of people executed will be the lowest since 1994, according to a new report.

The nonprofit Death Penalty Information Center reports 37 executions in 2008, with no more expected for the remainder of the year. That's down 12 percent from 42 in 2007 and a 30 percent drop from 2006.

The center estimates the total number of death sentences this year at 111. That is on par with the 115 death sentences imposed in 2007 that represented a 30-year low. It is more than a 60 percent drop from 1998, reflecting a steady decline over the last decade.

The report from DPIC, which opposes the death penalty, also indicates that executions in the U.S. have essentially become a regional phenomenon. All but four of the 37 executions this year occurred in the South and Texas, with Ohio and Oklahoma providing the exceptions. Half of the executions occurred in Texas, where 18 inmates were put to death.

Virginia executed four prisoners. Georgia and South Carolina executed three each; Florida, Oklahoma, Mississippi and Ohio each executed two and Kentucky executed one.

All of the executions in 2008 occurred after April 16, when a U.S. Supreme Court decision on the use of lethal injections ended what had been a de facto moratorium in place for almost seven months.

Experts differed on the moratorium's effect. Richard Dieter, the DPIC's executive director, had feared the numbers would spike in 2008 as states rushed to implement executions that had been on hold.

The fact that there wasn't a spike, he said, demonstrates the inherent problems with the death penalty, including the struggle to ensure a fair appeal process on issues like DNA evidence and inadequate lawyering.

But Richard Bonnie, a law professor at the University of Virginia and an expert on capital punishment, said it was expected that it would take some time after the moratorium was lifted for the normal pace of executions to resume, and he does not consider the drop in executions in 2008 as proof of a long-term decline.

What is more important, Bonnie said, is the drop in death sentences. That data is unaffected by the moratorium, which banned only executions, not death sentences handed down by judges and juries.

Death sentences have been on the decline for more than a decade. Bonnie said that while a majority of Americans still favor the death penalty, their fervor for it was waned as violent crime rates have receded.

Dieter also said that recent death-row exonerations prompted by DNA evidence have planted seeds of doubt in the public's mind about carrying out an irrevocable punishment.

On a state level, changes in the law have also made a difference. In Texas, for instance, a 2005 law gives juries the option of imposing a life sentence without parole. Before then, any sentence short of execution carried the possibility of parole after 40 years in prison, said Kristen Houle, executive director of the Texas Coalition to Abolish the Death Penalty.

As a result, Texas has imposed only 10 death sentences in 2008, according to Houle's organization, the fewest since the U.S. Supreme Court reinstated capital punishment in 1976.

Other states have made changes—North Carolina and other states have made it easier for prosecutors to seek a life sentence instead of a death penalty. New Jersey abolished the death penalty at the end of 2007. Maryland's legislature is expected to consider abolition in 2009.

Bonnie said he believes that public attitudes have softened on the death penalty in the last decade as the violent crime rate has receded.

"The real test will be what happens when violent crime goes back up again, if that will lead to a reversal of these trends," Bonnie said.

On the Net

Death Penalty Information Center:

http://www.deathpenaltyinfo.org

Application Exercise 8.1

Name of Student:________________

Student ID No.:________________

Course/Section No.:________________

Date:________________

1. Locate the most recent death penalty data available at http://www.ojp.usdoj.gov/bjs/dtd.htm. Use the interactive data online links to select three states, and compare death penalty trends for these states. What differences do you see?

2. What might explain these differences?

3. What alternate explanations might account for the trends in death penalty data?

4. Now consider the issue of death penalty by gender. Look up the most recent national statistics on death penalty sentences by gender. What do you see?

5. What explains the gender difference in the death penalty?

Exercise 8.2

Estimation of Individual Crime Rates from Arrest Records

Alfred Blumstein and Jacqueline Cohen

Journal of Criminal Law and Criminology
Vol. 70, No. 4, pp. 561–585, 1979

INTRODUCTION

This paper addresses patterns of individual criminality, a matter of fundamental concern for understanding and controlling crime. Despite an enormous volume of research into the causes and prevention of crime, very little is known about the progress of the individual criminal career. In particular, neither the number of crimes an individual commits each year, the crime rate, nor the changes in that rate as a person ages and/or accumulates a criminal record is known. Such knowledge about individual careers is basic to our understanding of individual criminality, and in particular, to our understanding of how various factors operate on the individual either to encourage or to inhibit criminal activity.

Basic knowledge about individual criminality also has immediate practical import for developing effective crime control policies. For example, incapacitation—physically preventing the crimes of an offender (e.g., through incarceration)—has emerged as a popular crime control strategy. But the benefits derived from incapacitation in terms of the number of crimes prevented will vary greatly, depending on the magnitude of the individual's crime rate; the higher an individual's crime rate, the more crimes that can be averted through his incapacitation.

One incapacitation strategy calls for more certain and longer imprisonment for offenders with prior criminal records. But if individual crime rates decrease as a criminal career progresses, there are fewer crime-reduction benefits gained from incapacitating criminals already well into their criminal careers than from incapacitating those with no prior criminal record. Clearly then, evaluating the crime control effectiveness of various incapacitation strategies requires information about the patterns of individual career criminality.

PRIOR RESEARCH ON CRIMINAL CAREERS

Prior research on criminal careers is largely limited to case studies and biographical or autobiographical sketches, which cannot be considered characterization of the typical offender. The major exceptions are the Gluecks' [1937; 1940] longitudinal studies of criminal careers in the 1920s and the Wolfgang [1972] study of delinquency in a birth cohort. Another major source of data on adult careers is the FBI Careers in Crime File. Some analysis of this data is published in the staff report of the President's Commission on the Causes and Prevention of Violence [Mulvihill, Tumin, and Curtis, 1969].

The Glueck studies found a steady decrease in the proportion of criminals who were still active offenders during successive follow-up periods. This was taken as evidence of an increasing dropout from criminal activities with the passage of time.

These results have served as the basis for the hypothesis that individual criminality declines with age, perhaps because of the aging process and its associated increased maturity and/or declining vigor. The Gluecks' "age of onset" theory represents further refinement of this hypothesis, where time until criminality ceases is determined by intervals after the start of a career, rather than as an explicit function of chronological age.

The available findings concerning the effects of aging, however, are based on measures of the incidence of arrests in the total population. They may result from changes either in the individual arrest rates of offenders with age or in the number of persons actively engaged in crime at any age. To the extent that the arrest patterns that have been observed are due to variations in the size of the criminal population at each age, these patterns do not reflect variations with age in the rate of criminal activity of active individual criminals.

DATA

The data to be used here are from the FBI computerized criminal history file. They include the adult criminal records through early 1975 of all those individuals arrested for homicide, rape, robbery, aggravated assault, burglary, or auto theft in Washington, D.C. during 1973. The data include the adult arrest histories of those 5,338 offenders and include records for 32,868 arrests. Despite the large size and richness of the data set, there are some features of the data that limit the generality of the results to the United States as a whole. Table 1 compares the characteristics of the Washington, D.C. arrestees with those of persons included in the reported arrests in the Uniform Crime Reports (UCR) for 1973 [Federal Bureau of Investigation, 1974]. The two populations are not directly comparable because persons with more than one arrest are counted more than once in the UCR arrest data. This multiple counting alone, however, would not account for the observed differences. The Washington, D.C. arrestees are clearly not representative of arrestees in the United States cities in general. Nonwhites are heavily overrepresented as they are in the general D.C. population. (In the 1970 census, the population of Washington, D.C. was 71% nonwhite compared to 12.3 percent nonwhite for the total population of the United States.)

TABLE 1 Comparison of Washington, D.C. arrestees with arrests in United States cities in 1973

	1973 Washington, D.C.	1973 UCR Arrests for Cities	
Race			
White	8.1%	69%	
Nonwhite	91.8	31	
Sex			
Male	89.7	84.4	
Female	10.3	15.6	
Age			
<18	0.1	26.5	—
18–20	18.6	13.9	18.9%
21–24	24.4	14.14	19.2
25–29	19.9	10.5	14.3
30–34	12.3	7.5	10.2
35–39	8.4	6.1	8.3
40–44	5.0	5.8	7.9
45–49	4.6	5.3	7.2
≥50	6.7	10.0	13.6

Federal Bureau of Investigation, Uniform Crime Reports: 1973 (1974).

It should also be noted that the arrestees used here are not drawn from the population of offenders, since there is no reasonable way of generating such a random sample. Only those offenders who come to the attention of the criminal justice system through the arrest process can be identified. As a result, as long as criminals differ in their crime committing activity and in their vulnerability to arrest, the arrestees in any year cannot be representative of all offenders in general. Offenders who are more criminally active and/or more vulnerable to arrest are more likely to be arrested at least once in a year, and thus, they will be over-represented among the arrestees in a year.

The arrestees, however, are representative of those offenders who are detected by the criminal justice system. From the perspective of direct crime control through incapacitation or rehabilitation, the criminal behavior of those offenders who are available for sanctioning should be the focus of stuffy, for it is their crimes that can be reduced directly.

METHODS

Several factors are considered as potentially influencing arrest rates during a criminal career. The first is age. It is well established that most criminals eventually stop committing crimes. What is not known is whether this dropout occurs suddenly or after a gradual decline in criminal activity. The second factor to be considered is the length of the criminal record. While it is not empirically substantiated, the traditional view has been that the presence of a criminal record indicates a higher than average criminal intensity, and thereby justifies harsher sentences. This idea has been given statutory form in a few jurisdictions. Individuals specializing in different crime types also might have characteristically different arrest rates.

The last factor considered is possible trends over time in arrest rates. These trends might reflect general increases or decreases in criminality over time that are independent of age, or they might arise from a cohort effect where different cohorts, i.e., groups of offenders all beginning their criminal careers at the same time, have characteristically different arrest rates. Such a cohort effect might, for example, reflect the effect of being socialized at different times.

To explore the import of each of these factors, individual arrest rates are estimated by the following:

- age of the offender,
- number of prior arrests in a record,
- crime type "specialties," and
- year of observation.

RESULTS

Analysis of variance was performed on the individual arrest-rate estimates. These results report that arrest rates vary with age, crime type, number of prior arrests, and time, with crime type, interacting with age and with prior arrests. The marginal means reported indicate that arrest rates increase with the number of prior arrests, decrease with age, and have been increasing generally over time. The particular approach used to characterize individuals by crime type makes very little difference in any of these results.

CONCLUSIONS

Using the arrest histories of cohorts of active offenders, this investigation isolated variation in the individual arrest rates during the careers of active offenders from variations in the size of the offender population. Contrary to previous findings of a decrease of arrest rate with age when rates per total population are used, it was found that individual arrest rates actually increase with age for burglar, narcotics and the residual category "all other" offenses, and that rates are trendless for robbery, aggravated assault, larceny, auto theft, and weapons offenses. At the same time, individual arrests rates are generally trendless with respect to the number of prior arrests in an individual's record, and tend to increase in later cohorts for all crime types except aggravated assault, auto theft, and narcotics.

Controlling for time served after sentence does not result in any meaningful differences in these results. The estimated time served of less than two months per arrest is not sufficiently long to significantly alter the variations in individual arrest rates observed during a career.

These results were obtained by using samples of active criminals (persons with at least one arrest before and after the observation period) and by controlling for variations in time served in institutions. Admittedly, the results must be regarded as only preliminary because of the limited number of years the cohorts were observed (from four to seven years). Further replications with other cohorts of active criminals are needed.

The findings increase in individual arrest rates with age, and increases for later cohorts can be reconciled with the prior findings of decline in criminality with age from cross-sectional analyses. First, the peak in arrests per capita previously observed at younger ages can be partially attributed to a large number of offenders actively engaging in crime at those ages. It is not due to significant variation in individual arrest rates over age for those persons who remain active as offenders. Also, the younger people at any time tend to be from later cohorts whose individual arrest rates were found to be higher. Thus, the cohort effect, where people beginning their careers in more recent years have higher arrests rates, would also contribute to the peak in arrests at younger ages. For the same reason, the decrease in per capita arrest rates as people get older is due to the combination of the greater dropout from criminal activity as people age (resulting in smaller numbers of active older criminals) and the lower arrest rates of older people who come from earlier cohorts.

References

Federal Bureau of Investigation. (1974). *Uniform Crime Reports: 1932.* Washington, D.C.: U.S. Government Printing Office.

Glueck, S., and Glueck, E. (1937). *Later criminal careers.* New York: Knopf.

_______ (1940). *Juvenile Delinquents Grown Up.* Cambridge, MA: Harvard University Press.

Mulvihill, D., Tumin, M., and Curtis, L. (1969). *Crimes of Violence.* Washington, D.C.: U.S. Government Printing Office.

Wolfgang, M., Figlio, R., & Sellin, T. (1972). *Delinquency in a Birth Cohort.* Chicago: University of Chicago Press.

Application Exercise 8.2

Name of Student:________________

Student ID No.:________________

Course/Section No.:________________

Date:________________

1. Read the article by Blumstein and Cohen from 1979 printed in Exercise 8.2. What do you think about the author's handling of *gender* in this study? What conclusions can be drawn about gender and arrest?

2. Locate one of the following in your school library or on the Internet: the Uniform Crime Report (UCR), the National Incident-Based Reporting System (NIBRS), or the National Crime Victimization Survey (NCVS). (*Hint:* The BJS has some helpful interactive tools at http://www.ojp.usdoj.gov/bjs/dtd.htm). Using the most recent 5-year period you can find, create a comparative table of annual arrest rates for race, gender, and age in rural and urban settings.
3. What is the general pattern of arrest rates for each category of crime?
   a. Homicide

   b. Rape

   c. Robbery

   d. Aggravated assault

   e. Burglary

   f. Auto theft

4. What are the general patterns of crime for rural compared with urban settings?

5. How do arrest rates compare for males versus females? What might explain this finding?

6. How do arrest rates compare for whites versus nonwhites in urban versus rural settings? What might explain this pattern?

APPENDIX

Random Numbers Table

	(1)	(2)	(3)	(4)	(5)	(6)
1	17603	11858	55651	24271	44970	56315
2	48838	71269	03976	05853	47106	49906
3	68064	13589	77014	33625	63792	26407
4	38561	75541	91159	70864	31748	22539
5	23607	20403	30016	01176	87695	01581
6	59924	11453	83423	14398	21471	26811
7	10789	58855	14657	73809	43238	34952
8	12926	52447	33884	16130	42833	62723
9	29611	28948	04381	78082	30420	73405
10	97567	25080	89427	22943	95836	03717
11	53515	30679	25743	13994	49242	43497
12	87291	29352	76609	87954	80477	02908
13	09058	37493	78745	81545	99704	18671
14	08653	65264	95431	31489	70200	07181
15	96240	75946	36829	54178	55247	52042
16	61655	32816	19335	33220	91563	16535
17	15062	46038	53110	58451	42429	90495
18	19739	05449	74877	40034	44565	84086
19	38965	47770	74473	94363	34693	60587
20	36020	09721	62060	05044	02649	56719
21	21066	54583	27475	35357	85154	35761
22	57383	45633	80882	75137	18930	60992
23	08249	93036	85559	07990	40697	69132
24	10385	86627	04785	50310	40293	96904
25	00513	63128	01840	12262	27880	07585
26	68469	85818	86886	83682	93295	37897
27	50974	64860	23203	48174	46701	77677
28	84750	90090	74068	22134	51379	37088
29	06517	71673	76205	15726	70605	79409
30	06112	99445	66332	92227	41102	41361
31	93699	10126	34288	88359	26148	86222
32	32557	66996	16794	67401	89022	77273
33	12521	80218	24012	92631	13330	24675
34	17198	39629	72337	00772	15467	18266
35	36425	81950	71932	28543	32152	94767
36	06921	43902	59519	39225	00108	90899
37	91968	88763	98376	69537	82613	96499
38	28284	79814	78341	09317	89831	95172
39	79150	27216	83018	42170	38156	03313
40	81286	20807	02244	84491	11194	31084
41	97972	97308	72741	73000	25339	41765
42	65928	19998	57787	17862	64196	98635
43	21875	99040	94104	82354	17603	11858
44	55651	24271	44970	56315	48838	71269
45	03976	05853	47106	49906	68064	13589
46	77014	33625	63792	26407	38561	75541
47	91159	70864	31748	22539	23607	20403
48	30016	01176	87695	01581	59924	11453

	(1)	(2)	(3)	(4)	(5)	(6)
49	83423	14398	21471	26811	10789	58855
50	14657	73809	43238	34952	12926	52447
51	33884	16130	42833	62723	29611	28948
52	04381	78082	30420	73405	97567	25080
53	89427	22943	95836	03717	53515	30679
54	25743	13994	49242	43497	87291	29352
55	76609	87954	80477	02908	09058	37493
56	78745	81545	99704	18671	08653	65264
57	95431	31489	70200	07181	96240	75946
58	36829	54178	55247	52042	61655	32816
59	19335	33220	91563	16535	15062	46038
60	53110	58451	42429	90495	19739	05449
61	74877	40034	44565	84086	38965	47770
62	74473	94363	34693	60587	36020	09721
63	62060	05044	02649	56719	21066	54583
64	27475	35357	85154	35761	57383	45633
65	80882	75137	18930	60992	08249	93036
66	85559	07990	40697	69132	10385	86627
67	04785	50310	40293	96904	00513	63128
68	01840	12262	27880	07585	68469	85818
69	86886	83682	93295	37897	50974	64860
70	23203	48174	46701	77677	84750	90090
71	74068	22134	51379	37088	06517	71673
72	76205	15726	70605	79409	06112	99445
73	66332	92227	41102	41361	93699	10126
74	34288	88359	26148	86222	32557	66996
75	16794	67401	89022	77273	12521	80218
76	24012	92631	13330	24675	17198	39629
77	72337	00772	15467	18266	36425	81950
78	71932	28543	32152	94767	06921	43902
79	59519	39225	00108	90899	91968	88763
80	98376	69537	82613	96499	28284	79814
81	78341	09317	89831	95172	79150	27216
82	83018	42170	38156	03313	81286	20807
83	02244	84491	11194	31084	97972	97308
84	72741	73000	25339	41765	65928	19998
85	57787	17862	64196	98635	21875	99040
86	94104	82354	17603	11858	55651	24271
87	44970	56315	48838	71269	03976	05853
88	47106	49906	68064	13589	77014	33625
89	63792	26407	38561	75541	91159	70864
90	31748	22539	23607	20403	30016	01176
91	87695	01581	59924	11453	83423	14398
92	21471	26811	10789	58855	14657	73809
93	43238	34952	12926	52447	33884	16130
94	42833	62723	29611	28948	04381	78082
95	30420	73405	97567	25080	89427	22943
96	95836	03717	53515	30679	25743	13994
97	49242	43497	87291	29352	76609	87954
98	80477	02908	09058	37493	78745	81545
99	99704	18671	08653	65264	95431	31489
100	70200	07181	96240	75946	36829	54178

Table developed from Random Numbers Generator, accessed October 7, 2008, at http://stattrek.com/Tables/Random.aspx